Guide to Historic Dublin *is the complete companion for the visitor to Dublin, or for anyone interested in the history, architecture and traditions of the city. Covering the entire area of the inner city, within the two canals, plus selected points of interest in the suburbs, the book takes the reader, street by street, on a tour of Dublin. For those who want to know the origins of a particular building or area, the architect involved and the people and traditions connected with it down the years, the* Guide to Historic Dublin *provides the answers.*

First published 1979 by
Gill and Macmillan Ltd
15/17 Eden Quay
Dublin 1
with associated companies in
London, New York, Delhi, Hong Kong,
Johannesburg, Lagos, Melbourne,
Singapore, Tokyo

0 7171 0938 0

Layout and design, Jan de Fouw, Dublin
Filmset by Keyspools Ltd, Golborne, Lancashire.
Printed in Great Britain by Fletcher and Sons Ltd, Norwich

GUIDE TO HISTORIC DUBLIN

Adrian MacLoughlin

Gill and Macmillan

TO MY MOTHER

Who provided the early encouragement

ABOUT THE AUTHOR

Adrian MacLoughlin was born in Dublin in 1936, and educated in O'Connell Schools. He has had over twenty-five years' experience as a working journalist in Dublin and is currently a sub-editor with the *Evening Press*. His working career has involved him in reporting, feature writing and as a critic of books, theatre and cinema. He has been a close student of the history and architecture, traditions and eccentricities of his native city for many years and has published many articles on these subjects in newspapers and reviews. A keen traveller, his extensive knowledge of major European cities lends a depth and perspective to his writings on Dublin.

ACKNOWLEDGMENTS

In the course of researching and writing this book I have drawn upon the help and advice of many people, all of whom I should like to thank. In particular, my thanks are due to the Office of Public Works; the Government Information Service; the staffs of the National Library of Ireland, Royal Dublin Society Library and Dublin Civic Museum; the public relations departments of Dublin Corporation and St James's Gate Brewery; the library staff of Irish Press Ltd; the Jesuit Fathers, Gardiner St, Dublin; Rev. R. D. Harman; Matt Farrell and J. J. Dunne of the *Evening Press*; Des Moore of the *Sunday Independent* and Professor Alan Browne.

PREFACE

This book attempts to fill a gap which is all the more surprising when one considers the wealth of material already available on Dublin. There has been, to date, no truly comprehensive work which attempts to pursue the historical development of the city from its earliest beginnings to very recent times, and which also divides it into reasonably compact areas for the benefit of visitors who may wish to use it as a practical handbook as they walk about. Indeed, the original idea for the book arose from the desire which so many of our visitors have, upon seeing a building or item of street furniture for the first time, to know 'what's that?'. In addition to answering that simple question, I have tried to anticipate others that might follow about the building's architect, its place in the history of the city and distinguished or infamous individuals who may have been associated with it.

It is hoped, however, that interest in this book will not be confined to tourists. There are many native Dubliners who are curious about their city and about areas and individual buildings in it that they have either taken for granted, or failed to notice, or concerning which they have had difficulty in getting details in the past.

Clearly, the breadth of the subject has not allowed me the luxury of dwelling at very great length on individual items, some of which could be — indeed have been — the subjects of separate books. Nevertheless, I have tried to give reasonably clear directions for the benefit of those unfamiliar with Dublin, even when tempted to drop these in favour of longer discussions of particular buildings and places. I hope that my fellow-Dubliners will bear with me in this exercise, and will be content to visualise their journey through familiar streets if they read this book in their own armchairs. At all events, I hope that I have pointed the noses of visitors and natives alike firmly in the right direction.

Adrian MacLoughlin May 1979.

PUBLISHER'S NOTE

The three major railway stations in Dublin were renamed in 1966, on the occasion of the fiftieth anniversary of the 1916 Rising. Although the new titles are always used officially, it is still common to refer to them by the older names. For the benefit of readers who might otherwise be perplexed, the following are the new titles, with the old given in parentheses: Connolly (Amiens St); Heuston (Kingsbridge); Pearse (Westland Row).

The titles of the chief officers of state in the days of British rule in Ireland are frequently a source of confusion, sometimes even to the Irish. As reference is made throughout this book to such personages, the following explanation may be of use to the reader: the *viceroy* or *lord lieutenant* was the representative of the crown; the *chief secretary* was the political representative of the London government, and the *under secretary* was the permanent head of the Irish civil service.

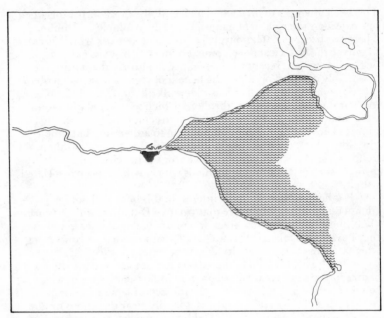

Medieval Dublin, c. 1200

Dublin, c. 1650

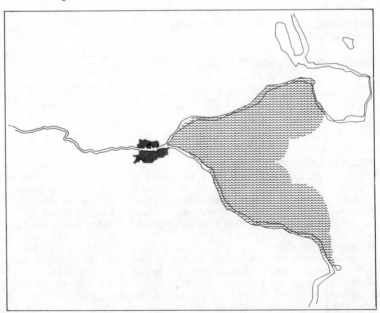

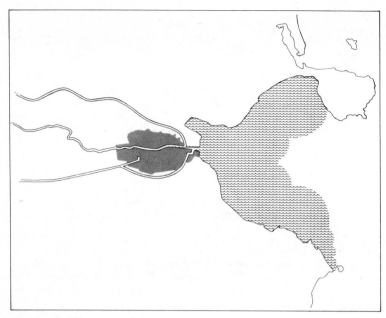

Georgian Dublin, 1750–1850

Modern Dublin, 1960–

CONTENTS

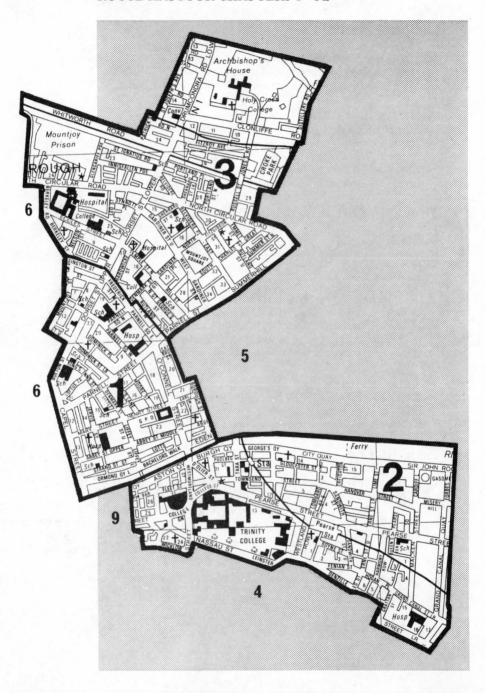

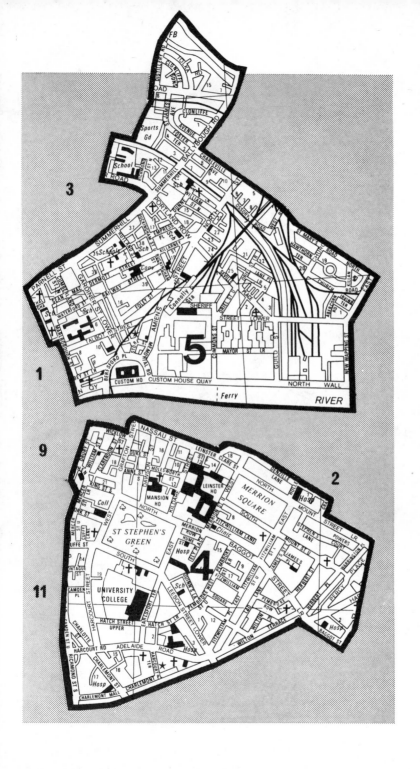

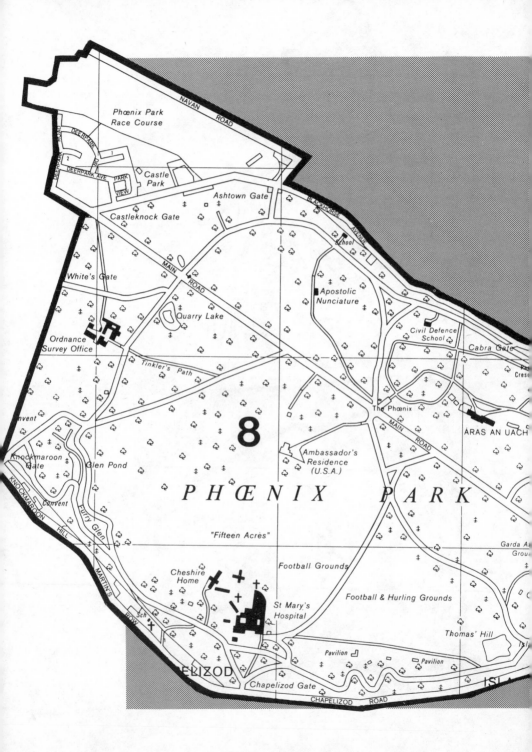

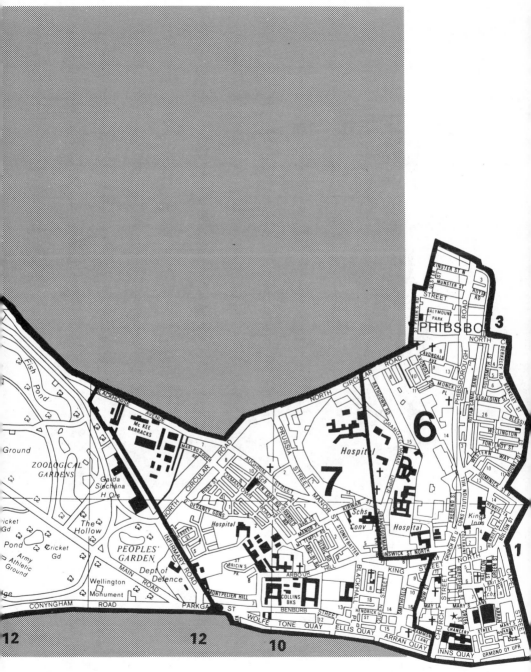

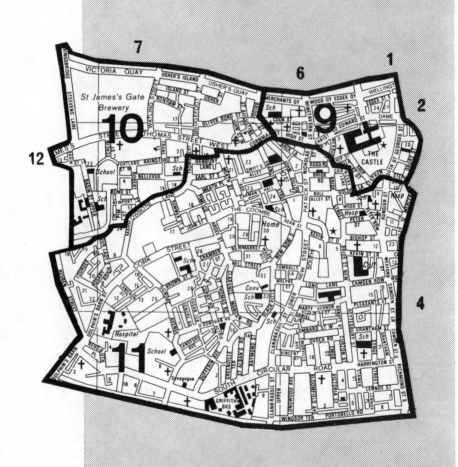

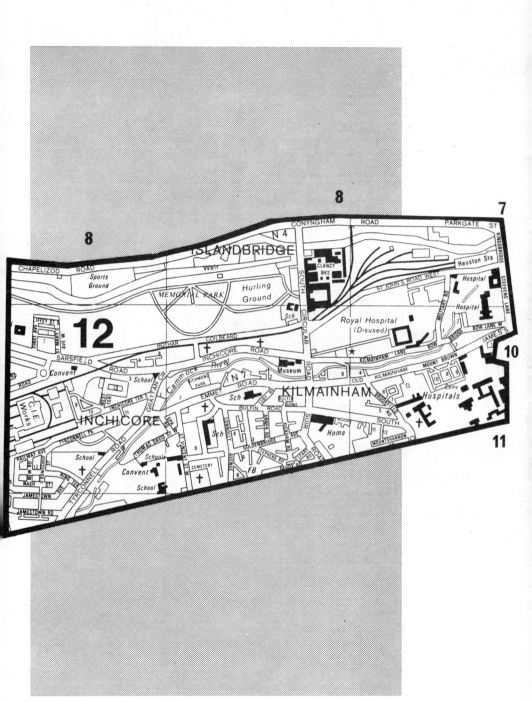

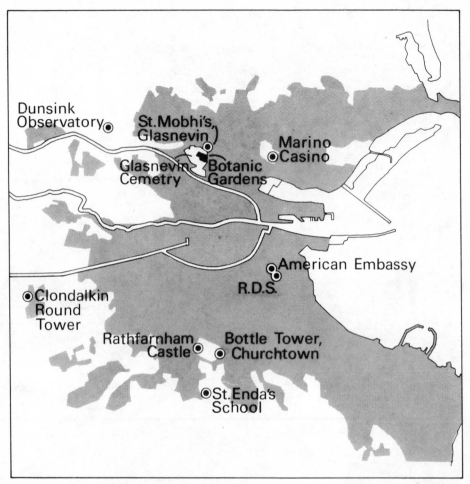

Location of main items discussed in chapter 13

LIST OF ILLUSTRATIONS

The cartoons on pp. 2, 15, 21, 28, 33, 43, 50, 66, 72, 83, 89, 95, 101, 112, 119, 126, 130, 140, 147, 163, 167, 172, 179, 191, 193, 200 and 203 are by Martyn Turner. Maps on pp. x–xv inc. are based on the Ordnance Survey by permission of the Government (Permit No. 3118).

Introduction

Dublin differs from the rest of Ireland in the admixture of cultures which formed it, and is still forming it. It has been in turn the most important of the Irish Viking settlements, a Norman stronghold, the second city of the British Empire and the capital of an independent state. Even when Irish was the predominant language of the country, Danish, Norman French and English in turn were widely spoken in the streets by the Liffey.

While its geographical position and the advantages of its bay to navigators were the physical factors that first led to its eminence, the eventual establishment of a large city here, somewhat more cosmopolitan in culture and commerce than the rest of the island, gave it its head start towards future development. Down the centuries the adventurous, the business-minded, the literary, the curious and those seeking refuge, who have come to Ireland, have always settled in Dublin in greater numbers than elsewhere.

Dublin was never a monumental city in the manner of London, Paris, Rome or Vienna, but the difference was merely one of scale. There are buildings here both big and beautiful, but not a proliferation of them, and none is very far from the River Liffey, whose eastward flow divides the city. The Custom House, Four Courts, Bank of Ireland and the west front of Trinity College are imposing by any international standard, but grand by ours. Merrion Square, Mountjoy Square, Fitzwilliam Square, Parnell Square, St Stephen's Green and some streets are Georgian or part-Georgian, and can still convey a feeling of grace and space, but this is relative to the percentage of the city's area they occupy. They could be scattered and 'lost' in a city of London's size.

While the more obvious features of Dublin, in a physical sense, mark it as a European capital, albeit smallish by continental standards, its many smaller facets and underlying habits make it unquestionably Irish, though in a distinctive way. By reason of its size, population and history, it cannot be fairly compared with any other Irish city or town. If the environs are included, there are about 900,000 people here, an urban mass unapproached elsewhere in the state. In Northern Ireland, Belfast comes near enough to this figure for a realistic comparison to be drawn, but other factors make such an exercise invalid. The antiquity of Dublin, its centuries of development, its years as the centre of the Anglo-Irish 'Pale', its present capital status and the differences — in size and character — of the hinterland make nonsense of any facile parallels with Belfast, a prodigy of the industrial revolution.

Capital status certainly gives a fillip to cultural and commercial life; apart from the ordinary proliferation of activity generated by the presence of the seat of government, presidential residence and headquarters of many corporations and associations, some of the more tangible advantages are the existence here of two university colleges, the National Library, National Gallery and National Museum, these last three all situated between Merrion Square and Kildare St, complementing but not supplanting the Municipal Gallery in Parnell Square, Civic Museum in South William St and many municipal public libraries. The national theatre, the Abbey, is one of the two Dublin theatres of international repute, the Gate being the other. University College Dublin is a constituent college of the National University, but Dublin University's Trinity College is far better known. It is in fact world famous. The city also has two Protestant cathedrals, one of which, St Patrick's, has national status.

Dublin is keenly aware of its past, but has often been lax in preserving the physical relics of it. There is an active Old Dublin Society but, despite this and the vigilance of the Irish Georgian Society and An Taisce (the national trust), many fine structures have disappeared. These have included some of the great Georgian houses which characterised the inner city, but repeated appeals to public conscience have now probably assured the future of most of the structurally sound ones that remain. Until the 1970s, however, nothing much was thought of the city's Victorian architecture, and such important buildings as Gilbey's of O'Connell St and Alexandra College in Earlsfort Terrace were casually toppled. The formation of an Irish Victorian Society and the rise of interest in industrial archaeology, with its many Victorian connections, have helped to slow indiscriminate demolition, but not to stop it. Dublin Victoriana embraces such important buildings as the churches at John's Lane, High St, Parnell Square and Arran Quay, Baggot St hospital and such others as the Richmond, Mater Misericordiae and Eye and Ear; Kingsbridge, Broadstone and Harcourt St railway stations, shop buildings in Upper Baggot St and South Great George's St, parts of Guinness's brewery and the Kildare St club.

It was in the 1970s that excavations at Wood Quay, between the Liffey and Christ Church cathedral, and the controversial decision to build municipal offices there, brought a new awareness of the city's Viking past. But long before that, more recent relics, the Dutch-style houses in Weaver Square, Chamber St, Longford St and elsewhere, built in the reign of Queen Anne and slightly later, had gone. Today the Tailors' Hall in Back Lane and Marsh's library near St Patrick's cathedral are among the few worthwhile Queen Anne buildings we have.

Dubliners are popularly supposed by outside analysts of the city to walk in the literary shadows of Dean Swift, Richard Brinsley Sheridan, George Bernard Shaw, Oscar Wilde, James Joyce, Sean O'Casey and Brendan Behan, who were all born here, but with the exceptions of O'Casey and Behan, the awareness of these giants touches the day-to-day life here as lightly as the knowledge that we also produced the Duke of Wellington and the mathematician Rowan Hamilton. O'Casey and Behan are different partly because they are more recent and partly because of their identification with working-class feelings and crises. To some, these two are folk heroes.

Dublin attitudes, Dublin priorities, Dublin mannerisms of speech and even the accent here, which often resembles that of Liverpool more than it does any Irish provincial one, often lead to the accusation that we are not totally Irish, and that our outlook is largely British. This is in part due to memories of the Pale and in part to the fact that a city of this size is unique here, while its hinterland is largely rural. Whereas, say, a Londoner, Mancunian and New Yorker can accept each other's urbanity without surprise or question, a Carlowman or Kildareman will always find that some of his pressing problems are of no interest or familiarity to a Dubliner.

The allegation of Britishness is not only directed in Ireland against Dubliners. Rural writers and public speakers sometimes refer to towns containing military barracks as 'garrison towns', meaning that they were formerly the bastions of a British military presence, and are somewhat un-Irish. This appellation is especially applied to towns where the 'English' game of association football is played on a wide scale, as it is in Dublin. In fact, the towns were there before the garrisons, and were the obvious places to billet soldiers, who would have been members of an Irish army had the British never come here. Dublin, in the minds of those who regard urbanity as not fully Irish, is the chief 'garrison town'.

The absence of a tradition of heavy industry has helped the city to retain a lot of its eighteenth-century charm, despite neglect and thoughtless demolition. Though ships and locomotives were built here, this never happened on such a scale as to destroy any amenity, or change the character of any but its immediate neighbourhood. Weaving of poplin, silk and wool, coachbuilding, brewing and distilling have been the traditions here, the last two being the most enduring. Guinness's brewery at St James's Gate, for many years the world's biggest, is still the largest in Europe. Its social significance to Dublin is almost as great as its economic importance, and St Patrick's cathedral, the gardens of St Stephen's Green and the Coombe hospital are among the amenities we might not have without it.

The widely-held impression of Dubliners as witty and fluent conversationalists is something on which each visitor must adjudicate for himself. Lovers of sport certainly abound here. The possession of beaches within a large bay, gently sloping hills to the south and one of the world's largest enclosed public parks, the Phoenix Park, may have helped to incline the Dubliner towards outdoor activities. The professional stage has never flourished here as much as the visitor might expect. The famous Abbey and Gate are state-subsidised, while our two largest theatres, the Olympia and Gaiety, have always had a strong music-hall slant. The Dublin theatre festival has had a history of financial struggle. But local amateur dramatic societies function with a village-like fervour, as do musical ones, as befits the city where Handel's *Messiah* was first performed. In this and other regards Dublin is still something of a collection of villages. Or as some would have it, a big village.

1   Going Down Sackville Street

Rotunda hospital — Parnell Square — Charlemont House — Findlater's church — Moore St — O'Connell St — GPO — Jervis St hospital — St Mary's church — Dominick St — Black Church.

'Why aren't yous in th' GPO if yous are men? It's paler an' paler yous are gettin'!

Bessie Burgess in The Plough and the Stars.

**Rotunda
Hospital
Parnell Square**

If you look at the main block of the Rotunda Hospital in Parnell Square with your hand over your eyes, so as to exclude the view of the tower and cupola, you will notice a distinct resemblance to Leinster House in Kildare St. There are differences in detail. The second floor windows in the Rotunda are deeper, the pillars in the engaged portico are Tuscan rather than Corinthian, the stained glass of the chapel over the main entrance interrupts the uniformity of the first floor windows. But each building is eleven bays across, three of them within the portico, each is of three storeys and each has a balustrade over the entrance and flanking bays.

**Richard
Cassels**

The similarity is no coincidence. Nor is it fully explained by the fact that both buildings were designed by Richard Cassels, sometimes called Castle, a German architect who came to Ireland about 1727 at the invitation of Sir Gustavus Hume, for whom he built Castle Hume, Co. Fermanagh, now demolished. Born in Hesse in 1690, Cassels married an Irish girl and, having arrived here, probably never left Ireland. He died in 1751, and his will was signed 'Richard Castle', explaining the later confusion about his name. Apart from designing Leinster House, which was begun in 1745, for the Duke of Leinster, he was responsible for Tyrone House (1740), Clanwilliam House in St Stephen's Green (1739), the dining hall and printing house of Trinity College in 1734, and some large houses in Henrietta St about four years before that. Outside Dublin he redesigned Carton House, near Maynooth, Co. Kildare, country home of the FitzGeralds, Earls of Kildare, in 1739, and designed Powerscourt House, near Enniskerry, Co. Wicklow, for the Wingfields, Viscounts Powerscourt, in 1731, Westport House, seat of the Marquess of Sligo, the same year, and Russborough, Co. Wicklow, in 1741 for Joseph Leeson, a brewer later created Earl of Milltown.

Cassels was within a year of his death when he came to design the Rotunda Hospital for Dr. Bartholomew Mosse in 1750. It had then been decided to call it the Lying-in Hospital, the circular assembly room which gave it its present name being a later addition. Cassels knew that Mosse had more pressing uses for his funds than paying a famous architect for a grand Palladian design, so he suggested using again the basic plan of Leinster House, and reducing his fee accordingly. The doctor agreeing to this, Cassels proposed to build the

**O'Connell St
Ambassador
cinema
Parnell St
Cavendish
Row**

hospital across the top of what is now O'Connell St, from the present Ambassador cinema to where the pleasing Victorian redbrick bank stands at the corner of Parnell St and Cavendish Row. That part of O'Connell St which runs from there to the corners of Earl St and Henry St had just been laid out by Luke Gardiner as Gardiner's Mall, and Cassels thought his building would be a suitable one with which to close the vista. Gardiner disagreed, possibly because it would impede some further development by him along what is now Parnell Square East, so the hospital site was literally pushed aside. The Rotunda that was built, and opened in 1757, has been described as a cold Palladian face hiding a warm Baroque heart.

Dr Mosse had opened his first hospital for 'poor lying-in women' in 1745 in George's Lane, in an old theatre where a Madame Violante had

The Rotunda Hospital, Parnell St

conducted her variety entertainments, including Peg Woffington in her company. Dr Mosse, a barber surgeon originally, was the fifth son of the rector of Portlaoise, then called Maryborough, and it was while returning to Dublin from medical duty with troops in Minorca that he visited several European hospitals, being impressed by the famous teaching hospital of Hôtel Dieu in Paris, where more importance was attached to careful midwifery than was common at the time. Mosse obtained a licentiate in midwifery in 1742 in the Royal College of Physicians of Ireland, which encouraged medical men to involve themselves in maternity care, and issued diplomas while other royal colleges forbade their fellows to engage in midwifery. Dr Mosse, apparently a man of forceful personality, prevailed on influential friends to enable him to obtain the four-acre site on which to build the present Rotunda, while he continued to administer the other in the converted theatre, which remained in commission until 1757.

The Rotunda is the oldest maternity hospital in the world, and the first one built as such. Since its inception, it has had worldwide importance as a teaching centre.

Mosse turned the hospital grounds into pleasure gardens, his plan being that the profits from these, and from an assembly room to be built

at the side of the hospital, would support the latter. He reasoned rightly that there were enough fashionable people in the vicinity to support these enterprises. The gardens in the grounds were called a 'Vauxhall', after London's Vauxhall Gardens, and even in the 1850s Phillip Hardy's *Tourist Guide to Cos. Dublin and Wicklow* recorded them as 'laid out in gravel walks and shrubberies, and affording a delightful promenade to the citizens, military bands always attending'. The Round Room, which gave the Rotunda its name and which is now the Ambassador cinema, did not come until after Mosse's death. Nor did the New Assembly Rooms, now the Gate theatre. The three-storey tower and copper cupola are often attacked as both architecturally unfitting and a ridiculous extravagance by Mosse and Cassels, but the tower, too, was built to earn its keep, Mosse's first idea being to have an astronomical observatory in it.

When Cassels died, the building of the hospital was taken over by his partner and former pupil, John Ensor, who later designed the Round Room, built in 1764, and houses in the east and west sides of Parnell Square. This 'square' has, incidentally, only three sides, the short north one and east and west ones of unequal length. The south side is really part of Parnell St, and the lower part of the east side is called Cavendish Row. The New Assembly Rooms were designed by Richard Johnston, brother of the more famous Francis, with advice from James Gandon, and built between 1784 and 1786. This became the Gate **Gate theatre** theatre in 1929. The theatre company had begun as the Dublin Gate Theatre Studio in the Peacock theatre, adjoining the Abbey, in 1928, with four directors, Hilton Edwards, Micheal MacLiammoir, Madame Bannard Cogley and Gearoid O Lochlainn. Among its earliest productions was the first public performance in these islands of Oscar Wilde's *Salome*. Though the Gate took over its new home at the Rotunda in 1929, it did not open there until 17 February 1930, with *Faust*. The Gate's early years were a struggle for survival, and financial aid came from the late Lord Longford, who later became a director, and even in the 1950s could be seen on the footpath in front of the handsome Tuscan portico, patiently holding a wooden collection box.

In 1969 the theatre qualified for a government grant. It had become internally shabby, and closed for repairs and decoration. The stage was enlarged, new seating and Waterford glass chandeliers were fitted, and the Gate reopened on 15 March 1971, with a Dublin Theatre Festival production of Jean Anouilh's *It's Later than you Think*, in which MacLiammoir appeared. The grant to the Gate is now administered by the Arts Council. Actors who gained early experience at the Gate include Orson Welles and James Mason.

Below the entrance to the Gate in Cavendish Row is a polished stone fountain, an unusually ornate example of this amenity, and not part of the original Rotunda facilities. The side facing the roadway contains a semi-circular drinking trough for horses, while on the footpath side, behind a tall screen, is a fluted niche which once housed a faucet and drinking cup for human beings. Both sides are now disused.

The original Rotunda was winged by colonnades, and the visitor will notice that on the west side the colonnade has been filled in and surmounted by a large extension to the hospital, with granite stones matching the older building. The hospital, like others in Dublin, is constantly needing more space. Inside the railings of the square there are modern buildings, those in the centre having a remarkable copper-sheeted top storey. On the square's west side, near the Parnell St end, is the Thomas Plunket Cairnes wing, a handsome redbrick block with terracotta mouldings and window dressings, built in this ornate Georgian-inspired style as late as 1895. Thomas Plunket Cairnes was one of a Drogheda brewing family who donated generously to the Rotunda. The new wing was planned in 1893 as an operative and gynaecological department. Albert E. Murray of Dawson St was selected as architect and an intensive search was made for funds. Lord Iveagh contributed £1,000 towards the building, which was opened on 27 November 1895. It was named after Thomas Plunket Cairnes — who is also commemorated by a school in Drogheda – in appreciation of his many cash gifts to the hospital and a large ward in the new wing was named the Iveagh Ward in appreciation of the Guinness donation.

One of the most memorable sights of Parnell Square is an indoor one, the chapel of the Rotunda, which was refloored in 1974. Here is arguably the best plasterwork in Dublin, executed by a French stuccodore, Bartholomew Cramillion. This really is the 'warm Baroque heart' of the Rotunda. The decoration flows on the exquisite ceiling, many of the figures being in high relief, and beautifully coloured, as they are in the altar piece and Allegory of Charity, which Cramillion completed in 1758.

Moore Lane

Facing the Rotunda in Parnell St, at the corner of cobbled Moore Lane, is the eighteenth-century tavern of Patrick Conway, its fine gold-painted nameboards, behind glass, topped by an ornate fringe of decorated spikes. Though the inn was founded in 1745, the facade is Victorian. The visitor may feel that an electric box sign at the corner of the building detracts somewhat from its character. Around the corner in Cavendish Row is Hawkins' tailor shop, another elegant timbered shopfront in traditional style. Dr Troy, Catholic archbishop of Dublin, lived in 3 Cavendish Row while the pro-Cathedral was being built.

The houses on the east side of Parnell (formerly Rutland) Square were all built by 1756, and the facing side was completed ten years later. On the east side, note the enormous, pillared door surrounds of numbers 10 and 11, the surviving wrought-iron framework of a large glass canopy at number 15, the episcopal crosses and the out-of-scale girth of two stone posts, like gateposts, outside number 4, where Cardinal McCabe lived in the 1870s and 1880s and which was the official residence of the Catholic archbishop of Dublin until 1890. Notice too the graceful outward curve of the iron railings at some houses, including number 5. This house is the birthplace of Oliver St John Gogarty, a surgeon who was also a novelist, playwright, poet, wit, aviator and athlete. Gogarty, who died in New York in 1957, was a friend of James Joyce, and he was the prototype of Buck Mulligan in *Ulysses*. He was born in 1878, and had a large practice as an ear, nose and throat specialist, besides being a member of the literary circle which included Joyce, Yeats and George Moore. He was a senator from 1922 to 1936,

Oliver St John Gogarty

and his autobiographical *As I Was Going Down Sackville Street* appeared in 1937.

The slope up this side of the square is dominated by the Abbey **Abbey** Presbyterian Church, with its clock tower and slender spire, which **Presbyterian** stands on the corner of the square's north side. This neo-Gothic church, **Church** built for a mere £20,000 and finished in 1864, is nearly always referred **'Findlater's** to as 'Findlater's Church'. There are many fine stone carvings on the **Church'** church, heads at the feet of window arches and others over the doorway, as well as demons and flowers. The Findlater of the name was Alex, a Scots grocer and brewer prominent in business here, who financed the church's building.

The rest of the north side of the square is occupied by schools, part **Gaelic League** of Coláiste Mhuire being the old Gaelic League building, and a dancehall, with the one notable exception of the striking building which **Municipal** now houses the Municipal Gallery of Modern Art. So striking is the **Gallery of** building that is once gave rise to the nickname of 'Palace Row' on this **Modern Art** side of the square. Known also as Charlemont House, it was built for the **Charlemont** earl of Charlemont between 1762 and 1765 to the design of Sir William **House** Chambers. Perhaps it is because of its grandeur, in a class apart from the other houses on the square, that we find John Ensor overlooked. Charlemont House, though magnificent, is statistically modest, with five bays and three storeys, flanked by curving screen walls with niches and balustrades, terminating in square lamps. There are four Ionic columns in the porch. Its fine interior is often taken for granted, hung as it is with art works.

Its present use is indeed fitting, as the earl for whom it was built was **Royal Irish** a keen patron of the arts and of literature. In 1785 he founded the Royal **Academy** Irish Academy, and his house was an important social and cultural centre, apart from gatherings there generated by his interest in politics. Among his friends were Henry Grattan, Edmund Burke, Sir Joshua Reynolds and Samuel Johnson. An indirect result of the building of Charlemont House was that the earl's old mansion, at number 14 Jervis St, was occupied by the Charitable Infirmary, and much later rebuilt as **Jervis St** Jervis St hospital.
hospital

Inside the railings at this end of Parnell Square is the Garden of **Garden of** Remembrance, commemorating Ireland's patriot dead. The modern **Remembrance** sculpture at its west end is by Oisin Kelly, and represents the Children of Lir, who, according to legend, were transformed into swans.

Parnell In the centre of Parnell St at the top of O'Connell St is the Parnell **monument** monument, with its message and gold harp, symbolic flame on top and the bronze figure of Parnell looking down the main thoroughfare. Charles Stewart Parnell was born in Wicklow in 1846, became an MP for Meath in 1875, became president of the Nationalist party in 1879, supported a policy of obstruction, encouraged the Land League and was imprisoned in 1881. He was one of the father-figures of modern Irish nationalism. An attempt by *The Times* in 1887 to implicate him in the Phoenix Park murders failed, but two years later a divorce scandal linking him with Kitty, wife of a Captain O'Shea, and his subsequent marriage to Kitty, led his party to depose him for fear of losing the support of Gladstone. Parnell is buried in Glasnevin cemetery, as is

Daniel O'Connell, the hero of Catholic emancipation. The Parnell monument is a triangular obelisk of polished salmon pink Galway stone. The statue was executed in the Roman Bronze Works, New York, by Augustus Saint-Gaudens, a Dubliner. If we follow the direction of Parnell's outstretched right arm up Parnell St, past the junctions with Dominick St and King's Inns St, we see the site of a second hospital in this street, Simpson's hospital, later a jam factory. It was a four-storey granite-fronted house facing the top of Jervis St, and from 1791 onward for more than a century, until its conversion to commercial use, it was a charitable institution, founded by a rich businessman for 'reduced gentlemen' suffering from failing eyesight, gout or both.

The hospital's inmates wore tall black felt hats and blue pilot cloth suits. It cost £6,500 to build, and occupied the site of a brick mansion, Rutland House, which had been demolished in 1787. At that time Parnell St, then Great Britain St, contained the residences of such wealthy men as Lord Mountgarret, the Earl of Altamont, Viscount St Leger and the Hon. A. Atcheson. The mansion that gave its site to Simpson's Hospital was vacated in 1775 by the Rutland family, who moved to Lower Mount St. The street was also noted for coachmakers, including Hutton's, the most famous Irish coachmakers, of whom Queen Victoria was a customer; but by her time they had moved eastward to Summerhill. Costello's, Coole's, Smyth's and Williams's were other leading coachbuilders here.

At number 59 Parnell St, near the corner of Moore St, is another fine surviving Victorian shopfront, that of Sullivan's, with a glass-fronted name-board between wooden consoles, sharp, slender gold lettering and scrollwork on the house numbers. An oval plaque below the ornamented top of the redbrick house gives its date, 1889. Such facades are becoming rare. Around the corner Moore St contains most of Dublin's surviving outdoor food stalls, full of people, colour, motion, and noise. Many butchers' shops are still here, though most of the west side of the street has been demolished. Adventurous Victorian styles of brick building persist among the surviving houses. Plunkett's shop, more than half way down towards Henry St on the left, has a curved brick top and a plaque with the date 1876; across the road, over a shop on the corner of Sampson's Lane, a pair of windows surmounted by carved heads and festoons can be seen in a front-gabled house, and a little further down a bar is housed in a narrow front-gabled house of five storeys and Flemish inspiration.

The part of Parnell St between the tops of Moore St and O'Connell St has revolutionary connections. Patrick Pearse surrendered to General Lowe at the top of Moore St after the Easter Rising of 1916, some of the first prisoners laid down their arms at the Parnell Monument, and some spent their first night in custody in the open, behind the railings of the Rotunda Hospital. The Round Room, three years before that, had been the venue of the first meeting of the Irish Volunteers.

O'Connell St is absolutely straight, but is saved from the mathematical dullness this sometimes entails by its width of 150 feet. Along its centre are forty trees and four monuments, if we exclude that

Jervis St

Parnell St

Moore St

O'Connell St

to Parnell. When Gardiner laid out Gardiner's Mall in 1750, trees, as the name suggests, were a prominent feature, and there was a row of obelisks along each side. Fashionable Georgian houses were built then in what is now called Upper O'Connell St, and the Catholic Commercial Club building, just below the Royal Dublin hotel, is a surviving clue to what it looked like. Below the present Henry St corner was a narrower street, a continuation of the earlier Drogheda St. In Upper O'Connell St the taste for ornamentation lingers in the four great green iron bollards below the Parnell Monument, which look like an outsize condiment set. Going down the middle of the street, the first statue is that of Fr Mathew, erected in 1890 as a centenary memorial to this famous temperance crusader. Further down, at the Abbey St crossing, are two white monuments, one on a limestone plinth to Sir John Gray, and the other, below it, on a granite plinth to William Smith O'Brien. Gray, who lived from 1815 to 1875, was the owner of the *Freeman's Journal* newspaper, and was MP for the city of Kilkenny. The reason for his commemoration, however, is that he was, from 1863 until his death, chairman of the Dublin Corporation waterworks committee which introduced the Vartry water supply to the city and its suburbs. Smith O'Brien, a nationalist, lived from 1803 to 1864, surviving a death sentence for treason imposed on him in 1848.

Upper O'Connell St

**O'Connell
Bridge**

At the bottom of the street, fronted by seats facing out over O'Connell Bridge, is the big monument to Daniel O'Connell, the Liberator, after whom the street was renamed from Sackville St, and the bridge from Carlisle Bridge. Topped by a commanding bronze figure of O'Connell, the monument is the work of Irish sculptor John Henry Foley, and was erected in 1854, the foundation stone laid by Mr John Power, the distiller of one of Ireland's best-known whiskeys. Around the drum are the arms of the four Irish provinces and 30 figures executed by Foley, the central one, a female figure, representing Eire or Ireland, with a harp. In her left hand is a copy of the Catholic Emancipation Act of 1829. The other figures are drawn from various aspects of O'Connell's life. The four winged figures seated around the monument are often mistaken for angels, but are the four Victories, and they represent Courage, Eloquence, Fidelity and Patriotism as qualities of the Liberator. The winged Victory facing toward the Ulster Bank will be seen to have a bullet hole in her right breast, a legacy of fighting at some time between 1916 and 1922.

There is a small religious shrine under a tree in Upper O'Connell St, opposite the junction with Cathal Brugha St. It contains a statue of the Sacred Heart, and for many years the shrine has been tended by taxi drivers. In the days of Gardiner's Mall this part of the street had a strip of grass down the centre.

The fighting between 1916 and 1922 left the street largely in ruins, and considerable rebuilding was done in the 1920s, some in the style then known as 'modern'. While this has been criticised as unworthy of the main street, O'Connell St, it still has much to offer. Near Henry St on the west side, there are the slender brown Corinthian columns in the Northern Bank. The six columns are crowned by a pediment with a fine carved group of figures in the tympanum, but the ground floor of the bank has been modernised, so that it is possible for a casual passerby to miss the nineteenth-century part above. The dominant building on the

Gresham Hotel

east side of Upper O'Connell St is the Gresham Hotel, with its incongruous stone sphinxes, which now extends back to Marlborough St and is totally different from the building it replaced. The canopy replaces a more elegant glass one with a scalloped finish. The hotel dignifies an otherwise rather dull block. Below the Gresham is the Savoy cinema, built in 1929 as the biggest 'picture house' in Ireland. Directly facing it is the 1937 Carlton, one of the more thoughtful pieces of cinematic architecture. Below the Savoy, the very ordinary-looking Hammam Buildings, containing civil service offices, perpetuate in their name the Hammam Hotel, in and around which fighting took place.

**General Post
Office**

O'Connell St is dominated by the massive General Post Office, designed by Francis Johnston and always known in Dublin by its initial letters. This is where the 1916 Rising began on Easter Monday, when Patrick Pearse read the Proclamation of the Irish Republic from outside the building. It is regarded by many as the physical birthplace of the modern Irish state. Reviewing stands for parades are erected here, and for many years political parties have held final election rallies outside the GPO, while other politically-oriented groups use the location for meetings.

The building is 223 feet wide and 50 feet tall, to the top of the cornice. When it was built in 1815 it was 150 feet deep. The portico is 80 feet long, and the pediment is supported by six massive fluted Ionic pillars. The three statues by John Smyth on top of the GPO represent Hibernia, with spear and harp, Mercury, holding a purse, and Fidelity. The building, apart from the Portland stone portico, is of mountain granite. There is a balustrade around the top of the cornice, giving the place an elegant finish. In the tympanum of the pediment, the stonework was originally decorated with the British royal arms, and their removal has not been quite complete. Mortar marks remain, and the outline of the imperial decoration is clearly visible from the street below. Nevertheless, the absence of this central decoration leaves the building with a vaguely bare look, as the rest of it is unusually plain for a construction of its size, especially a classical one. Protruding from the facade are two huge octagonal lamps on long, stout brackets. Between them, a clock is surmounted by a gold harp, and below this a legend records the 1916 Rising. At the feet of the pillars, which are at the extremity of the pathway, are six enormous iron studs, and there is a curious octagonal iron bollard at each end of the portico. Inside the post office, one is struck by a preponderance of green and red marble in an otherwise functional setting. The centrepiece of the main office is a memorial of the Rising, a bronze statue by Oliver Sheppard of the dying Cuchulainn, leader of the Red Branch Knights in Irish mythology, with a raven on his shoulder. On the statue's green marble plinth the Proclamation of 1916 and the names of its signatories are reproduced. A large octagonal writing table in front of the statue has a faintly martial motif, smaller decorations being feline heads, and larger ones resembling Roman shields.

The site of the GPO had lain bare since 1796, after demolition for widening of what was then Drogheda St, and the Catholic ecclesiastical authorities had decided to buy it, to build the church which is now the pro-Cathedral in Marlborough St. But fear of a Protestant backlash at the sight of a Catholic church in such a prominent position dissuaded them.

The pro-Cathedral

By the time the GPO came to be built, the site's importance had been enhanced by the building of Nelson Pillar in the centre of the road, between Henry St and Earl St. This monument stood on its fortress-like cube of a pedestal from 1808 until 1966. Its building had been financed largely by merchant shippers and it was a graceful Doric column, designed by William Wilkins of Norwich under the supervision of Francis Johnston. A trek up the 134 steps of its spiral stone staircase to the viewing platform below the statue of Lord Nelson was standard procedure for visitors to Dublin who felt energetic enough, and the best view of the city was available from it, there being then no taller building in the vicinity.

The Pillar was the source of considerable controversy. Ranged against those who claimed that it added dignity and vitality to O'Connell St were those who complained that it was a traffic hazard or that it was politically objectionable. The more vigorous proponents of the latter view got their way by simply blowing it up in the small hours

Some

of a March morning in 1966. The present garden layout has exactly the same significance to the traffic flow as the Pillar had.

Below the GPO, the British Home Stores, with a functional grey marbled facade and canopy, replaces both the Metropole cinema and ballroom and the ornate Capitol cinema. The Metropole in turn replaced the Metropole Hotel, and the Capitol was earlier the La Scala opera house. Below the BHS, Eason's shopfront, with red marble pillars and steps, is a tasteful 1919 construction. Towards the bottom of this side of the street we notice a tall, pale green building whose gracefully curved top could be in Amsterdam. It contains an old clock, oddly marked with compass points, which are totally inaccurate.

Across the road, the domed Ulster Bank, with its pillars and heavy balcony, looks extravagantly Victorian, but it bears the date 1923. Above it, on either side of Lower Abbey St junction, are two pleasantly ornate buildings, one a bank and one the office of the Irish Permanent Building Society, the latter adorned with a balustrade and carved heads; its interior is equally impressive. Both these buildings are surmounted by corner turrets, as is the Irish Press office across the street.

Going up the street, the bulk of Clery's store, with white engaged pillars in fluted Ionic, and eleven quarter spheres of biscuit-coloured awning along the front and more down the side, adds strength to the scene. Part of Clery's site accommodated the Imperial Hotel, from one of whose windows Jim Larkin, the Irish labour leader, best known for the general strike of 1913, addressed the workers.

Middle Abbey St

Going west along Middle Abbey St we pass the imposing premises of Independent Newspapers. This is the site of the old *Nation* newspaper, founded by Thomas Davis. Beyond it is the 1939 Adelphi cinema. Further on, we turn off Upper Abbey St to the right and are outside Jervis St hospital, a redbrick cliff with classical timber-framed fanlights over two great doorways, once regarded as a skyscraper. In a sense the hospital is Dublin's oldest, having been in continuous existence since 1718, though not on the same site. It was founded by six surgeons as the Charitable Infirmary in Cook St, across the Liffey, quickly outgrew its premises and transferred to a house on Inns Quay in 1728. The birthplace of Sir Patrick Dun, founder of another Dublin hospital, was next door to this house. When the Earl of Charlemont moved from his residence at 14 Jervis St it was taken over by the infirmary, but this seems to have retained its Inns Quay premises for a few years, probably until the building of the Four Courts, and the Jervis St house seems not to have been fully altered for hospital use until 1796. In 1854 the internal management and nursing were taken over by the Sisters of Mercy, and in 1877, as the old mansion began to crumble, the rebuilding which led to the present hospital began, accelerated by the need to adapt to new treatments and new legislation. By 1906 the hospital was treating about 1,400 patients in the wards and 25,000 in its dispensary annually.

Jervis St hospital

Wolfe Tone Park St Mary's church

Facing the front of the hospital is Wolfe Tone Park, and the street that runs along the park's other side, formerly Stafford St, is now called Wolfe Tone St after the patriot, who was born there, in number 44, on 20 June 1763. The park is the former burial ground of St Mary's church, which adjoins it in Mary St. This seventeenth-century building became the parish church of St Mary in 1697 when St Michan's parish was divided in three, due to a population influx into the area. St Mary's took over its eastern extremity and St Paul's in North King St, its western end. After that St Mary's became the north side's most fashionable parish. In the Mary St church were baptised Richard Brinsley Sheridan in 1751, Theobald Wolfe Tone in 1763, Sir William Rowan Hamilton, the renowned mathematician, in 1805 and playwright Sean O'Casey in 1880, not forgetting the Earl of Charlemont in 1728. Arthur Guinness and Ann Lee were married in it in 1793: the 'Lee' we find in Sir Benjamin Lee Guinness's name was thus introduced to the brewing family. Dean Swift was a visitor to the church, and John Wesley preached there in 1747. Thomas Brinsley Sheridan and Lord Norbury are buried in what is now the park, as are Mrs Mercer, foundress of Mercer's Hospital across the river, and Mrs Simpson, one of the founders of Simpson's Hospital, already mentioned. Lord Norbury was a judge who boasted that he had begun his legal career with a brace of

pistols and £50. His family had come to Ireland with Cromwell. His Lordship voted for the Act of Union in 1800 and after that, as Chief Justice, his unionist zeal proved too much for his judicial impartiality. The church has box pews, a fine galleried interior and carvings on the organ case of early eighteenth-century figures. In its east end is a large ornate window with Baroque scroll adornments, but the Georgian doorway in the west front is a later addition.

Mary St

Turning back along Mary St towards O'Connell St one sees on the left, over Penney's store, a magnificent Victorian brick front with terracotta mouldings, one of which, a circular one, has been defaced by piercing the centre of it with the end of an advertising sign bracket.

Capel St

The west end of Mary St leads into Capel St, which runs from the river up to Bolton St, forty feet wide and with a leisurely, old-world air, despite the crowds. Some of the shops add to this atmosphere, such as Brereton's, with its gold-painted pawnbroker sign, antique front and jewellery showcase on the footpath. Most of Capel St was originally built between 1675 and 1710 and peat, called turf in Ireland, was sometimes used as a building material. Brereton's stands up from the corner of Little Britain St – so named because Parnell St was Great Britain St.

Lower Dominick St

Going up Capel St and along Bolton St we come to Lower Dominick St on the right. The newer buildings of the priory, carefully matching the Gothic original nearby, are visible from beyond the corner. A short way down the street on the left is the Dominican church of St Saviour, one of the better examples of the neo-Gothic of the second half of the last century. The church and priory were designed by J. J. McCarthy, sometimes called the 'Irish Pugin', and the church was begun in 1858 and opened for worship in 1861. It has a fine rose window in its west front, and good carvings, a pleasant nave and a graceful east end reached by a side passage. The front originally had four slender spires, purely decorative, but an extension to its lower side included a fifth. The asymmetry created by the addition makes it less than perfect, and the profusion of small spires qualifies it for the description of 'spiky' Gothic.

Four doors below the church is the superb five-bay Georgian house which now accommodates St Saviour's orphanage for boys. From 1857 until 1926 this was a Church of Ireland school for St Mary's parish, but it was originally the home of Robert West, stuccodore and builder. West built the house for himself in about 1753, and decorated it with some of Dublin's finest plasterwork, which is still intact. Walls and ceilings are lavishly ornamented with mouldings, which include slender birds' necks protruding 17 inches from the base.

William Rowan Hamilton was born in number 36 Lower Dominick St on 4 August 1805. When aged 12 he compiled a Syriac grammar, and the following year, when he was proficient in Sanskrit, Persian, Arabic, Hindustani and other languages, his father complained of the difficulty he experienced in finding Chinese books in Dublin for his son. In 1843 Sir William discovered quaternions, while walking with his wife near Broomebridge, on the Royal Canal.

Joseph Sheridan le Fanu was born in number 45 Lower Dominick

St in 1814, and was a grandnephew of Richard Brinsley Sheridan. As well as writing of the supernatural he owned the *Evening Mail* newspaper. His first novel, *The Cock and Anchor*, was set in Dublin, and *The House by the Churchyard*, one of the sources of Joyce's *Finnegans Wake*, in Chapelizod, just up the Liffey from the city.

Number 12 Upper Dorset St, birthplace of Richard Brinsley Sheridan, is around the corner from Dominick St in the opposite direction to Bolton St, and adjoins the priory. After his departure to Harrow at the age of eleven, Sheridan never returned to Dublin. The house bears a commemorative plaque, but for many years the brass plate of a window cleaning firm has been rather more prominent.

Proceeding along this street, past the redbrick fire station, we come to the corner of St Mary's Place on the left, where we see the striking needle spire of John Semple's chapel of ease for St Mary's, colloquially called the 'Black Church', as its dark calpstone gives it a black hue after rain. Semple also designed churches in Monkstown and Rathmines. His St Mary's Place work, built in 1829–39, has unified walls and ceiling, giving a beautiful parabolic curve to the interior. **'Black Church'**

Around the corner from here, in Mountjoy St, is the unpretentious brown brick convent of the Irish Sisters of Charity, which includes an orphanage and has a fine entrance. Poet Austin Clarke spent some of his boyhood in this street, and his autobiography, *Twice Round the Black Church*, recalls in its title a local superstition about meeting the devil if one walked around this church, which happens to be on an island in the roadway, a certain number of times. In this tradition, the number of circuits required for the apparition varies from person to person, three, seven and ten being quoted, three being the favourite.

21

Trinity College, west front

2 Learning, Civility and True Religion

Trinity College — Bank of Ireland — College Green — St Andrew's church — Pearse St — Westland Row church and station — Kildare St club — Provost's house.

Here lies our good Edmund whose genius was such
We scarcely could praise it or blame it too much.

— Goldsmith, proposed epitaph for Burke.

College Green

College Green was originally called Hoggen Green, and lay to the east of the medieval walled city. In the Middle Ages a great pageant was enacted here each year on the feast of Corpus Christi by the city's craft guilds. A stage was erected on the green and religious plays were performed, each trade taking the parts best suited to it, fishermen being the Apostles, mariners dealing with Noah's Ark, butchers acting as tormentors. The nearest city gate to the green was Dame's Gate at Cork Hill, and Hoggen Green remained common pasture until the seventeenth century. Two Augustinian establishments adjoined it: All Hallows Priory was to the east, where Trinity College now is; and the convent of St Mary de Hogge to the south, at the top of Trinity St, formerly known as Nunnery Lane. The priory was founded in 1166 by Dermot McMurrough, king of Leinster. Its steeple became a landmark for navigators, and stood between the present west front of Trinity and

Trinity College

the college's campanile. Trinity College itself is another royal foundation, that of Elizabeth I, and dates from 1592, the first stone being laid on 13 March 1592, the site of the suppressed priory being a gift from the Corporation. The first students arrived in the college in 1594.

In the time of James II, the college finances were poor, and Archbishop William King writes of an incident in 1689 when 'King James and his party . . . seized upon the furniture, books and public library, together with the chapel, communion-plate and all things belonging to the college . . . In the house they placed a Popish garrison, turned the chapel into a magazine, and many of the chambers into a prison for Protestants.' He also gloomily recorded that they turned out the vice-provost, fellows and scholars.

For many years Trinity College was regarded as exclusively Protestant, and even as a forcing ground for proselytes. According to its Elizabethan charter, it was founded for 'the planting of learning, the increasing of civility, and the establishing of true religion within the realm'. True religion in this context meant Protestantism, and in the years before the Cromwellian occupation, the population of Dublin was two-thirds Protestant, so that the rest of the country saw it as a Protestant stronghold, and Trinity College became accepted as a mainspring of Puritan Dublin thought. The provosts were appointed by the crown. In the mid-nineteenth century the college was much frequented by English students because of its cheapness, the permission of non-residence, and the admissibility of 'dissenters'.

The Rubrics

The visitor to Trinity will find no physical traces of the Elizabethan foundation, the oldest part of today's college being a row of Queen Anne buildings, used as residences, called the Rubrics. These were begun in 1700. On 10 January of that year Queen Anne signed a warrant granting £3,000 to the college, money which had been raised by increasing the duty on tobacco. The college authorities used it as a building fund, along with £1,200 bequeathed to them by George Browne, a former provost. The present redbrick buildings are the survivors of three ranges of such residences. Originally the Rubrics, which we see facing us in the distance behind the campanile as we enter the college grounds from under the west front, had a central arch which

Trinity College, the old and the new

College Park

New Square

Edmund Burke
Oliver
Goldsmith

led to College Park. Three bays at each end are missing, having been demolished about 1840, and the attractive Dutch-style gables, strongly reminiscent of Queen Anne times, are in fact 1890s replacements of the original dormer windows. The east side of this range of buildings, facing into the part of College Park that became New Square, has had a coat of concrete dashing. Yet much of the character of the original Rubrics remains, especially in the narrowness of the windows.

Beginning at the front of the college, in College Green, we have a graceful curve of railings around lawns on which stand statues of Burke and Goldsmith by John Henry Foley. This space was leased by the college from the Corporation in the 1680s for half a crown (12½p) a year, and 'a couple of fat capons at Christmas yearly to the Lord Mayor'. A condition of the lease was that railings be erected on both sides.

Although Burke and Goldsmith were contemporaries at Trinity and were almost of the same age — Burke having been born in 1729 and Goldsmith in 1728 — they were not friends at college: indeed they may not have been even acquainted. Yet they became close friends in later life, and were both original members of the 'Literary Club' that grew from meetings in the house of Sir Joshua Reynolds in London in 1764. Edmund Burke, whose statue is on the left as one faces the entrance of the college, settled in London in 1750, and first won literary fame six years later with his *Essay on the Sublime and Beautiful* and *Vindication of Natural Society*. Oliver Goldsmith was the second son of Rev. Charles Goldsmith, a parson whom he later described in his poem, *The Deserted Village*, and was born in Co. Longford. Less than two years after Oliver's birth, the family moved to Lissoy, Co. Westmeath, possibly the original of 'Sweet Auburn', and some scenes depicted in *The Vicar of Wakefield*.

The west front of Trinity, behind these statues, has been described as the only piece of monumental collegiate architecture in these islands, apart from the front of Christ Church, Oxford. Its design has often been wrongly attributed to Sir William Chambers, and Dr Edward McParland, arts lecturer, suggests that the attribution of it to Henry Keene and John Sanderson of London is wrong. Its real architect, he believes, was Theodore Jacobsen, amateur architect of the London Foundling Hospital. If the Trinity west front is indeed amateur architecture, it is not unique as such in Dublin. The pro-Cathedral in Marlborough St was designed by an amateur. Trinity's front is one of the finest Palladian facades in these islands; Dr McParland allows for the possibility that Keene and Sanderson provided the working drawings for it from a design submitted by the amateur. There is no record of payment to Jacobsen, and that would be consistent with his amateur status. However, there is record of payment to the other architects. At either end of the front are pavilions with Venetian windows and festoons, and balustrades. While construction was going on between 1752 and 1760, it was suggested that cupolas be erected over these, and that a dome should crown the central projection. A cupola was erected over the north pavilion in 1756 and demolished in 1759. Preparations were also made for the dome. These, as Dr McParland points out, can be seen in the masonry piers of the octagonal entrance vestibule. By 1758, however, their continuation into the floor above was demolished, and replaced by the present graceful room known as the Regent House.

Going through the vestibule and entering Parliament Square, with its lawns and the cobblestones beyond, one discovers that the east facade, or 'back', of the west front is similar to the other side, with a central projection, Corinthian engaged columns and pilasters, and pediment with clock in the tympanum. The buildings on either side as we face the campanile have unadorned shallow central projections, but end in deeper projections, each with a Corinthian portico, which face each other and narrow the square. That on the left is the chapel, that on the right the examination hall, originally the public theatre. These buildings were designed by Sir William Chambers, and they mark the limit of the formal classicism of the Trinity layout. They are similar, but not identical, buildings. Each has a low-slung barrel-vaulted ceiling, and each has plasterwork by the celebrated firm of Michael Stapleton. The theatre, or examination hall, was completed about 1785. Christopher Myers was the executive architect for Chambers never came to Dublin. Work on the chapel went on from 1787 until 1800, under Graham Myers, Christopher's son.

Parliament Square

the Chapel the examination hall

Trinity College, the 1937 Science Reading Room

Midway between the classical fronts of the chapel and examination hall was once a five-storey bell tower erected by Richard Cassels, and the campanile is the natural successor to this centrepiece.

the campanile

The campanile was erected in 1852 to the design of Charles Lanyon, though the bell tower, along with an old hall and chapel, had been demolished almost 60 years earlier. Beyond the campanile is Library

Library Square

Square, with its antique lamp standards, its shaven lawns and big Oregon maple trees, and the massive block of Burgh's 1712 library on its south side, its severe, granite-fronted upper storeys and long balustrade contrasting sharply with its near-contemporaries, the Rubrics, at the eastern end of the square. In a Dublin context, not merely a Trinity one, this is a notable building. Thomas Burgh built it with £15,000, the money coming in three equal parliamentary grants in 1711, 1717 and 1722.

the library

Burgh planned it to house, as well as the library, an observatory, philosophy school, librarian's room and manuscript room. In 1860 Deane and Woodward made considerable alterations to the building. The foundation stone of the library was laid on 12 May 1712. The dark limestone ground floor originally had open arcades along its north and south sides, and the upper storeys were of white sandstone. The sandstone was later covered in granite, and the arcades were glazed in the 1890s, probably to avoid pneumonia among the students, who would tend to gather more in the bleaker 'inner' one, that with the northerly aspect. The main room in the building is 210 feet long, 41 feet broad, and was 40 feet high even before Deane and Woodward considerably raised the level of the ceiling. The room was originally divided into one tier of compartments by oak partitions, each terminated by fluted Corinthian pilasters. Above these ran a cornice and carved oak balustrade, which formed the front of a gallery that ran all around the room. It was called the grandest room in Ireland, and was the biggest library reading room in Europe. Deane and Woodward left the lower part as it was, but removed the flat ceiling, inserted more transverse book compartments above the cornice, and gave the room a high, barrel-vaulted timber ceiling, springing from the tops of the new compartments, in neo-Romanesque style. This explains the high pitch of the building's roof. What had been huge now became immense. This room is the usual home of the Book of Kells, and the Books of Durrow and Armagh. The pilasters are fronted by facing rows of busts, including one of Dean Swift. The original fourteen of these are by Peter Scheemakers, and others are by Vierpyl and Roubilliac. Beside the library is another, modern, library, designed by Paul Koralek, who also designed the new Arts block in the Fellows' Garden. **Book of Kells**

Arts block

Beyond the library, and on the south side of New Square, with its several trees, is the museum building, designed by Deane and Woodward and erected in 1854 by Gilbert Cockburne and Sons, builders, for £24,000. This beautiful building, with grouped windows and tall chimneys rising from the edges of the roof, owes its design to the influence of John Ruskin. The style was often called Ruskinian, and also referred to as 'fenestral architecture' because of its insistence that windows should be the dominant features in buildings of merit. The Trinity museum building led to Woodward's Lombardo–Venetian style being copied in other parts of Dublin. He later designed the Kildare Street Club and also a museum, debating hall and curator's house at Oxford, all of which led Ruskin to describe this Corkman as 'the only architect in Europe'. But Benjamin Woodward, who was born in 1815 and died in 1861, when his partnership with Thomas Deane was in its tenth year, was ably assisted in his work at Trinity, Kildare St and Oxford by two other Corkonians. **the Museum building**

These were the O'Shea brothers, James and Richard, stone carvers. The very detailed carvings in the museum's interior comprise their work and that of a Mr Roe of Lambeth, London. The hall with its twin staircases is decidedly Moorish, slim marble pillars supporting spreading capitals with bold leaf designs, the arches having broad stripes of alternating shades, spaces between arch and wall being filled with mosaics, as are the surrounds of domes. The outside of the building is adorned with medallions of marble, in rows, and those on the ground floor are copied from the Ducal Palace in Venice, those on the upper storey from the Palazzo Dario. The originals of these were illustrated in the first volume of Ruskin's *Stones of Venice*.

With this delightful building and the back of the Rubrics forming two sides of New Square, the remaining sides are filled by two long unassuming granite buildings, similar to each other and erected in the 1830s by Frederick Darley, then resident college architect. Darley also designed a Greek Doric pavilion called the magnetic observatory, which has been taken down and transferred to the grounds of University College, Dublin. Partly overlooked by his New Square buildings was the temple-like printing house of Richard Cassels, which was designed **printing house** in 1734 and built in the following two years. This has a Tuscan portico and, in keeping with this classicism, it produced in 1738 the first book totally in Greek to be printed in Ireland, an edition of Plato's *Dialogues*.

Graduates' Memorial Building

Botany Bay

Re-entering Library Square on the north side, we pass the front of a long grey building in fine Elizabethan style, with tall chimneys. It is the Graduates' Memorial Building, designed by Sir Thomas Drew of the Royal Hibernian Academy and erected before 1900, about the same time as the science buildings went up at the east end of College Park. Behind the memorial building is an area called Botany Bay, whose tennis courts are overlooked on two sides by long, monotonous four-storey blocks of limestone apartments. The site was formerly the kitchen garden, balancing the fellows' garden behind the library, now the site of the Arts block, and work on the new students' quarters went on from the mid-1780s until about 1815. At one time it was proposed to abandon the residential scheme in favour of an examination hall in Botany Bay, but this came to nothing. Neither did a suggestion to build the Wellington Monument, now in the Phoenix Park, in College Park, although this was seriously considered in 1814. In 1775 public access to this park 'from the town' had been barred by Provost Hely Hutchinson on the grounds that it had become a 'public walk for company of the lowest and worst kind'. The company referred to was obviously unfit for students who were allowed to play cards on Christmas Day only.

the dining hall

Set back between the memorial building and the chapel at the north-west corner of Library Square is the dining hall, with a facade that looks like a smaller, modified version of the college's west front, with four Ionic pilasters and a clock in the tympanum. This is not the dining hall of Cassels. His was demolished after a series of mishaps during and after its slow building. A storm blew down part of it in 1744, and three years later some vaults collapsed. This happened again in 1758, when the foundations of an adjoining kitchen were being laid, and the entire building was condemned and taken down. The replacement was designed by Hugh Darley, who was supervising the bigger work in College Green at the time, hence the similarity. Some of the material from the demolished hall was used, including a great fireplace surround in black Kilkenny marble, which Cassels had had carved by David Sheehan. Simple but striking, this was salvaged from the dining room of the old building and fitted in the common room of the new one, which is over the entrance. It is still there. The more ornate and less attractive white marble one in the new dining room is by George Darley. Dr McParland says that this cost £55 15s. 8d. in 1765, and that this included £8 for a Carlow marble tombstone laid as a hearthstone.

Bank of Ireland

The noble limestone and granite facade of Trinity College looks across College Green and a little to its right to an even more imposing Portland stone one, that of the Bank of Ireland, formerly the Irish parliament house. This is one of the finest buildings in Ireland. The grand portico facing College Green is 147 feet in extent, and has 22 Ionic pillars, 16 of them free-standing. The tympanum of the central pediment bears the royal arms, and over its apex is a figure of Hibernia, with those of Commerce and Fidelity on the right and left respectively.

The middle door under this portico led, in the days when it was a parliament house, directly into the House of Commons, passing through a large hall known as the Court of Requests. The Commons comprised a circle 55 feet in diameter, within a square of walls. Seating was in concentric circles, rising from the centre. An elaborate central dome was supported by 16 Corinthian columns.

Bank of Ireland from College St

A narrow public gallery, described as 'handsome' in old accounts, ran between these pillars, and an ornamented corridor connected by three doors with the committee room, coffee room and other facilities. The House of Lords, which is largely unaltered, still has its Corinthian columns at each end, is 73 feet long and 30 feet wide, with a fine barrel-vaulted, coffered ceiling. Two large tapestries on the walls represent the Battle of the Boyne and the Siege of Derry, and are still well preserved, even to their colouring. These were hung in 1735 by John van Beaver and his staff, working for the firm of Robert Baillie, and we are told that it took one man one month to weave a square foot of this tapestry. The bill to the Lords was £436 6s. 8d. In a recess at one end of the room is the speaker's mace from the old Commons, silver with gold plating, and over a long table, replacing that at which the Lords deliberated, is an exquisite glass chandelier, also a relic of parliamentary days. Both the chandelier and mace had been sold into private ownership, and were bought back by the governors of the bank at an auction in London in 1931.

House of Lords

The old Commons room is now the bank's cash office. It has undergone two important alterations, the first by Vincent Waldré. In 1792 a fire destroyed the dome. The present cash office was executed by Francis Johnston between 1803 and 1808. The bank brought with it new names, and the original Lords became the Court of Proprietors. In a room called the La Touche room, after the Right Hon. David La Touche, who became first governor of the Bank of Ireland — formerly the La Touche bank — in 1783, is an exquisite Venus ceiling attributed to the Francini brothers, Paul and Philip, who brought to Ireland this kind of rococo plasterwork in 1739, taking over from the late Louis XIV style then still being executed here.

Foster Place

On the bank's west side is a cul-de-sac called Foster Place, where trees grow in the cobbled roadway, their bases surrounded by granite circles. Here we pass under the bank's west portico, also Ionic and tetrastyle, and originally one of James Gandon's designs, though it was actually executed by Robert Park in 1797, and his plans were said to have been partly the work of an MP for Maryborough (now Portlaoise) called Samuel Hayes. Across the road from it is the smaller portico of the Allied Irish Bank, surmounted by a balustrade and six urns. The western extremity of the Bank of Ireland closes this street, and over it is a magnificent carved trophy of cannon guns.

Thomas Burgh, designer of the Trinity library, sometimes is credited with the original design of the parliament house. But work began on it under his successor in the surveyor-general's chair, Edward Lovett Pearce, in 1729. Lovett Pearce was given a knighthood in 1732, died the following year, and is usually spoken of as the main architect of what is now the Bank of Ireland. One school of thought persistently claims that Richard Cassels was the designer, and that his plans were plagiarised or stolen by Lovett Pearce. Some of the pillars in the House of Lords are wooden; Cassels used wood to simulate masonry when he decorated a hall in Burgh's library, but that was in 1750. Thomas Sadleir, who made a study of the Cassels theory, credited Lovett Pearce with the design, pointing out that he had visited Italy and had produced drawings with his own hand. But Mr and Mrs S. C. Hall, writing of their Irish travels in the mid-nineteenth century, complain that the identity of the building's architect is 'wrapt in obscurity almost approaching to mystery'. According to them, it was at that time usually attributed to a 'Mr Cassell or Castell'. And they quote from Harris's History of Dublin that it was executed 'under the inspection' of Sir Edward Lovett Pearce, and completed by his successor as surveyor-general, Arthur Dodds, in 1739.

There is no confusion, however, about the later addition of an east portico of the bank in Westmoreland St. It was done by James Gandon in the Corinthian style and is surmounted by figures of Fortitude, Justice and Liberty. Gandon was commissioned in 1785 to create here a 'more convenient' entrance to the House of Lords for the peers. He has often been criticised for departing from the Ionic order already existing on the building, and creating a mish-mash of styles, especially as his plan for the west portico had conformed to the earlier order. It is more likely, however, that the peers, having decided to distinguish themselves with a separate entrance, insisted that the distinction be emphasised by the richer order of capitals. The Ionic engaged columns were added to the bank's curving screen wall by Francis Johnston in 1803.

Henry Grattan is the statesman whose name is best remembered from the Irish parliament of College Green. His bronze statue now stands, arm upraised, in the roadway opposite. Like those of Goldsmith and Burke outside Trinity, which it faces, it is by John Henry Foley. Below the statue there stands a pair of elegant iron brown-painted lamposts on concave triangular bases, each lamp adorned with three seahorses and each side of the bases with the city arms and a shamrock. Grattan was born in Dublin in 1746 and entered the parliament that became known as 'Grattan's parliament' in 1775. Through his able campaigning as leader of the opposition, the claims of the British parliament to legislate for Ireland were withdrawn in 1782, although the Act of Union, nineteen years later, set his life's work at nought.

A little further up College Green is Edward Delaney's modern and controversial statue of Thomas Davis, poet and patriot of the Young Ireland movement and a founder of the *Nation* newspaper. The statue is roughly on the site of an ill-fated equestrian one of William of Orange. This was given a coat of black paint soon after the abortive rebellion of Robert Emmet in 1803. Before that it was customary for Orangemen to adorn it with orange lilies, and for Catholics to deface it. Two Trinity students were once fined £100 and jailed for six months each for the latter activity. The statue was blown up in 1836 but restored, and blown up, this time conclusively, in 1929.

Dame St

The buildings of College Green facing the Bank of Ireland, and further west into Dame St, have a pleasant polychromatic range, yellow, red, grey and pink. From the remarkable fussy angles of a yellow sandstone building on the corner of Grafton St we come to the broad front of the old National Bank, built in 1842 and now a branch of the Bank of Ireland, with its two iron balconies, one very long. Over the building a headless figure of Ireland sits with harp and wolfhound. Below her are engraved the words 'Eire go brath' (Ireland forever), and below that again two coronets and three shamrocks. The patriotic slogan is piquantly placed opposite the royal arms on the erstwhile parliament house. The tall classical facade of the Ulster Bank adjoins this building.

Church Lane

At the top of Church Lane is the rather cumbersome Gothic church of St Andrew, with its arcade and dominant spire. There are St Andrew's churches of both major persuasions. This Protestant one is a design by Charles Lanyon, begun in 1860 and finished in 1873. The nunnery of St Mary de Hogge was here, and across the road, in what is now the angle of Suffolk St and Church Lane, earlier stood the Thingmote, the ceremonial meeting place of the Vikings, a mound 40 feet tall and 224 feet in circumference, on which laws were promulgated. Henry II met the Irish chiefs on it in 1172, and he possibly later had a palace built there. In 1661 the Bishop of Meath, Dr Jones, leased the mound, which was still standing, from Dublin Corporation, but that body cut it down to fill in the marshy Patrickswell Lane, now Nassau St, and left him with level ground. Inside the railings of St Andrew's a crowned marble monument commemorates a more recent matter, the deaths of members of the 74th (Dublin) company of the Imperial Yeomanry in the Boer War.

In College Green, beyond Church Lane, we find another large Victorian building, the Ulster Bank, and beyond it a red sandstone bank which will recall the Romanesque cathedral in Worms to anyone who has been there, by its circular tower. This terminates in a black candlesnuffer top; there are engaged Corinthian columns, festoons, a dormer window, a balustrade and a very tall sandstone chimney, extended in brick. The interior of this rich specimen is a glorious example of the solid wooden furnishings used by Victorian bankers to inspire the confidence of depositors. Bank failures were not unknown in Dublin. The top of the tower balances an octagonal grey turret of 1890 over the Pen Corner at Trinity St, and in between the Guinness, Mahon bank is a strong, five-bay brick building in a modified Queen Anne style. Across the street, at number 52 Dame St, there is a small-paned bay window, with concave side panels, extending for two storeys.

Crow St

Crow St, a turn to the left below this, was the site of a school of medicine attached to the Catholic university. The school occupied the site, at the Dame St end of Crow St, of another Augustinian friary, founded here in 1259. It comprised a church and college for friars of the order's Irish province, but was a mendicant institution without adornment, lacking the possessions and influence of All Hallows. Its remains are buried under the top of Crow St. In Crow St also a famous theatre operated from 1758 to 1820. The patentee was at one time

Frederick (Buck) Jones, also a one-time city sheriff and a compulsive gambler, after whom Jones's Road, the border between Drumcondra and Ballybough, is named. Spranger Barry was the theatre's first manager, and it stood on the site of a 1731 music hall. Mrs Delany, well-known Dublin society hostess in the eighteenth century, wife of Dr Delany, chancellor of St Patrick's Cathedral, fellow of Trinity College and friend of Dean Swift, regularly attended the theatre. She had also patronised the earlier music hall, where, we are told, she heard Geminiani play the violin. She lived in Glasnevin, and northsiders like her, wishing to visit Crow St, had often to make the Liffey crossing by ferry. In 1816 an Alerman Beresford and a William Walsh bought the tolls of the ferry and built Wellington Bridge, the graceful iron footbridge above O'Connell Bridge. The footbridge had its name later changed to Liffey Bridge, but is more often referred to as the 'metal' or 'ha'penny' bridge. Though it was erected primarily as a short cut to Crow St, it remained a toll bridge until 1919.

Midway down Crow St, on the left, it is worth pausing to look at a shop with a very high and elegant Victorian window, and long wooden consoles. Going back up to Dame St, we see at the corner of Fownes St the Hibernian insurance building, an unusually adventurous essay in the Venetian style popularised by Woodward. At number 9 College Green, near the modern Central Bank building, whose erection caused a storm of protest, as it is out of scale with all its surroundings, is another insurance building with a charming granite and yellow sandstone facade, red marble discs and decorative balconies. In Anglesea St, near the Stock Exchange, is a lovely narrow brick house whose long consoles incorporate carved wooden heads.

Around at the corner of College St and Westmoreland St is another **College St** florid Venetian construction, lacking the pointed dormer windows of the Hibernian, but with medallions and long, deep balconies, now the Armstrong, Lloyd and Ramsey building. Between this and the side of the college front is the bronze statue of Thomas Moore, notebook in his hand. Moore lived from 1779 to 1825, and was once regarded as the national poet. Modern opinion has been more hostile and he has been accused of bowdlerising the traditional ballads which he used as material. In *A Portrait of the Artist as a Young Man*, James Joyce refers to this College St statue: 'He looked at it without anger, for, although sloth of the body and of the soul crept over it like unseen vermin, over the shuffling feet and up the fold of the cloak and round the servile head, it seemed humbly conscious of its indignity.' One of Moore's most popular melodies, *The Meeting of the Waters*, has given its name to this site in popular Dublin speech: there are public toilets directly underneath!

A little further down College St is a splendid building of the Allied Irish Bank, designed by W. G. Murray and opened in 1862. Looking up, we notice in the tympanum some stone figures, splendidly carved in high relief, in an earnest commercial encounter. Ahead of us is the Pearse St garda or police station, in rough granite, contrasting with the vivid yellow glazed bricks, including those on an enormous chimney, of the travel agents' building at the confluence of D'Olier St and Hawkins St. Over the entrance to the police station's detective office the heads of two officers are carved in the stone, wearing flat caps. A little to the east, over the main office, are two corresponding heads of policemen, in the beehive helmets no longer worn here, and wearing the moustaches that were popular in the days of Dublin Metropolitan Police. The DMP was founded in 1836 and College St was one of its earliest establishments. Facing the western end of the station, a lawn marks the location of the Staine, or long stone, Viking pillar denoting possession. Such pillars were usually erected by the Norsemen near their landing places. The one in College St was about fourteen feet tall and stood until the 1790s. From it, the land from this point eastward to the River Dodder in Ringsend, south of the Liffey, was once called the Staine or Stein. The street running eastward from the northern side of the police station is Townsend St, and the land between that and the Liffey, eastward to Ringsend, was under water or mud until 1607, when its reclamation was begun by Sir William Carroll. In 1646, when Owen Roe O'Neill and his ally General Preston were threatening to lay siege to Dublin, and part of the city wall which had collapsed in 1641 was still unrepaired, an attempt was made to fortify the city with earthworks. The marchioness of Ormonde and other titled ladies, having consented to carry baskets of earth, levelled a Viking burial mound that had stood beside the Staine, thinking it a convenient earth supply. In the event, it was an unnecessary piece of vandalism. The would-be besiegers withdrew due to shortage of provisions, Owen Roe contenting himself the following year with burning all crops around Dublin. In 1648 the city wall was repaired.

Hawkins St

From here we go down Hawkins St towards the Liffey. The Hawkins commemorated here was the builder of a great wall in 1663, to help reclaim land from the Liffey. The tall office block on our right, Hawkins House, occupies the site of the Theatre Royal, demolished in 1962. This theatre held over 4,000 people, and was claimed to be the biggest in Europe. It was the automatic choice for such visiting artists as Danny Kaye and Joan Hammond. Circuses were performed on its enormous stage. It was the third theatre to occupy the site. The first Theatre Royal was built there by Samuel Beasley in 1820 and opened on 18 January 1821. This was accidentally burned to the ground on 9 February 1880. In 1886 the site was taken over by Mr M. Gunn, who had had architect C. J. Phipps design the Gaiety in South King St for him in 1871, and he employed the same architect to build a new theatre on the old Royal site, calling it at first the Leinster Hall, later reverting to the old name. It looked somewhat as the Gaiety does now, with the same old-world elegance, but more luxury. It too came down in the middle 1930s, to make way for the third Royal.

Leinster Market

Facing the theatre site is the arch of Leinster Market. Over it, there is a preserved tablet with the words 'Dublin Gaslight Company, 1825', reminding us that gas lighting came to the city in that year.

Poolbeg St

Beside the site of the theatre, Poolbeg St runs eastward. Detour for a moment and go along it past the back of the Irish Press newspaper office, which stands where the Tivoli music hall stood, the Tivoli in turn being a replacement of the Conciliation Hall. The Tivoli, when it opened in 1897, was first called the Grand Lyric Hall. Beyond this, on the left, Mulligan's bar was a meeting place for company and patrons alike of the Royal, Tivoli and Queens Theatre. It was founded in 1782, and was known both to James Joyce and John F. Kennedy, who had a drink there in his youthful obscurity in 1947.

Going back and down Hawkins St, we see in the centre of the roadway where it joins Burgh Quay a curious Edwardian monument, on the back of which is a disused drinking fountain. This was erected in 1906 in memory of a policeman and a Corporation worker who died when overcome by fumes below a nearby sewer entrance the previous year, the policeman trying to rescue the other. To our right on Burgh Quay is the former corn exchange, and to our left we see O'Connell Bridge, with its handsome wrought iron lamps, four along each balustrade and three trefoils across the river in the centre of the roadway. This centrepiece has been restored after its removal to make way for a concrete flowerbed as part of a short-lived tourist festival known as An Tostal. The flowerbed was intended to be faced with marble, but never was. Halfway along it, two tubular steel arches supported a plastic flame called the 'Bowl of Light'. The construction became almost universally known as 'the thing', was lampooned in humorous journals, and dubbed by Dublin comedian Jimmy O'Dea 'the tomb of the unknown gurrier'. A student flung the plastic torch into the Liffey, which pleased popular opinion more than it did the judge who convicted him. Subsequently the flowerbed was dismantled.

Burgh Quay

O'Connell Bridge

O'Connell Bridge replaces a similar, but narrower one designed by James Gandon and built in 1794. Then known as Carlisle Bridge, it was rebuilt in its wider form in 1880. The Corporation intended to rename it O'Connell Bridge then, but influential objectors took the matter to court, and on 19 June 1885 vice-chancellor Chatterton granted a permanent injunction forbidding the Corporation to change the name. Butt Bridge, below it, was built in 1879, and the rebuilt form of it was officially renamed Congress Bridge in 1932, after the Dublin Eucharistic Congress of that year, but the name never gained popular currency.

Butt Bridge

Going down Burgh Quay — named after Thomas Burgh, architect of the old library in Trinity — towards Butt Bridge, we pass the front of the erstwhile Corn Exchange, and that of the old Tivoli, the ground floor of the theatre's facade being preserved. Turning up Tara St, we find at its top on the left a pleasant piece of Edwardian architecture, the fire station, opened officially on 13 September 1907, having been completed the previous year at a cost of £21,840. It has a commanding redbrick clock tower, and notice the stepped brick consoles, or corbels, supporting the platform. Directly across Pearse St from here are two modern office buildings. The one on the left replaces the old Queens theatre. The Queens was noted for variety, but from 1951 to 1966, after the fire in the Abbey theatre, it housed that company.

Tara St

Pearse St

Further east is number 27 Pearse St. A plaque sculpted by Albert Power in 1951 is on the wall over a shop, bearing effigies of the Pearse brothers, Patrick and Willie, whose family home this was. The father of the 1916 leaders, a Londoner, had a monumental sculpture works in this street. Two doors further on, under two brick arches, is the small

**St Mark's
Church**

door of the Grace Baptist Church and Brunswick Hall, almost hidden. Further on again is St Mark's Church, where Oscar Wilde was baptised, with its churchyard and vaults. Although the foundation stone was laid in 1729, it was not consecrated until 1757 and its pulpit is believed to have been made from the poop of a ship that sank in Dublin Bay. The cinema just beyond it was originally the Antient [*sic*] Concert Rooms, but its fine ceiling has now been covered over by another. It was built in 1824 as the Dublin Oil Gas Station.

Passing the corner of Westland Row, which runs off to the right, we notice a stone-walled roadway running up to the railway station from street level, and beyond that again the railway crosses South Cumberland St and then Sandwith St Upper. In the latter street, near the corner of a narrow side street with picturesque cottages, is a low drinking-trough with one end extended upward into a fountain. On its granite side is inscribed the name 'Metropolitan Drinking Fountain and Cattle Trough Association', a reminder that it once watered not only horses but cattle, when these were unloaded from the trains that reached Westland Row from the west, and driven down a ramp across the road at Devlin's Place, to be herded down to the nearby docks for export.

Crossing Pearse St, and going down Lower Sandwith St to its end, where Hanover St East runs off to the right, leads to a street with the intriguing name of Misery Hill. There is no need to go there, as it is almost uniquely unimpressive, being a strip of road between blank walls, but the name is worth remembering, and is an excellent choice. The place was formerly a leper colony, and once the site of a municipal gallows for maritime and other offenders. We cross the intersection and head down Creighton St towards the docks, passing the L-shaped Windmill Lane on the right, where the ruin of a tall windmill stood in the corner until the early 1970s. On the lower left-hand side of Creighton St, just off the docks, the houses have tiny gardens in the front basement areas. It is a refreshing surprise to see geraniums and shrubs growing in the ground within a few yards of the ships. At the end of the

**Sir John
Rogerson's
Quay
Pearse Square**

street turn right and go down Sir John Rogerson's Quay. This forms part of the South Wall, an older quayside than the one facing it, and first planned as a dock in 1707. Turn right again and go up Lime St, then straight on up Lower Erne St to Pearse St, and turn left. Soon Pearse Square with its little park is encountered on the left; it has, notice, only three sides. This was formerly Queen's Square, the recognised centre of theatrical lodgings. Pearse St leads on to Grand Canal Docks, across which it is connected with Ringsend Rd by a lifting bridge formerly called Victoria Bridge, of which there were two in Dublin. Beyond the bridge, on the right, is the tall bulk of Boland's Mills, where Eamon de Valera commanded a garrison in the 1916 Rising, but we stop short at Macken St, on our right, head south along it, and beyond the railway crossing come to Grand Canal St.

**Sir Patrick
Dun's hospital**

Across the road to the left is Sir Patrick Dun's hospital, opened in 1808. It had taken five years to build, the foundation stone having been laid in 1803 by the provost of Trinity College, Dr Kearney. The hospital has been extended since then. A right turn off Grand Canal St leads into

Eblana Villas. Going down it, we find Island Villa, Hogan Avenue, Rostrevor Terrace, Greenore Terrace and Carlingford Parade grouped between the main road and the railway wall, a quaint hidden community. Emerging from it, turn right, then right again at Upper Erne St, which leads back to Pearse St, where a left turn leads back past Sandwith St to the corner of Westland Row. This time, go up Westland Row. **Westland Row**

The bridge crossing the street here is high Victorian railway architecture, with its iron coffered sides and balustrade. But despite a little red and yellow brickwork, the station looks like a shed. As a former mainline terminus, it is certainly the poor relation of Amiens St, Kingsbridge, Harcourt St and Broadstone stations, all of them splendid buildings. Yet Westland Row is enshrined in history, as the first railway service in Ireland began from here on 17 December 1834. The station was then the Dublin terminus of the Dublin and Kingstown Railway. Its present appearance is largely due to the building of the City of Dublin Junction Railway in 1891, when the line was run through the front of the station to bridge the street on its way to the north side. The 1834 opening, incidentally, gave Ireland a railway service before Germany had one. Beyond the station the Christian Brothers' school is a warm Victorian building of granite and marigold-coloured bricks with some purple courses, but number 21 across the street is a sparrow-brown Georgian house, birthplace of Oscar Wilde in 1854.

Crossing the street again we are at St Andrew's Catholic church, also known as All Hallows, designed by Patrick Byrne and built between 1832 and 1834. This has a splendid granite Doric facade, though there are only two pillars in the portico, behind which are fine oval pink marble fonts. Similar marble is used in the Corinthian pillars of the big high altar screen. In a side chapel there is a Pietà executed by Willie Pearse.

Pass the Royal Irish Academy of Music on the left near the top of Westland Row, and go right into Lincoln Place, whose north side is largely fussy Victorian redbrick, including the dental hospital and training hospital for students. Emerging from this street, we see over to our left one of the best Victorian shopfronts in Dublin, that of Price's Medical Hall. Heading west along Leinster St and into Nassau St, the **Nassau St** spire of the Protestant St Andrew's dominating the view ahead, we pass the magnificent Kildare St club on the corner of that street, an 1859 **Kildare St club** redbrick essay by Deane and Woodward, with stone carvings by the O'Shea brothers. In the 1970s some excellent parts of the interior of this grand building were removed. But we can still see the almost incredible wealth of carving on the exterior, and though this is somewhat time-ravaged, we may identify birds, a hare being chased by a hound, monkeys, leaves, branches and berries. The building is now occupied by the cultural institute of the French embassy.

Further on, at the corresponding corner of Dawson St, is the domed neo-Classical Lombard and Ulster bank, bearing carvings of an Irish harp and the arms of Dublin and the four provinces. In the vestibule is a ceiling where the provincial arms and harp are displayed in colour. This was the site of Morrisson's hotel, where Parnell was

39

**The provost's
house**

arrested in 1881, and where he sometimes was a guest before and after that. Heading towards Grafton St, notice a charming little Venetian facade over the Berni Inn, with carvings on seven panels, including two dragons. Around the corner, going right towards the college, is the Palladian house of the provost, inside its separate entrance. Trinity's most famous provost, Narcissus Marsh (of Marsh's library), never lived in it, for it was built in 1759 for provost Francis Andrews. The facade design was supplied by Lord Burlington for a house in Old Burlington St, London — that of a General Wade — in 1723, and the same design was used by Frederick the Great for a house in Potsdam in 1755. This design is said to have been by Palladio himself. The provost's house is the sole survivor of the trio. Notice that it is three storeys at the sides and two in front. It has a splendid interior, and is one of Dublin's finest houses. Among those who enjoyed the interior was John Pentland Mahaffy, noted Dublin acerbic wit, who was provost of Trinity for the last five years of his life.

Kildare St Club, a detail

3   Mountjoy Fields and Leopold Bloom

Mountjoy Square — Fitzgibbon St — Free Church — St George's church — Belvedere — North Great George's St — Eccles St — Mater hospital — Mountjoy jail — Gardiner St church.

Quick warm sunlight came running from Berkeley Road, swiftly, in slim sandals, along the brightening footpath. Runs, she runs to meet me, a girl with gold hair on the wind.

— James Joyce, *Ulysses.*

**Mountjoy
Square**

Mountjoy Square is the only one of Dublin's great squares which literally qualifies for the title. It was originally intended to emphasise its mathematical accuracy by having each side look like a unified building, with a pillared portico in the centre and architectural decorations at each end, while each house behind the facade retained its isolation, but this was found to be too costly. Also, it would have hampered the internal arrangements of the house in the centre of the range. The first reference to the square in *Wilson's City Directory* appeared in 1791, and it

Luke Gardiner

was then called Gardiner's Square, after Luke Gardiner, Lord Mountjoy, whose family had laid out Gardiner's Mall. In 1792, the year building began, the name had been changed to Mountjoy Square. The west side was built first, with William Pemberton, a builder, being the square's first resident. The next two occupants were John Russell, another builder, and Michael Stapleton, a builder also, but more famous as a stuccodore. The east side of the square was built last, and was not completed until 1818. Originally each side of the square was numbered separately, and the address incorporated the compass point, but this was changed in the middle of the nineteenth century. In its first five years the square became a popular address for members of the legal profession.

In 1798 Lord Mountjoy was killed while leading a Dublin brigade against the insurgents at the battle of New Ross. A census of Mountjoy Square taken in that year shows that 100 people occupied ten houses on the north side, with three vacant plots, 67 people occupied nine houses on the west side, with six vacant plots, 190 people lived in sixteen houses on the south side, with two vacant plots, and nobody as yet lived on the east side. In this context a vacant plot may mean either what is literally suggested, an open space, or a house built but not yet occupied. At his death Luke Gardiner was site owner of numbers 19, 20, 21, 22, 23, 24, 28, 29, 30, 31. Charles Thorp, the plasterworker remembered for his ceiling in the Bluecoat school, built numbers 19 and 22. Builders of large houses sometimes left their signatures, and when research was being carried out in the 1930s into the origins of Mountjoy Square, Thorp's name as builder was found on a beam in the back of number 22.

For a long time the centre of the square was waste ground and hillocks, a dump of builders' rubble having done nothing to improve its original wild condition. This had been part of Mountjoy Fields, where tradition says that Brian Boru pitched the tent in which he was killed at the battle of Clontarf on 23 April 1014. Logic is on the side of tradition, the area known as Clontarf then being much further west than it is today, and Mountjoy Square being a plateau. In May 1801 the residents met in St Thomas's Church, Marlborough St, and decided to petition parliament for an act to close in and improve the centre of the square, each resident paying five guineas towards parliamentary expenses. Thus was founded a commission to administer one of Dublin's most exclusive parks, and it was to remain in existence for over a century. The first trustees included Lord Baron Ventry, Rt Hon. Richard Annesley and the Hon. Hugh Howard, and the treasurer was Jeremiah D'Olier, who lived in number 26, one of a Huguenot family originally known as Olier. D'Olier St is named after him.

John and James Clarke supplied the railings for the new central park, and they apologised for their inability to obtain Swedish iron, and for having to make do with British. The park was lit by eighty-four globe irons, at a total cost of £47 15s. 6d. Richard Dunne of number 49 Capel St was the first painter of the railings, for which he was paid £34 2s. 6d., and the only blot on the stately proceedings was a request by one of the Clarke brothers to lease the park for six months as a potato patch!

A survey of 1787 by Mr Thomas Sherrard of number 60 Capel St shows that the church of St George in Hardwicke Place was originally intended to be built in the middle of the new Mountjoy Square. It would have been approached by four paths, one from the middle of each side of the square, dividing the grass area in four segments. An inner path would have followed the line of the square, and an oval path would have run around the church.

But the centre of the square never got its church, or any other architectural endowment, and had to make do with a large ash tree, around which was a circular path. Four gates were placed in the railings in 1805, and 100 keys were issued to residents. There was some disquiet among residents about misuse of the square after this. In 1808 Lord Glenawley sold his house. In 1809 an 'assistant gardener' was appointed to 'keep out improper persons' and a sentry box was put up at the north gate, while a gardener's rest house was built at the north east corner. In 1811 the problem was obviously as bad as ever, and the residents resolved to 'procure four stout constables to attend in the square on Sunday evenings to preserve order and protect the square'. The park in

these days opened at six a.m. in summer and daylight in winter, and a bell at night clanged to warn of closing time. In 1830 financial strain obliged them to open the park to residents of neighbouring streets, at a fee of a guinea a year per family, the families to be first approved by the commissioners. The treasurer, Thomas Tilly, had made no reports since 1824, and a select committee of William Lunelle Guinness, Col. Pelly and Thomas Forde was set up to investigate his activities: they found £100 missing from the accounts. So bad were things in 1832 that the gas company was told to cut off the lighting in the park, as the bill could not be paid. It was then decided to be more businesslike, and open an account with Ball's Bank in Henry St. In 1835 the square park still boasted merely an iron railing on a granite base, lights and walks, but no seats or shelters. That year the gardeners were instructed to 'prevent the young gentlemen who frequent the square from playing at football, hurl or prisoner's bar, or any other game tending to injure the grass plot'. They were further instructed to eject the young gentlemen if they persisted. In 1836 the general public were admitted to the park for the first time.

Throughout the nineteenth century Mountjoy Square continued to be a most fashionable address. The earl of Annesley lived in number 61, the dean of Down in number 56, Archbishop Hawkesley in number 1 and Dr D. Murray, Catholic archbishop between 1823 and 1852, in number 44. Alderman John Campbell, twice lord mayor of Dublin, was at number 27, and owned other houses on the square. Under his chairmanship the commissioners banned smoking in the park. (Wine drinking, presumably, was not banned: the Campbells were wine merchants.) Richard Dowse, baron of the Court of Exchequer, lived in number 38 until 1890, and Piers Geale, crown solicitor, in number 65. So assiduously did he encourage titled young men to court his daughters that his residence became known as the House of Lords.

The footpaths around the park did not become public thorough-fares until 1890, the same year that this change of status occurred in Rutland (Parnell), Merrion and Fitzwilliam Squares. The character of the square had then begun to change. In 1914 it could still boast a knight, Sir John Edmond Barry, a magistrate, Mr K. McInerney KC, several clergymen, surgeons, solicitors, two private hospitals and a private nursing home, the Distressed Irish Ladies' Home and the famous Mountjoy School. At number 29 lived Frank Hutton, of the celebrated coachbuilding family. Its tennis club was the foremost in Dublin, and a new pavilion was still being erected in 1927. But by now the city fathers were anxious to take over the park. A suggestion that it be turned into a public playground was turned down by the commissioners in 1933. Mr Esmond W. Little, of number 22, was the last treasurer of the commissioners, and in 1938 Dublin Corporation took over the park. In 1947 it was turned into a playground, and the character of the square changed again, the number of tenements having shot up, the private hospitals gone, but the distressed ladies' home, the school and the Church of Ireland hostel for Divinity students still there. These have all since disappeared. A wine merchant has restored number 25, one of the Divinity hostel's houses on the east side, and the

Irish Georgian Society has taken over one on the south side. Mountjoy School's premises became Dublin Corporation offices.

The original number 35, on the south side of the square near the corner of Mountjoy Place, has been demolished. Here Sean O'Casey lived for five months in 1920. He was not raised in the slums, as we shall see shortly, though it is often romantically supposed that he was. He used a mythical Hilljoy Square as the setting for *The Shadow of a Gunman*, and we can reasonably suppose that this was inspired by his experiences of this house. Such houses, when divided into tenement rooms or even bigger residential units, retained in the parlance of the new tenants references to their former functional divisions; the floors, from the basement up, were still called kitchen, parlour, drawingroom, two-pair and top, with the extension at the back being the return room.

Running downhill from the north-east corner of the square is Fitzgibbon St, now mostly rebuilt. The eleven-year-old James Joyce came to live here with his family in 1893, in number 14. Below the russet brick Victorian garda station is a gate which formerly led to a bakery's stables. Number 14 stood almost opposite, and was demolished long before the rest of its range, indicating that even when Joyce lived there it was past its heyday. For many years afterwards a one-storey vegetable store occupied the site. Joyce's father, John, humiliated at having had to remove his son from the Jesuit college of Clongowes Wood because the fees were beyond his reach, sent the boy to O'Connell Schools in North Richmond St while they lived in Fitzgibbon St, but after six months, believing that Irish Christian Brother education produced socially inferior citizens, managed to transfer him back to the Jesuits, this time in Belvedere College, beyond the far side of Mountjoy Square.

Fitzgibbon St

From Fitzgibbon St cross the North Circular Rd into Russell St. On the left beyond a lane a store occupies the site of number 14, childhood home of Brendan Behan, whose grandmother owned five houses in this street, and another in Fitzgibbon St. Further on is the site of the Mountjoy brewery, founded by Alex Findlater in 1852. Mr John Lloyd Blood, one of Findlater's partners, put the name Mountjoy on the enterprise because of the prestige of the nearby square. One of the brewery's progressive features was a miniature tramway on which wagons brought malt from the kilns to the malt bins. The Mountjoy survived to be the last Dublin competitor of Guinness's brewery. It was best known for its 'invalid' or 'nourishing' stout, though it also brewed pale and brown ales and barley wine. It had a large export trade, notably to British troops in the Mediterranean. Beyond the brewery site the Royal Canal is bridged, and Jones's Road runs down towards the gate of Holy Cross College in Clonliffe Road. Jones's Road was laid in the eighteenth century by Frederick 'Buck' Jones as a short cut to his house, which is now the Dublin diocesan press office in the grounds of the college. He was reluctant to ride down Clonliffe Road, then called Fortick's Lane, at night for fear of ambush. This Fortick was Tristram Fortick, founder of an almshouse in Little Denmark St in 1755, who previously owned Jones's house, and who planted Fortick's Grove, now the college grounds, as a garden showpiece, cutting yew and box hedges into the shapes of men, animals and birds.

Russell St

Holy Cross College

45

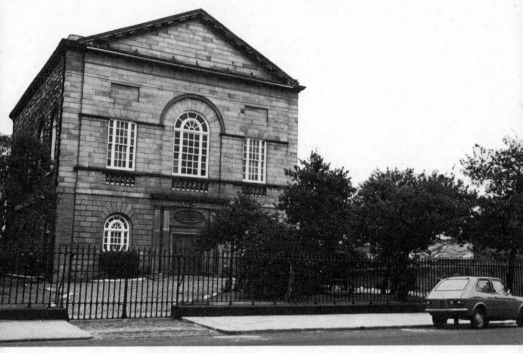

Free Church, Great Charles St

Great Charles St

In Great Charles St stands the Church of Ireland Free Church, adapted in 1828 from a Methodist building of 1800 to dominate the view along another Georgian street, Upper Rutland St, with its smaller but still stately houses. This church stands in railed grounds on a site chosen in 1823 for a Jesuit church. The Jesuits had almost completed negotiations for the purchase of the site for £2,000 when the landlord decided, on finding out that it was to be used as a site for a 'mass house', not to sanction the deal. The present spireless church never fully exploited the advantages of its situation. Number 21 in this street was the ordnance survey office in which the poet James Clarence Mangan worked. He composed his poem, 'The Woman of Three Cows' here. Mangan began working in this office in 1833, at the age of 30, having been a copying clerk and Trinity College librarian. He is best remembered for his lyric 'Dark Rosaleen'. At number 50 Great Charles St, and also at number 1 Mountjoy Square, lived Timothy Michael Healy KC, who was born in 1855 in Bantry, Co. Cork. He was the first governor-general of the Irish Free State, and earlier had been a bitter opponent of Parnell at the time of the O'Shea divorce scandal.

Running from the north-west corner of Mountjoy Square to the north-east one of Parnell Square is a line of streets divided into Gardiner Place, Great Denmark St and Gardiner's Row.

The first of these brings us to the corner of Temple St, on the right **Temple St** with the children's hospital run by the Irish Sisters of Charity, in which some plasterwork is still beautifully preserved. Temple St was another street of elegant Georgian houses, as was Hardwicke Place beyond it, which is now dominated by the church of St George, completed in 1814, **Church of St** possibly Francis Johnston's finest work. A turn to the right between the **George** hospital and church leads to St George's Place, now laid out in municipal flats parallel to Hardwicke Place, but formerly a cul-de-sac of smaller Georgian houses, which in its declining tenement years was known as 'George's Pocket'. Facing the church, Hardwicke St, running towards North Frederick St, is another former Georgian street. Notice that the blocks of flats facing the church on either side of Hardwicke St entrance are in a crescent, also part of the old Georgian plan.

The church is a replacement of an older St George's, built by Sir John Eccles in 1714 or thereabouts in Hill St, a continuation of Temple St down toward Parnell St, of which only a castellated tower of dark calpstone remains. It was decided in 1787 that this needed rebuilding, and that in the meantime a replacement should be erected. It is not clear why both rebuilding and permanent replacement were considered necessary. It was never rebuilt, but was gloriously replaced. St George's at Hardwicke Place, standing on an island, is a Greek Ionic gem, with four fluted columns in the portico and a five-storey clock tower terminating in a slender spire, bringing the height of the church to nearly 200 feet. This church has often been likened to St Martin-in-the-Fields in London, and is sometimes attributed to Sir Christopher Wren, who was eighty years dead before it was begun.

For St George's, Johnston designed a roof with a huge span of sixty-five feet. This explains why, on entering the church, we are so struck by its breadth that we feel it is running the wrong way.

In 1836 two Dublin engineers, John and Robert Mallet, inserted iron arches in the roof after a great chime of bells, presented by Johnston himself, had been installed in the clock tower. The sound of these bells has long been familiar to many north side residents.

The Georgian Hardwicke St, then called Beresford St, contained a building that had begun in 1752 as a Poor Clares convent, when it was isolated amid fields and connected by an avenue to Drumcondra Lane, as Dorset St was then known. It became in turn a Jesuit church, Jesuit college, Methodist church, Protestant national school, theatre and finally the home of the Dun Emer guild of craftworkers, before its demolition with the rest of that range of houses in the mid-1950s. Piquantly, it was Luke Gardiner's death in New Ross that forced the nuns to leave; as landlord, he had intended to renew their lease on favourable terms, but their new landlord felt differently. The Jesuit college vacated the building for something more spacious in 1841. They moved to Belvedere House and established Belvedere College, now one of the city's best known schools, not least in rugby circles.

If we go back along Temple St, turn right into Great Denmark St, with Findlater's church dominating the view ahead, we find the impressive detached former mansion facing the top of North Great George's St.

Belvedere House

Belvedere House was begun in 1775 for George Rochford, who had succeeded to the title of Lord Belvedere the previous year. He bought the land from Nicholas Archdall, an Ulsterman who had purchased it as part of the Eccles family estate in 1748. The Rochford roots were in Co. Westmeath, where George's father had imprisoned his second wife for his lifetime in his mansion near Gaulstown, for allegedly having an affair with George's uncle. George Rochford may have preferred town life to the grim memories of this country house. He engaged Michael Stapleton to design and build Belvedere House, and execute the plasterwork. Stapleton came from Mecklenburgh St, but later, as we know, was to live in Mountjoy Square.

Belvedere House has five bays and a very handsome brick and Portland stone front, a fine entrance reached by steps, and a view which was once among the most important in Dublin's townscape, but is no longer so. It contains some of Stapleton's richest and most colourful plasterwork, including the Apollo, Venus and Diana rooms. The Diana room is now a library, and the Venus room's centre-piece was removed when the building became a boys' college. The staircase handrails have bronze medallions with an Apollo motif, and there are fireplaces by Bossi, the Venetian master.

When Lord Belvedere died in 1814 his widow married Mr Abraham Boyd KC of Gloucester (now Sean MacDermott) St, and her son by this marriage, George Boyd, sold it to the Jesuits in 1841, through the precautionary third party usual in those dying days of bigoted opposition to sales of important property to Catholic clergymen. In this case the middle man was Sylvester Young, brother of one of the priests.

Belvedere College has expanded physically in three directions since then, the Victorian purpose-built school section — which can be seen behind the old mansion — having gone up in 1884. For many years the training ground for the college's feats on the rugby field has been at Jones's Rd, behind the Gaelic Athletic Association's Croke Park headquarters, and formerly a part of it.

North Great George's St

At the corner of North Great George's St, facing Belvedere, is a hotel which includes number 2 in that street, the former home of John Dillon, last leader of the Irish Nationalist party in Westminster. In number 20, on the same side, was the home and literary salon of Sir Samuel Ferguson, poet and historian. Across the road at number 38 is Mahaffy House, with a big halldoor and generous fanlight, with two ornate sphinxes in its surround. Here lived Sir John Pentland Mahaffy, classical scholar and wit, who ended his days as provost of Trinity College. Mahaffy was a noted conversationalist, teacher of Oscar Wilde, friend of Oliver St John Gogarty, pioneer of the Georgian Society which compiled five volumes of data on the architecture of eighteenth-century Dublin, accomplished bird shot and cricketer, expert on horse racing and author of a book on angling. He has been described as one of the rudest men who ever lived, but this was acceptable when one was established as a 'Dublin character' in the nineteenth century, just as it was later acceptable elsewhere from W. C. Fields. Mahaffy is credited with the remark, upon hearing that someone he disliked was ill, 'God grant that it's nothing trivial'. Further up this

Sir John Pentland Mahaffy

St George's Church, Hardwicke Place

49

side of the street, from number 41 to number 46, is the Loreto convent school, the best kept part of the street, a phenomenon sometimes encountered where Georgian houses are in the hands of religious communities.

North Frederick St

St George's church

Sean O'Casey

Going down Denmark St from Belvedere we pass through Gardiner's Row and turn up North Frederick St at the corner of Parnell Square. Here there is a fine view of the side of Findlater's church, with its big diamond-paned windows. The walk up North Frederick St takes one past the end of Hardwicke St, giving another perspective on St George's church, and leads to the corner of Upper Dorset St. Across and down the road, at the corner of St Joseph's Place, is a bank building which incorporates number 85, birthplace of Sean O'Casey. It has been said that O'Casey's father was caretaker of this house when Sean was born there in 1884, but the city directory of the time listed him as the occupant. O'Casey subsequently had many Dublin addresses, but his birthplace, at this corner, was a substantial residence. (The bank nowadays also incorporates number 86). The nearest the playwright came to 'slum life' in Dublin was going to live on the south side of Mountjoy Square for five months.

Surprise is sometimes expressed that O'Casey, a Protestant, should have had to work for a time as a builder's labourer, and that a man of his religious persuasion should have been a member of James Connolly's Irish Citizen Army. It has been suggested that he deliberately chose to live among working-class people, either to improve his standing in socialist circles or to gather material for his plays. It might be remembered, however, that Dublin in the early twentieth century did have a substantial Protestant artisan population.

Further on, on the left, is Eccles St, straight and stately, but with some of the houses now missing from its lower end, including number 7, where Leopold and Molly Bloom lived in *Ulysses*. Gerard O'Flaherty, writing on why Joyce picked this house, says that Joyce's frequent visits to the house to see his friend J. F. Byrne, the prototype of Cranly in *A Portrait of the Artist as a Young Man*, who lived there, made him aware of when the house was empty. Thus he knew it was safe to make it Bloom's house on 16 June 1904. Joyce wrote *Ulysses* with the help of a 1904 *Thom's Directory*, a map of Dublin and his memory of the city's physical features. When unsure of a detail, he wrote to his Aunt Josephine in Dublin and asked her to check it. O'Flaherty relates that one such errand entrusted to the aunt was to see whether a man of average height could easily climb over the railings of number 7 Eccles St and drop into the basement area, as Bloom does. In fact, number 7 was one of the smaller houses in Eccles St, and its front railings were remarkably low.

Eccles St number 7

Numbers 10 and 11 were the Bertrand and Rutland high school for girls, now incorporated with the Mountjoy boys' school in Mount Temple at Malahide Road. A little further up, several houses still accommodate the Dominican convent school. Here we find an unusually beautiful, simple fanlight, and notice the graceful granite curve of the domed chapel front, suspended above the street. Across the street we find decorative panels on the front of number 64, including a reproduction of Michelangelo's Moses. Francis Johnston lived in this house, and it was later the home of Isaac Butt, lawyer and founder of the Home Rule movement in 1870.

Number 63 Eccles St was occupied in the eighteenth century by Sir Boyle Roche, described as the clown of the Irish parliament. Though perhaps most noted, and quoted, for his statement that no man could be in two places at once unless he was a bird, Roche's most excruciating talent was for grinding metaphors together. Thus he 'smelt a rat, saw it floating in the air and nipped it in the bud', and warned parliament, on the occasion of a threatened French invasion, that the French would 'break in, cut us to mincemeat and throw our bleeding heads upon that table to stare us in the face'. His most cynical remark, however, whether unwitting or not, must surely be: 'What has posterity ever done for us?'.

Sir Boyle Roche

Number 59, the tallest house in Eccles St, was the residence of Cardinal Cullen, and later a presbytery. Seven doors up is the corner of Nelson St, where Behan's play, *The Hostage*, is set, in the house of a Madame Rogers. Behind part of Nelson St and off St Joseph's Parade is May Cottages, at the corner of whose footpath water is still drawn from a stubby iron pump.

At the top of Eccles St on the right is the neo-classical granite facade of the Mater Misericordiae hospital, known simply as the Mater. The foundation stone of this was laid in 1852, and it was opened on 24 September 1861. It was built to relieve the poor of Dublin and elsewhere of cholera, typhus and typhoid. There had been frequent outbreaks of these diseases in Dublin in the mid-nineteenth century, especially among the poor, who had least resistance. The Sisters of Mercy had been founded by Catherine McAuley in Baggot St in 1831, and they took over the running of an emergency hospital in Townsend

Mater Misericordiae hospital

St the following year. Mother McAuley's long-term plan was to replace this with a large permanent hospital in Dublin. The Mater was the eventual fulfilment of this plan, but by the time a firm decision was taken to build it, in 1851, the superioress of the Baggot St convent was Mother M. Vincent Whitty. The site was bought on behalf of the nuns by the president of All Hallows college, Dr Moriarty, and the architect of the new hospital was John Bourke of Charlemont St. It had been decided to build in sections, as funds allowed, so Mr Bourke's facade is in dressed granite, but his east wing of 1868 is in calpstone, an economy measure. The west wing, along Berkeley Rd, was designed by John L. Robinson in 1884 at a cost of £68,000, Bourke having died in the meantime.

During the 1866 cholera epidemic, the Mater on the north side and Sir Patrick Dun's hospital on the south were the principal centres of treatment. By then, the Sisters of Mercy were well established as nursing nuns, some having been in the Crimea with Florence Nightingale. The Mater training college for nurses opened in 1891 in part of the present private nursing home, moving to the newly-built six-storey fireproof building on the North Circular Rd, in 1954.

Across Eccles St from the hospital, a triangular park contains a Celtic cross memorial, with trilingual inscription, to the Four Masters, Franciscan friars led by Michael O'Cleary, who chronicled, between 1627 and 1637, the history of the ancient kingdom of Ireland. Beyond the park in Berkeley Rd is the square-towered neo-Gothic **church of St Joseph**, designed by the firm of Ashlin and Coleman and begun in 1875, opening in 1880. This had been part of the parish of St Michan, and the church in Berkeley Rd was built to serve an influx into the area caused by the building of houses between the Royal Canal and the North Circular Rd, below Mountjoy prison, an area previously occupied by orchards and ropewalks (factories). The church replaced a wooden chapel.

Going back along Berkeley Rd, past the side of the Mater, we see the North Circular Rd ahead, with big chimneys beyond the facing side. These chimneys mark the centre of that part of the prison now known as St Patrick's. The prison was put up in the middle of the nineteenth century to the plan of London's Pentonville. Because of executions, and the number of political prisoners it has held, **Mountjoy jail** is an emotive subject in Ireland. Behan's play, *The Quare Fella*, is set there, and is based on an incident that happened while the playwright himself was an inmate. The Royal Canal, along whose banks the 'ould triangle' went jingle jangle, flows behind the prison, the triangle referred to in the ballad being that struck to call prisoners to meals, and to duties.

Luke Gardiner had planned the Royal Circus for this area, and it would have been the greatest Georgian glory of Dublin. John Taylor's 1828 map of the city includes the circus, the cartographer obviously assuming that something would have been built by the time his map was published. But no new sponsor was found after Gardiner's death. The circus was intended to occupy the present site of the Mater hospital, swinging around in the direction of the present Goldsmith St and taking

Entrance to Mater Hospital, Eccles St

in what are now St Vincent St, Sarsfield St, O'Connell Avenue and Geraldine St, then returning across the present Berkeley Rd and along Nelson St, taking in the church site. The biggest town houses would have been built in this ring, probably all detached, and Eccles St would have been one of several radial arms, with another called Cowley Place — where the prison officers' houses were later erected — going all the way to the canal, another to a terrace with a full-length lawn facing the North Circular Road at Florida — or Florinda — Place, where the nurses' home is now, then running down St Joseph's St to meet Synnott Place. Another curved street, behind the circus, would have run roughly from Blessington St across Eccles St and the top of Eccles Place to the Florida Place arm. The centre of the circus would have been a railed park, with keyholders, and it probably would have resembled Royal Circus in Edinburgh, though bigger.

Below the nurses' home we cross the end of Leo St and at the corner of a lane beyond it see a four-storey brown house named Sean O'Casey House. O'Casey lived here immediately before leaving for England, and in it he wrote *Juno and the Paycock* in 1925 and *The Plough and the Stars* in the following year. It was then, and for a time afterwards, literally a tenement, but there is no evidence that it was ever a slum. Turn left at Lower Dorset Street's junction with the North Circular Road and walk towards Drumcondra.

(These 'uppers' and 'lowers' of Dublin streets can puzzle visitors. Here, for example, we have Upper Dorset St, Lower Dorset St, Lower Drumcondra Road and Upper Drumcondra Road in that sequence. A simple guide is that the 'lower' is always nearer to the mouth of the Liffey).

Going towards Binns Bridge and the canal, pause at Innisfallen Parade on the left. A minute's detour allows us to see number 9, a single-storey house, yet another former address of Sean O'Casey. Between Innisfallen Parade and the canal is a plain two-storey redbrick building, now a community centre, formerly a Jesuit school. In the last century this was called Kellett's school. A Miss Kellett had left money for the building of a Protestant school in Navan, but her executors breached the terms of the will by taking over an existing school on this site. A commission of inquiry found that it did not meet the terms of the bequest, it was sold to the Jesuits and they replaced it with the present structure.

Binns Bridge

Binns Bridge commemorates 'Long John Binns', and a bridge on the Grand Canal at Robertstown is also named after him. The Royal Canal Company was founded on 24 October 1789, and Binns was among the first subscribers, in such company as the Duke of Leinster, Lord Longford and Sir William Newcomen. He was also a director of the Grand Canal Company — hence his other commemoration on their bridge — but had walked out of a board meeting at which, he said, he was insulted over his lowly station, that of shoemaker, and vowed to start a rival canal and syphon off the traffic. Shrewdly, he remained on the board of the Grand until early in 1790, when the Royal's future was assured.

Just before crossing Binns Bridge, notice the quaint stile on the left,

54

between a towpath gate and the water. This was for use when the gate was locked. Beyond the waterway, the bridge also crosses a low-level railway which goes to the docks at the North Wall. As we go up Drumcondra Road, we pass under a high level railway bridge. Look at the side of the last building on the right before the bridge, and see the marks of where another house once joined it. This road and others had houses demolished to build this line, the Drumcondra link line, which was begun in late 1897 and finished in April 1901. It is now part of a main line. Just beyond it on the left the brickwork of an old station can still be seen. This station was opened in 1901 as part of a commuter service between Inchicore and the North Wall, and it was said that rarely did more than two passengers use a train. It closed in 1907. **Drumcondra Road**

Further up the road a left turn leads to St Alphonsus Road, opposite which on the main road one of Dublin's last turnpikes stood up to about 1850. This area was then called Clonliffe, with Drumcondra further out. Going up the side road, we see a long wall on our right, behind which is the Redemptoristine nuns' present convent and chapel, built in 1872, using the same foundation stone as had been laid on this site ten years earlier for a college of the Catholic university. This college, through lack of funds, was never built. Further up, in Iona Road, is the neo-Romanesque church of St Columba, designed by the firm of Ashlin and Coleman and opened on 15 October 1905. The intended spire was never added, and the squat tower gives the church an appearance similar to some mediaeval French and Spanish churches. **St Alphonsus Road**

Iona Road

Coming back to Drumcondra Road, turn right. Walk back towards the city, and turn left into Upper Gardiner St and come to the corner of Upper Sherrard St, named after the Thomas Sherrard who surveyed Mountjoy Square with a view to building St George's Church there. He was also secretary of the Wide Streets Commission, founded in 1757. In number 53 Upper Gardiner St, where these streets meet, lived **Upper Sherrard St**

Denis MacCarthy, who published a translation of works of the Spanish dramatist Calderon, and was one of the *Nation* poets. Down the street to the left is the St Francis Xavier hall, where the Radio Telefis Eireann orchestras rehearse and sometimes perform, and ahead of us is the church of the same name, to which the Jesuits moved from Hardwicke St after they failed to acquire the site in Great Charles St. The Gardiner St church was designed by John B. Keane of Mabbot St, now Corporation St. This architect's other works include the church of St Laurence O'Toole in Seville Place, and Longford cathedral, which is worth a visit. The foundation stone at Gardiner St was laid on 2 July 1829, and the church was opened three years later. The large brown brick presbytery between it and the garden adjoining Sherrard St was built in 1834. The church has a tetrastyle granite portico, with Ionic columns 50 feet tall. Its coffered ceiling, with moulded high-relief rosettes, ends over a high altar with pediment surmounting 25-foot Corinthian pillars. The entire altarpiece was shipped from Leghorn, and while the pillars have the appearance of green marble, each is built around a wooden core by an Italian process called *scagliola*, using powdered marble and paint. Below them, the altar is decorated with marble and lapis lazuli. One piece has been removed. It was described in William Fitzpatrick's *History of Dublin Cemeteries* as being a gift to the Jesuits from Major Sirr, called the 'terrorist of 1798', who was town-major of Dublin and led the arrests of most of the conspirators in the insurrection of that year.

The brown brick convent on the other side of the church, that of the Irish Sisters of Charity, with its school behind it, will be seen to have an extra storey over part of its length. This was added between 1832 and 1834 as a sanatorium, during a devastating cholera outbreak in the city. The school lane leads to Belvedere Place, where Cardinal Cullen lived in number 3 before moving to Eccles St.

Thomas Sherrard, despite his failure to have St George's erected in Mountjoy Square, is worthy of commemoration, if only because he was an executive of the Wide Streets Commission. This remarkable public body, whose achievements included laying out the quays east of what is now O'Connell St and west of Capel St, widening Dame St, bringing O'Connell St to the Liffey, bridging that with the old Carlisle Bridge and laying out Westmoreland St and D'Olier St, was set up about the time Berlin was starting its rapid growth, and almost 60 years before John Nash laid out London's Regent St. It had the authority of parliament to stipulate the height of houses, the width and the number of windows per facade, so that even where a terrace was built piecemeal over a number of years, there would be uniformity. Though the commission lasted well into the nineteenth century, its most important work was done in the days of the great classical awareness among architects. Georges Haussmann's Paris programme of widening streets, laying out parks and planning boulevards was not so lucky. Haussmann's prefecture of the Seine did not begin until 1853 and he has been accused of over-planning; no such charge can be made against the Dublin commission.

Wide Streets Commission

4 The Second City of the Empire

St Stephen's Green — College of Surgeons —
Newman House — UCD — Shelbourne hotel —
St Stephen's church — Merrion Square —
Fitzwilliam Square — Grand Canal —
Government buildings — National Gallery —
Leinster House — Mansion House — St Ann's
church — Grafton St.

Each chimney's vapour like a thin grey rod,
Mounting aloft through miles of quietness,
Pillars the skies of God.

— Æ, *Homeward.*

St Stephen's Green

St Stephen's Green is reputedly the biggest city square in Europe, and one of the biggest in the world, and conscious efforts to preserve it as an open space date from the reign of Charles II. The 'common land' that is now the green was first enclosed in 1663, probably at the instigation of Sir William Robinson, architect of the Royal Hospital in Kilmainham and surveyor-general of works and fortifications in Ireland. Before and after the enclosure the west side of the Green was a place of execution. A bishop of Waterford, John Atherton, was executed there for bestiality in 1640. After the enclosure, which comprised a wall emphasised by a deep ditch, it was decreed that twenty acres or thereabouts should be kept as a park, and the adjoining lands divided into eighty-nine allotments, for which lots were drawn by leading citizens who wished to build town houses there.

A walk around the green, on the park side, helps to capture its atmosphere before entering the park, and before examining the built-up part of the square. Opposite Dawson St is a fountain, with two horse troughs, presented by Lady Laura Grattan in 1880. Running away on either side are trees, graceful yellow lamp standards and low granite posts, and all of these continue right around the Green. Notice that the posts are topped by small iron capstans, a reminder that chains were hung from one to the other around the Green in the days when the park was the preserve of the residents, up to 1880. Two tall trefoils of lamps stand outside three corners of the park, the south-west corner being the exception.

memorial arch

The magnificent memorial arch which forms the entrance at the north-west corner, at the top of Grafton St, is a monument to the officers and men of the Royal Dublin Fusiliers who were killed in the Boer War, and if we look upward as we pass under it, we can see the names of the dead engraved in the vault. Going along the Green's west side brings us to a statue of Robert Emmet outside the railings. Emmet's birthplace was number 124 St Stephen's Green and we can see it by looking across the road from the monument. The ground floor is occupied by an antique shop. Passing on, we see inside the railings a seated statue of Lord Ardilaun, the brewer, who opened the Green to the public in 1880 and laid it out as a park. This statue, the work of Thomas Farrell in 1891, was erected in 1892, the commission paid for by public subscription. The likeness appears to be glancing casually across at the College of Surgeons. But — and this can only be an amusing coincidence — the statue, head slightly inclined, is looking straight in the direction of Lord Ardilaun's Guinness's brewery at St James's Gate.

Continuing along the path, we find a charming front-gabled redbrick lodge with decorated black timber eaves inside the south-west entrance, and an iron water pump beyond it. Going along the Green's south side, there is a seat opposite Newman House, dedicated to the memory of James Joyce, Dubliner, and his father John Stanislaus Joyce, Corkonian. At the south-east corner of the Green and just inside the gate is a group of three bronze female figures over a fountain. The work of the German sculptor Josef Wackerle, this is a gift to the Irish government from that of West Germany, in appreciation of Ireland's help after World War II. The female figures represent the three fates, spinning and measuring the thread of man's destiny. A walk along the east side of the Green ends at Edward Delaney's bronze statue of Wolfe Tone, backed by a curved line of carved stone pillars. The gates at this corner were removed to accommodate this monument, which is unloved to the point of ridicule by many Dubliners. Theobald Wolfe Tone, a barrister born in 1763, was the leader of the United Irishmen; he accompanied a French expedition to Ireland in 1798, in support of the insurrection, but was captured and condemned to death, and said by his captors to have committed suicide in his cell by cutting his throat. The reported suicide was greeted in Ireland by the assertion that he had been murdered in prison.

Theobald Wolfe Tone

Before entering the park itself, it is best to walk along the footpath on the north side of the Green to arrive back at the memorial arch. Once inside, one immediately notices a large rough stone bearing a likeness of the Fenian leader Jeremiah O'Donovan Rossa, whose activities in the cause of Irish separatism drew him a sentence of twenty years penal servitude. Its closeness to the Boer War arch is a neat illustration of two strands in nineteenth-century Irish history: at the same time that many Irishmen were giving their lives in the Imperial cause, there were others who dedicated theirs to the destruction of Ireland's connection with the Empire.

Much of the northern half of the park is occupied by an artificial lake, crossed by a rustic bridge. The promontory on the south side of the lake contains a series of small cobbled terraces and the William Butler Yeats memorial, by Henry Moore. Yeats, born in 1865, lived to become the greatest poet of his day in the English language and is generally recognised as the leader of the Irish literary revival which led to the foundation of the Abbey theatre. As director of the Abbey, he is frequently blamed for 'driving Sean O'Casey into exile' by his rejection of O'Casey's play, *The Silver Tassie*, but this is unjustified, as O'Casey had already settled in London when the Abbey rejected that work. Yeats won the Nobel Prize for Literature in 1923 and was, in the words of T. S. Eliot, 'one of those few poets whose history is the history of our own time, who are part of the consciousness of their age, which cannot be understood without them'. The memorial was erected in 1967. Nearby are three bronze busts, one of the poet James Clarence Mangan, with high relief marble medallion of Roisín Dubh (Dark Rosaleen or Ireland, literally 'small black rose') beneath it. Mangan lived at number 6 York St, off the Green's west side, and also worked as a solicitor's clerk in that street. Another of the busts commemorates Countess Markievicz, who was born Constance Georgina Gore-Booth and married a Polish count in 1900. Prominent in both the Irish Citizen Army, James Connolly's organisation, and the Irish Volunteers, she helped feed hungry women and children during the long strike and lock out of 1913–14. During the 1916 Rising, as a colonel in the volunteers, she was leader of a group who attempted to hold St Stephen's Green. It is said that when they were forced to withdraw to the College of Surgeons, the countess asked immediately where the scalpels were kept, so that the volunteers could use them in hand-to-hand fights. In 1918 she became the first woman ever to win election to the British House of

William Butler Yeats

Countess Markievicz

Commons but did not take her seat. The third bust is that of Tom Kettle, described on the plinth as poet, essayist and patriot. As well as being all these, however, Kettle was a soldier and an economist. Born in 1880, he was killed in action in World War I at Givenchy during the battle of the Somme.

Near these busts we see a stone seat, placed there in memory of Anna Maria Haslam (1829–1922) and Thomas Haslam (1825–1917) in recognition of their public service, and their work for the enfranchisement of women. A little to the east, a memorial to Louie Bennett (1870–1956), one of the foundresses of the Irish Women Workers' Union, takes the beautiful form of a garden for the blind. It is small and fairly simple, and there are no flowers; the plants are of the robust kind, which can withstand a lot of handling. As blind people feel the plant, they identify it from an accompanying metal label in braille.

South of this group of monuments is a children's play area, and between it and the south-east gate stands a monument to members of Fianna Eireann. One of the Green's most celebrated monuments is no longer there. This was a statue of George II on horseback by John van Nost, erected in 1758 and described as one of Europe's best equestrian statues. It stood near the centre of the park. It was blown up in the 1930s.

By now the visitor will have noticed, by looking across the road, that three of the Green's sides were developed to a more sophisticated level than the fourth, the west side being the laggard. The north side, dominated by the Shelbourne hotel and the dining clubs, was first to be built up. In the early eighteenth century viscount Molesworth's mansion stood across what is now the top of Kildare St, a street which this family was later to help develop. Sir James Ware's mansion stood immediately west of Molesworth's, on a site later occupied by numbers 25 and 26 of the green. Kerry House stood where part of the Shelbourne hotel now is, and east of it the house of viscount Lanesborough, originally owned by his brother, Mr Theophilus Butler, MP. Kerry House was owned by the first Earl of Kerry, Thomas Fitzmaurice, then by his son, the first Earl of Shelburne, then by Shelburne's second son, the Hon. Thomas Fitzmaurice, upon whose death in 1793 it passed to a Mr Luke White for £6,000. Abuse and neglect had reduced it to a poor state. It is probable that tenants would have been hard to find, especially in the next decade, after the Act of Union. The union did not ruin Dublin; it is often supposed that there was a mass exodus of Anglo–Irish, fearful of disturbances or dismayed at the city's reduced status. Some people of influence did move out, just enough to quieten the property market. Mr White had already solved his problem, however, by renting Kerry House to the British government in 1798 as a billet for troops sent over to quell the rising.

The troops remained his tenants for twenty years, until one of them unwittingly burned the mansion down. With his government compensation White erected numbers 27, 28, and 29 St Stephen's Green and number 12 Kildare St on the site. In 1824 Martin Burke, a Tipperaryman, leased the three houses on the Green from White for £3,000 and an annual rent of £300, and started the Shelbourne hotel,

Shelbourne hotel

originally known simply as Burke's hotel. A clause in the lease forced him to retain separate halldoors, as White, whose family had made its money from state lotteries, was anxious to disguise the fact that he had leased his property to a hotelier. There had been an outcry in 1798 when the Ware mansion was sold to William Binns for an ironmongery store. 'Trade' was thought to lower the tone of the Green. Burke later leased numbers 30 and 31 on the Green, and the Kildare St house, as his business expanded.

Martin Burke died in 1863 and his family sold the Shelbourne for £13,000 to William Jury, Charles Cotton and Christian Goodman. This Jury owned a hotel in College Green, and the family name still appears in Jury's hotel in Ballsbridge. Goodman had managed the Railway hotel in Killarney, and Cotton was owner of the Imperial hotel in Cork. In 1866, having bought numbers 30 and 31 on the Green outright from their owner, a Dr Carroll, the new syndicate demolished the hotel and replaced it with the Shelbourne we know today, which opened in January 1867. Luke White's heir had become Lord Annaly, and he waived the stipulation in the lease referring to the separate halldoors. But when he found that the houses built by his father could no longer be identified in the new building on the enlarged site, he angrily demanded that the former dividing line between numbers 29 and 30 be marked by a row of arrows down the new Shelbourne's facade. This hideous idea was countered by a suggestion from the new hotel's builder, a Mr Bolton, that a stone ridge on the roof could act as marker of the old boundary. This was accepted by his lordship. Bolton put up the ridge, let a suitable interval elapse, then 'lost' it by adding a few more ridges. The ridges are still on the Shelbourne's roof.

Architecturally, the hotel is obviously a high Victorian interloper in a Georgian neighbourhood, but its scale ensures that the intrusion is a pleasant one. The redbrick building has bands of cream-coloured stucco and similar window mouldings, and a parapet runs along the top. Deep two-storey bays flank the heavy porch, with its balustrade, and the projecting porch has been supplemented by a long glass awning, to shelter guests' journeys to and from vehicles on rainy days.

The Shelbourne's heavy iron scrollwork railings are punctuated by four big granite Egyptianesque cubes, on each of which a bronze female figure holds aloft a torch-shaped lamp. These figures have now been painted. The inner pair, with Egyptian-style headdresses, are Nubian princesses, and the others Nubian slave girls. The slave girls' status is emphasised by fettered ankles, but the sculptor seems to have been a good democrat, as they are considerably better-looking than the princesses.

The houses immediately east of the main hotel, which are now its annexe, were built by Lord de Montalt, who bought the mansion they replaced when its owner, the second Lord Lanesborough, died in 1768. With the houses, de Montalt passed on to the Shelbourne, via the La Touche banking family, who owned it for a time, some beautiful plasterwork for the Georgian cocktail bar later installed here. Number 32, the part of the annexe nearest the main hotel, has had two storeys added since the peer's day.

61

The interior of the Shelbourne has been noted since its building for luxury and spaciousness. Care was taken to ensure that the doors were wide enough to accommodate a lady's bustle. From the outset it was the haunt of titled people, leaders of fashion and army officers, British and Irish. George Moore set much of his novel, *A Drama in Muslin* there, and also deals with the hotel in his trilogy *Hail and Farewell*. Thackeray was a guest in the old Shelbourne in 1842, and later wrote of it as a 'big red house'. The Shelbourne is also traditionally associated with the social functions of Dublin's horse show week each August, as it formerly was with those of the winter 'Dublin Castle season'. The constitution of the Irish Free State was drafted in the Shelbourne, in room 112 in the front of the first floor.

Going from the Shelbourne to the top of Grafton St, we pass the Friendly Brothers' house at number 22; note the long-roofed wrought iron balcony, perfectly preserved. Number 17 is the University Club, with the stone-fronted St Stephen's Green Club further along at number 9. Sir Walter Scott stayed here with his son and daughter-in-law in 1825, remarking that it was a large and noble house and that its builders never foresaw its use as 'garrison lodgings'. (His son was an army officer.) Scott also criticised the Protestants of his day for dropping the 'Saint' from the Green's title. Number 8, the Hibernian United Service Club, is a splendid building, with its gracefully curved double sweep of steps and balustrade, and lamps, and unusually pale brickwork. Beside it, numbers 6 and 7 formerly housed 'Smyth's of the Green', one of Dublin's most exclusive grocery shops.

Walking along the built-up west side of the green, we see more clearly the disparity between it and the other three sides. It was neglected during the eighteenth century, being socially undesirable for domestic building, partly because of a history of executions, partly because of a cemetery there, partly because a haunt of criminals called Raparee Fields was adjacent to it, and no police force had jurisdiction there. The compelling reason for its unpopularity, however, was most likely the former presence of a leper house, where Mercer's Hospital now stands. We can see this hospital, at the end of Lower Mercer St, by looking up South King St from the corner of the Green. The leper asylum, which incorporated a church of St Stephen, had been there since the early thirteenth century. Though it was closed in 1698, eighteenth-century speculators probably found that a tradition of nearly 500 years takes some time to be forgotten. In 1724 a charitable lady named Mary Mercer built a house and school for '20 poor girls or other persons' on the old leper house site, which did nothing to endear the neighbouring side of the Green to Georgian builders. In 1733, finding the area unsuitable for the school, possibly because of the criminals and lack of police supervision, she decided to move to a rural setting, and the following year the school was handed over to trustees for the accommodation of 'sick and diseased poor'. This was the beginning of Mercer's hospital, but in terms of reference probably revived memories of the leper asylum.

The west side is dominated by the Royal College of Surgeons, a handsome building by William Murray on the site of the old cemetery

Mercer's Hospital

The Royal College of Surgeons

62

with a balustrade and ten engaged Tuscan columns, erected between 1825 and 1827, and with a large modern extension running along York St. A new police force, with jurisdiction extending beyond the city boundaries, had been established in 1808, so that criminal encampments, to survive, would have to be far removed from the Green. The only criminals to bother the surgeons were body-snatchers, anxious to bring bodies into the premises — and sell them — rather than remove anything. Further along this side of the green is the Unitarian church of 1863, with its slim, slated spire. The church, an unpretentious Gothic building, incorporates the Damer Hall, a small but enterprising Irish-language theatre.

Unitarian church

The south side of the Green is dominated by buildings of University College, Dublin — including University Church — and by Iveagh House, now the headquarters of the Department of Foreign Affairs. For many years the Centenary Methodist church of 1842 and the Russell Hotel were the outstanding features of the south-west corner. But the church was destroyed by fire, although the heavy facade remains, and the hotel was pulled down by property 'developers'. Also gone from this end of the Green is Wesley College, which was set back behind the streetline and possessed the curious postal address of 94½.

Dublin's first university was established in 1312, as a national university, at St Patrick's Cathedral by a Papal Bull issued from Avignon by Clement V. But rules for its administration were not drawn up until eight years later. In 1358 its students were granted the protection of Edward III, but in 1363 it appears that there were no students. Yet in 1364 Lionel, Duke of Clarence, presented land for the endowment of a lecturer in theology, an Augustinian friar, and in 1496 stipends for lecturers were mentioned in a decree of the Irish Synod. This university, though it may have functioned only spasmodically owing to civil disturbances, was in existence until the dissolution of the cathedral's Catholic establishment by Henry VIII. Unsuccessful attempts were made to revive it as a Catholic university in 1568 and 1585.

The establishment of the Catholic university in what is now Newman House at number 86 St Stephen's Green was an entirely different matter. The Catholic hierarchy was dissatisfied with Trinity, complaints being that the measure of religious freedom there still denied Catholics the most lucrative honours, and that, in any case, many Catholics of moderate means could not afford to attend it. It was recalled that in the 1585 attempt to revive the St Patrick's Cathedral university, Sir John Perrot, the Lord Deputy, had envisaged the establishment of separate universities in Dublin, but that this plan had been successfully opposed by the Lord Chancellor and Protestant archbishop of Dublin, Adam Loftus. A second, and Catholic, university was the bishops' ideal. A second university was established in 1849, under an Act of 1845, when three 'Queen's Colleges' were opened in Belfast, Cork and Galway. These, constituting the Queen's University, were nondenominational, their professors being forbidden to teach any doctrine, or to make any statement derogatory to the religious convictions of any of their students. The new university was empowered to grant degrees in the usual faculties, except in theology.

Instead of solving what had become known as the 'Irish university question', the new university was condemned by the Catholic bishops as a 'godless institution' and in 1854 they voluntarily established the Catholic University of Ireland, with neither aid nor recognition from the state. It had only one college, the Catholic University College, at 86 St Stephen's Green. This impressive granite house, with a great stone lion sprawled on the lintel, is now called **Newman House**, but has also during its university career been known as St Patrick's House and University House. Built in 1765 for Richard Whaley MP, a notorious priest hunter who was nicknamed 'Burn-chapel Whaley of Whaley Abbey, Ballinaclash', it passed, on his death in 1769, to his son **'Buck'**, a flamboyant rake and gambler, who became an MP at the age of 18, and was a regular at the card tables in Daly's club in College Green. 'Buck' Whaley has been described as a layabout, but the description ill fits a man who walked from Dublin to Jerusalem to win a bet. Newman House has a wonderful array of plasterwork birds, 63 in all, on walls and ceiling, executed by Robert West. Next door, number 85 has a smaller stone front, and is also part of UCD. This was built in 1739 as Clanwilliam House to the design of Richard Cassels. Its beautiful plasterwork is by the Francini brothers, and their Apollo panel on a chimney breast there, in the late Louis XIV style, is exquisite.

John Henry (later Cardinal) Newman was the Catholic university's first rector, but he won only lukewarm support from the Irish bishops, who were anyhow divided on the project, Archbishop Murray of Dublin having been totally opposed to it. They were uneasy about Newman's Englishness, and about his reluctance to regard this college as one for Irish Catholics only. After Newman returned to England, the Catholic university eventually came under the academic wing of Jesuits, but there was still opposition from the hierarchy to lay appointments. The poet Gerard Manley Hopkins was professor of Greek from 1884 to 1889, and Aubrey de Vere and the Gaelic scholar Eugene O'Curry also held appointments. James Joyce was a student from 1899 to 1902. But in the meantime, the university's status had altered. The University Education (Ireland) Act of 1879 provided for the dissolution of the Queen's University, though the Queen's Colleges were unaffected. A royal charter of 1880, granted under the authority of this act, established the Royal University of Ireland.

This was established, on the lines of London University, merely as an examining body, and it occupied buildings in Earlsfort Terrace, off the Green, which had been erected for international exhibitions in 1865, 1872 and 1873. The Catholic University became an 'approved college' of this university, and fifteen of the Royal University's twenty-nine fellowships were assigned to it. In 1908, with the passing of another act, the Catholic University became University College Dublin, a constituent college of the National University of Ireland. A new main building was erected in Earlsfort Terrace between 1914 and 1919, designed by R. M. Butler. The long facade of limestone, with its Ionic pillars, while not exactly enhancing the neighbourhood, does not detract from it. UCD retains some faculties in Earlsfort Terrace, but the new campus is in suburban Belfield.

Dr Newman's neo-Byzantine University Church stands to the west **University** of Newman House, linked to it by a floating canopy over a redbrick **Church** entrance that does not even hint at the lovely interior. Newman brought John Hungerford Pollen from England to design it as a collegiate church, and it was built between 1854 and 1856.

Iveagh House, at numbers 80 and 81, was occupied by a Bishop **Iveagh House** Clayton, then by Lord Mountcashel, who called it Mountcashel House, then, after a period of dereliction, by Sir Benjamin Lee Guinness. It was presented to the Irish government in 1939 by the second earl of Iveagh, a descendant of Sir Benjamin.

The Green's east side retains more of its Georgian character than any of the others, but some of this is due to rebuilding. Towards the south-east corner, Sean Lemass House, named after a former taoiseach (prime minister), replaces the huge St Vincent's hospital. When it was announced that the hospital site was to be rebuilt, fears were expressed that the hospital's Georgian facade would be lost, but it then transpired that the hospital authorities themselves had altered the eighteenth-century character of the place in the nineteenth century.

The new builders have gone some way towards restoring it to its original form. Henry Grattan and earls of Meath are among former residents of this site. In the lane behind the former hospital is a great brick outbuilding, unknown to most Dubliners, with a former dispensary. These now house a state laboratory. Going along Leeson St, **Leeson St** with its restaurants, towards the Grand Canal, the Catholic University School on the left offers another fine example of a reconditioned Georgian house. At Leeson St bridge turn right, follow the canal for a moment, turn right again into Adelaide Rd, with the synagogue and the tiny Lutheran church of St Finian on our left, where an Irish-speaking Church of Ireland congregation was formerly established. Beyond it, on the same side, is Harcourt Terrace, Dublin's finest group of Regency **Harcourt** houses. To the right stands the florid Royal Victoria Eye and Ear **Terrace** hospital of 1897. This was built under the terms of an act of that year **Royal Victoria** which amalgamated two older hospitals, the national eye and ear **Eye and Ear** infirmary of Molesworth St and the ophthalmic and aural hospital of St **hospital** Mark in Lincoln Place, which had been founded in 1844 by Oscar Wilde's father William. If we continue along Adelaide Rd we will reach Harcourt St, a stately Georgian row. Immediately on our right is the **Harcourt St** former railway station, referred to simply as 'Harcourt St', with a little piazza of sixteen Tuscan pillars, broken in the middle by a large round arch surmounted by a pediment. The arch is flanked, over the cornice of the piazza, by large inverted consoles. Despite its small scale, and the fact that brown bricks are used in the upper part, the station has a noble classical look. It was designed by G. Wilkinson and opened in 1859, as the Roman numerals on the centre tablet tell us. It was then the terminus of the Dublin and Wicklow Railway, on whose construction Isambard Kingdom Brunel had worked. The station was built for £8,502, and the first train ran from it on Monday, 7 February 1859. For lovers of statistics, the last train ran from it at 4.25 p.m. on 31 December 1958, and within a year all trackwork for three miles out of the station had been lifted. The closure is still an emotive subject and is generally admitted now to be one of the worst mistakes made by the national transport company, but it came at a time of dismal official thinking, which looked on public transport as a luxury not to be tolerated unless it 'paid its way'.

Across the road, the building now known as the Television Club was erected as Four Provinces House and was designed by Michael Scott to blend in with its surroundings. Near it was the High School, where Yeats was once enrolled, yet another academy to have moved to the suburbs. At one time, Shaw lived directly opposite, at number 61. The gentle curve of Harcourt St still retains a sedate eighteenth-century air, more appropriate to the casual stroller than to the businessman in

Bram Stoker

a hurry. Nor do its literary connections stop at Yeats and Shaw. Bram Stoker, the author of *Dracula*, lived at number 16 on the left going down towards St Stephen's Green. Not a name commonly bandied about in discussions on Irish writers, he was probably the most successful of them all, simply in terms of sales. Number 15 was the home of John Scott, Lord Clonmell, a notorious judge and scoundrel known to his

'copper-faced Jack'

contemporaries as 'copper-faced Jack' on account of his complexion. This was encouraged not least by his dissipated lifestyle in the company of his bosom pal Buck Whaley. Across the junction of Montague St,

Sir Jonah Barrington

at number 14, lived Sir Jonah Barrington, the feckless and charming chronicler of late eighteenth-century Dublin. Lady Barrington was accustomed to sit in the huge first-floor bow window on the side of the house, overlooking the Clonmell establishment and noting the proceedings therein. It was Barrington who recorded that Buck Whaley twice accepted bribes during the Act of Union debate in the Irish parliament in 1800, once to vote for the Union and once to vote against.

The big building across the road is the National Children's Hospital. Number 12 is now Kennedy's art suppliers. It was rebuilt in 1884 and has an attractive Oriel window and Dutch-style top, best seen from across the road. It is also worth pausing outside number 9 and looking back along Harcourt St at the great dome of Rathmines church, which is directly south of here. After that, it is best to retrace your steps as far as the corner of Hatch St, where you turn left. Beyond the junction with Earlsfort Terrace in Lower Hatch St is the startling University Hall in red-brick Victorian Gothic. It clashes with everything about it but at least demonstrates the freedom with which Victorian architects experimented. University Hall and the Eye and Ear are almost back-to back. From here, cross the junction of Leeson St and follow the curve of Pembroke St into the quiet of Fitzwilliam Square. **University Hall**

Fitzwilliam Square's first appearance is on a plan submitted by Viscount Fitzwilliam of Merrion for the approval of the Wide Streets Commission in 1791. On this, the square is marked out for building. The first leases were granted in that year, and building began on the square's north side, with the west and east sides being begun in 1798. After that, building was spasmodic. Though the houses are not as large as those on Merrion Square nor as ornate inside, they are remarkably well finished. The square lacks associations with the notabilities of the eighteenth century. It first found favour with members of the legal profession. **Fitzwilliam Square**

It was later popular with the medical profession as it still is, and is the only Dublin Georgian square whose central park is still reserved for residents. It was finished in 1825, the latter part of a spate of Georgian building begun in 1762 by viscount Fitzwilliam of Merrion, as the development of the 'town end' of his sprawling estates. Notice that much of the pathway on the inner, or park, side is below the level of the roadway, and that on the west side of the square there is a double path, the outer one being higher. A gateway stands in the centre of the railings on each side, those in the longer north and south sides being elegantly arched. Inside, an ornamental fountain has been installed in the south-east corner for the use of the residents, while near the north-west corner is a once-common pump for the use of the gardeners. Walking around the square, we go back up Pembroke St. In the lower end of this street, at number 5, is the cabinetmaking premises of James Hicks; much of the furniture for Titania's Palace, the unique doll's house sold in January 1978 for £135,000 by Christie's of London, was made here when the firm collaborated with the fairy-tale writer Major Sir Neville Wilkinson to build the palace, whimsically said to be for a fairy his three-year-old daughter Guendolen said she saw at the bottom of their garden in Mount Merrion.

Coming back to Leeson St and returning to the east side of St Stephen's Green, we pass Sean Lemass House, Loreto girls' college at numbers 53 and 54, with its high steps and a fine doorway at number 53, and the Office of Public Works at number 51, a building of heavy dignity, its broad steps rising between stout balustrades with a circular motif; the steps begin between granite Egyptianesque pillars supporting slim posts topped by white globes, and the front balustrade is

punctuated by six more of these pillars in limestone, with a granite one at each end. Further down, the houses on either side of Hume St entrance are modern, but were built in Georgian style following a protest and a student occupation of the houses they replaced, dubbed the 'battle of Hume St' by the popular press and television. Hume St was begun in 1768. Sir Richard Griffith, called the father of Irish geology, was born in number 8 in 1784. Suitably, the offices of the Irish geological survey are at number 14, across the street, facing the City of Dublin Skin and Cancer hospital. Going into Ely Place, the big red house facing up Hume St is number 8, Ely House, headquarters of the Knights of St Columbanus. The novelist George Moore lived at number 4 Upper Ely Place from 1901 to 1911.

Hume St

Ely Place

Emerging at the lower end of Ely Place, we have Merrion Row on our left, going back towards the Green, with its Huguenot cemetery of 1693, close to the Shelbourne; this cemetery seems not to have inhibited building on that side of the Green, as another did on the west side. It is a neat, almost square, enclosure. To our right is Lower Baggot St, a meandering Georgian mall, which curves off in a south-easterly direction towards the canal at Macartney Bridge. Walking along it, one finds the trees in the centre its most pleasing feature nowadays, since its Georgian character has been interrupted by demolition and the erection of some unsuitable modern blocks. The dark bulk of the Bank of Ireland building on the left, with its glass and grey steel, is an obvious intrusion. Cross the canal bridge and go a little way along Upper Baggot St, whose later period is obvious from its ornate Victorian architecture, rising to an irregular skyline over the shops on the left, and in the highly colourful Royal City of Dublin hospital's redbrick and terracotta. The hospital was founded in 1832, and rebuilt to an enlarged plan in 1893.

Merrion Row

Lower Baggot St

Going back to the city side of the bridge, turn right down Herbert Place, where Georgian houses with front gardens face the Grand Canal. Opposite a house called Assumpta House we find steps leading down to the towpath, but one must take care, turning left along the path at the bottom of the steps, not to trip over the protruding roots of the trees which shade the path. This is one of the 'leafy-with-love banks' celebrated by poet Patrick Kavanagh. The rustic track should be taken slowly. It is quite a transition from the high urbanity of the hundred-foot-wide Baggot St. The canals of Dublin, unlike those of Amsterdam, give a sense of detachment, best captured, perhaps, on the towpath on the other side of Macartney bridge, which leads one up towards Leeson St. Incredibly, there are regular suggestions of filling in the canals. Coming to Huband Bridge, with its 1791 up-country hump, we find the towpath wider and more even. On the left we see the apse of St Stephen's Church in Mount St Crescent, but before taking a closer look at it, we may wander further along the canal to Mount St bridge, on the far side of which is a cut stone memorial to volunteers killed in fighting here in 1916.

Herbert Place
Grand Canal

St Stephen's Church

The terrace facing the canal between Mount St and Huband bridges is Warrington Place. Coming back up it, turn right into Mount St Crescent, another quiet retreat. St Stephen's is nicknamed the

St Stephen's Church, the 'pepper cannister'

'pepper canister church'. Standing on its island, its classical facade and domed tower dominate the view along Upper Mount St, in front of it, as can be seen upon reaching the other end of the street. The church, designed by John Bowden and built in 1824 and 1825, does not deserve its undignified soubriquet. Off the crescent, on its south side is Herbert St, whose other end we have already seen. In number 2, near the crescent and on our left looking towards Baggot St, Sir Charles Villiers Stanford, the composer, was born in 1852. Upper Mount St contains the headquarters of both the Fianna Fáil and Fine Gael political parties. The Fianna Fáil building is at number 13, on our right going from the church, and is now called Áras de Valera (de Valera House) after the former Irish president and party founder. The Fine Gael building is on the far side at number 51.

Pause at the south-east corner of Merrion Square. Look down the east side of the square towards the national maternity hospital at the top of Holles St, the street itself being just out of sight. The line that begins at the hospital and passes us, comprising Merrion Square east, Fitzwilliam St, Fitzwilliam Square east and Fitzwilliam Place, over a half-mile long, was once the longest unbroken line of Georgian houses in Europe.

Herbert St

Upper Mount St

Merrion Square

70

The beauty of the stretch was enhanced by the pleasant view of the Dublin hills to the south. The view to the north from the southern part of this stretch is dominated by a large gasometer, usually the subject of discreet silence. It can be seen rising behind the hospital. The Electricity Supply Board, in 1961, decided to demolish seventeen houses in Lower Fitzwilliam St and build a new office block, and violent opposition from the public and Dublin Corporation failed to stop the plan, though it delayed it. If we look south, we see the office block on the left.

The central park in Merrion Square was acquired by the Catholic hierarchy as the site for a cathedral that was never built, and is now a public park, which so far has not suffered too much artificial development. The square was originally intended by viscount Fitzwilliam to be much bigger than it is, running onto a new street to be laid down east of the present long Georgian stretch whose mutilation has been noted. On the square's east side, number 39 has been restored to its original form after another sort of mutilation. As the British embassy, it was burnt down a few years ago. Going along the south side of the square, we pass number 56, known as Argyle House, where the Liberator, Daniel O'Connell, lived; number 65, where the Viennese physicist Erwin Schrodinger, winner of a Nobel prize in 1933 for his studies of wave mechanics, worked; number 70 where Joseph Sheridan Le Fanu lived; number 77 where Andrew O'Connor, the American sculptor, died in 1941; number 82 where W. B. Yeats lived from 1922 to 1928, and number 84, which housed the office of George Russell (Æ), Yeats's ally in the Irish literary revival.

Daniel O'Connell

W. B. Yeats

In Merrion Square

Upper Merrion St

The next turn left is Upper Merrion St. Number 24, Mornington House, an enormous five-bay Georgian mansion on the left, occupied by the Land Commission, is generally recognised as the birthplace of the duke of Wellington, Arthur Wellesley, though he is sometimes said to have been born in Trim, Co. Meath. Wellington, despite his huge monument in the Phoenix Park, has never been a popular memory in Ireland, largely because of his opposition to Catholic emancipation, which, as British prime minister, he was forced to concede, though unwillingly. However, he never inspired the hatred felt here for another one-time occupant of number 24 Upper Merrion St, Robert Stewart Castlereagh. While this son of an Ulster landowner is blamed in England for the 'Peterloo' massacre at St Peter's Fields, Manchester, in 1819, and remembered with distaste accordingly, his memory in Ireland is linked with his part in the suppression of the 1798 rising, and his manipulation of votes to secure the passage of the Act of Union. Neither he nor Wellington is accorded a commemorative plaque on the house.

Government Buildings

Across the road are Government Buildings. Though the ironwork of the gate bears the date 1922, we notice an inscription on the building furthest from us, stating in Latin that it was begun in the reign of Edward VII and finished in that of George V, and George V is likewise commemorated in the high stonework over Merrion St. The main building was designed by Sir Aston Webb as the Royal College of Science, and opened by George V when he visited Dublin in July 1911. Adjuncts to it became offices of the Ministries of Agriculture and Local Government, still in British days. In the upper stonework of the front screen we see the names of the ministries borne on scrolls by carved cherubs under outsize crowns. Going down towards the west side of

Merrion Square, we find it mainly occupied by Leinster Lawn, with Leinster House in the background.

Leinster House

Leinster House was designed by Richard Cassels for the earl of Kildare, who in 1766 became duke of Leinster. The house was begun in 1745 and finished in 1748. It was the biggest and most lavish of the city mansions, and its position was a splendid fillip to the development of the south-east of the city. The house will be better viewed from Kildare St, but it is worth noting here that Lord Kildare was forced to lease land from viscount Fitzwilliam, on which to lay out Leinster Lawn. The land on which the house stands was formerly part of Mychen's Fields, once the property of the convent of St Mary de Hogge, and the earl had bought it in 1744 from the Molesworths.

In 1814 the Royal Dublin Society, then simply the Dublin Society, bought the house from the duke of Leinster. The museums, gallery and library which now bear the prefix 'national' followed later in the century. The National Gallery was built between 1859 and 1864. The design was by Francis Fowke, but some additions, including the rather forbidding portico, were made by Sir Thomas Newenham Deane. This is at the lower end of Leinster Lawn, and beside it is a statue of William Dargan, organiser of the 'Great Exhibition' of 1853 on Leinster Lawn. This wealthy railway builder, who had donated £26,000 to the Dublin Society, mounted an elaborate industrial exhibition which eventually forced him almost to quadruple that contribution. Sir Joseph Paxton, with some advice from Prince Albert, had built the original Crystal Palace for the great London exhibition of 1851, and similarly Sir John Benson built a great steel and glass structure on Leinster Lawn, with a 300-foot frontage on Merrion Square. Benson's was a more pleasing building than Paxton's. At the end of August 1853, Victoria and Albert visited the exhibition. A collection of paintings assembled for this exhibition formed the original nucleus of the National Gallery, and thus justifies the statue of Dargan. On the other side of Leinster Lawn is the Museum of Natural History, outside which is a statue of Surgeon Major T. H. Parke, an Irish explorer associated with H. M. Stanley. Dail Eireann, the new Irish parliament, moved into Leinster House in 1922, the RDS moving out to Ballsbridge. An obelisk in the centre of Leinster Lawn commemorates Michael Collins and Arthur Griffith, signatories of the treaty of 1921, and Kevin O'Higgins, Minister for Justice in the infant Dail. Across the road, inset in the railings of Merrion Square, is the Rutland fountain, long neglected but now restored. It was designed in 1791 by Baker, Gandon's pupil, and commemorates the duke of Rutland, a former viceroy, and his wife. Its urns are from the Wedgwood works in Burslem, Staffordshire.

The National Gallery

Viscount Fitzwilliam originally intended to build a bigger Merrion Square than that which actually emerged from the drawing board, running onto a new street to be laid down east of where Fitzwilliam St was built. John Ensor, the experienced Georgian designer, was engaged. John and George Ensor had finished the north side of Merrion Square by 1764. It is noticeable that some of these tall houses have less grandeur in their doorways than Georgian buildings elsewhere.

Oscar Wilde lived in number 1 Merrion Square, at the corner of Lower Merrion St, as a child. His father, Sir William, owned this house from 1855 to 1876. He was an eminent physician and, like his son in later years, found himself on one occasion at the centre of a sensational trial. But whereas Oscar was the plaintiff in his case against the marquess of Queensbury, father of Lord Alfred Douglas, Sir William found himself in the uncomfortable position of defendant in an action brought by one Moll Travers, a mistress of his who had borne his child and later claimed that he had chloroformed and raped her while she was under his medical care. Wilde arranged for the adoption of the child and arranged for Moll to go to Australia, but she wanted him to divorce his wife and marry her. Wilde's wife, Speranza, who lived in Bohemian style and dressed in traditional Irish shawls embroidered with Celtic designs, was trapped into sending a damaging letter to Moll's father. Moll's libel damages came to one farthing, but Wilde's legal expenses came to about £2,000. Moll Travers, who had been a persistent caller at number 1 Merrion Square, usually delivering a scurrilous letter when

William Wilde

Wilde refused to see her, disappeared, but only temporarily. William Wilde had a brilliant career. Having studied eye and ear surgery in Vienna, he became a famous doctor, wrote books on surgery and on travel, became surgeon-oculist to Queen Victoria, was an archaeologist and was knighted. Before he died, Moll Travers, black-clad and veiled, came every day to see him, sitting motionless and silent for hours, simply looking at him. She waited there until he died, then left, still without speaking to anyone, and was never heard of again.

Kildare St

Royal College of Physicians

From Merrion Square north, we go west by way of Clare St and South Leinster St to the corner of Kildare St, turning left into this street around the club we have already encountered in Chapter 2. Up the street from it, on the same side, is the handsome Royal College of Physicians, designed by William G. Murray, son of the designer of the College of Surgeons, and completed in 1864. The College of Physicians had been granted its charter by Charles II in 1667. The college building in Kildare St occupies the original site of the Kildare St club. The club had been established here in 1782, and in the late 1850s bought the bigger site at the bottom of the street. In 1860, before they had moved, the old club was burned down. The Kildare St club, described as a landlords' club by its critics, was generally conservative and aristocratic.

Leinster House

Continuing up Kildare St, once called Coote St, we have a fine view of the front of Leinster House, across what is sometimes mistakenly called Leinster Lawn. We note the similarity to the Rotunda. In front of Leinster House a large statue of Queen Victoria by John Hughes was unveiled in February 1908, and was removed in 1948. The seated figure is now in the Royal Hospital, Kilmainham. A spate of jokes accompanied its removal from Kildare St, the humorous journal *Dublin Opinion* carrying a cartoon showing Nelson shinning down his pillar at night, reading of the removal on an abandoned newspaper poster and exclaiming: 'Good Lord, I must have a word with Dan O'Connell immediately'.

National Library

To the left of the open space is the National Library, with its

Leinster House, Kildare St

pavilions and semi-cycle of columns, resembling somewhat the parliament house in Oslo. It and the National Museum facing it were designed by Sir Thomas Newenham Deane and his son, Sir Thomas Manly Deane, in 1884, and finished before 1890. Further up Kildare St, in Kildare Place, is a statue of William Conyngham, fourth baron Plunket, who was Church of Ireland archbishop of Dublin from 1884 to 1897.

National Museum

Crossing the road and going up Molesworth St, we see the yellow sandstone Masonic hall on our right, a sextant in the tympanum being one of the symbols derived from the tools of masonry. There are about 2,700 freemasons in Dublin. The first recorded meeting of a grand lodge of the oath-bound secret society in Ireland was on 24 June 1725. Henry Grattan was a member of the order, as was Daniel O'Connell, the latter leaving it when a ban issued by Pope Clement XII in 1738 very belatedly took effect in Ireland. In the Molesworth St building are an enormous grand lodge hall, a Knights Templars chapel with altar and a Royal Arch room with dais and plaster sphinxes.

Masonic hall

Across the road were St Ann's parochial school and hall, demolished despite protests, in 1978. The school, in an unusual type of fenestral Gothic, was designed by Deane and Woodward. Around the corner to the left in Dawson St is the imposing St Ann's church, with a

Dawson St St Ann's church

75

neo-Romanesque appearance, built in pale granite and decorated with single red courses. It looks up South Anne St. To the left of the altar in its galleried interior is an unusual shelf. This was erected to hold bread for the poor, under the terms of a 1723 bequest of Lord Theophilus Newtown of Newtown Butler, leaving £13 a year to the poor of St Ann's parish, to be distributed in the form of five shillings' worth of bread per week.

Royal Irish Academy

Mansion House

Number 19 Dawson St, beside the church, is the Royal Irish Academy, with one of Dublin's finest libraries. Beyond that again, set back from the roadway, the plaster on the Mansion House's facade disguises the fact that it is a Queen Anne brick house, built in 1710 by Joshua Dawson, after whom the street is named. The city arms surmount the building, with its wrought iron and glass canopy, and eight fine lamps, and the same motif is on each gate into the round room, on the left. This round room was built at the Corporation's expense in 1821 for the reception of George IV. Dawson had had a large garden surrounding his residence, but in 1715, the Corporation deeming it necessary to have a permanent residence for the lord mayor, they bought the property and contents from him for £3,500, no rent being payable after that, but 'one loaf of double refined sugar of six pounds weight' to be paid to Dawson's representatives every Christmas, if demanded.

This pleasant street also contains the large Royal Hibernian hotel, and there is a vividly colourful Victorian facade over Brown Thomas's shop further down. Between these two is Duke St, and going along it towards Grafton St we pass between the celebrated hostelries of Davy Byrne's, on the left, and the Bailey. It was in Davy Byrne's 'moral pub' that Mr Leopold Bloom ate a cheese sandwich, smellsipped his cordial juice and was pestered by Nosey Flynn. But Grafton St, gay with housed

Grafton St

awnings, lured his senses. Grafton St is Dublin's most fashionable shopping street, and its meandering curves are a relief from the rectangular rigidity we have left. Bewley's cafe, above the narrow Johnston's Court, has mosaics and rich mahogany oddly juxtaposed in the facade. There are three Bewley's 'oriental' cafes in the inner city, here and at Westmoreland St and at South Great George's St. The firm, owned by one of Dublin's leading Quaker families, began as tea and coffee merchants in Sycamore St, sometime before 1842. This side of the business continues, but the idea of opening cafes came because customers insisted on sampling the product on the spot before purchase.

Near the top of Grafton St on the right, we pass Harry St and McDaid's bar, a former Bohemian and literary haunt, especially in the forties and fifties. From here, Balfe St leads around to Chatham St. Balfe St commemorates Michael Balfe, composer of *The Bohemian Girl*, who was born here in 1808. In Chatham St, Neary's has one of the finest pub fronts in the city and is a theatrical gathering place, for its back door is opposite the stage door of the Gaiety theatre. The theatre itself faces on to South King St and its yellow bricks and interior of 'theatre baroque' are known to all Dubliners. It was designed by C. J. Phipps and opened by Mr M. Gunn in 1871. For many years it was closely identified with Jimmy O'Dea, probably the greatest of all the Dublin

Mansion House, Dawson St

comics, who drew audiences from all walks of life, including those who never manifested any interest whatsoever in ordinary 'straight theatre'. In earlier times Ellen Terry, Beerbohm Tree, Henry Irving and Martin Harvey all appeared here.

Turn right at the end of South King St and go down South William St, passing the absorbing Civic Museum, which is well worth a visit. **South William St** Just beyond it is Powerscourt House, not to be confused with the house of the same name near Enniskerry which was designed for the same family by Cassels in 1731. This town house was built in 1771 to the design of Robert Mack, who had previously designed Essex — now Grattan — Bridge, linking Capel St and Parliament St. Powerscourt House passed **Powerscourt** into the hands of a wholesale textile firm in 1835 but still contains some **House** splendid plasterwork by Michael Stapleton.

The area we have covered in this chapter is the most fashionable in the inner city in terms of commerce, the medical and legal professions, clubs and social pursuits. It contains not only the seat of government and seats of learning, but the lord mayor's official residence and two of the city's most prestigious hotels. It also has a high proportion of the surviving domestic Georgian architecture, including three of the city's five Georgian squares.

The importance of the eighteenth century to the history of the city lies in the fact that it involved a conscious exercise in town planning, a deliberate experiment in urbanity, of which we had no experience before the Georgian period and which, lamentably, we have failed to repeat since. Georgian Dublin is small by modern standards, but in its own time was larger than any British city, except London, and was in every respect the second city of the empire. It is a reminder to modern Dubliners, and indeed to urban dwellers everywhere, that the word 'city' need not be a synonym for pollution and motorised horror. The serenity of the great squares and the canal walks is still there to remind us of the higher possibilities.

5   From Anna Livia to Bella Cohen

Custom House — North Wall — Busaras —
Connolly Station — Aldborough House —
O'Connell schools — Summerhill — Monto —
Pro-cathedral — Tyrone House.

I went down to Monto town to see young Kit McArdle,
But he wouldn't lend me half a crown to go to the Waxies'
Dargle.

— Dublin ballad.

The Custom House

The Custom House is one of Dublin's most splendid buildings. Its classical beauty not only enhances the quay on which it stands, but has enabled this building to continue to dominate this stretch of the river despite the appearance, down the years, of several unsuitable neighbours. It is often called the most beautiful building in the city, and dissenters from this opinion are usually those who reserve the title for the Four Courts, another creation of the peerless James Gandon. The Custom House scores over its rival in that its Palladianism, though clearly defined, is not overstated, so that its long facade has a unified impact, spearheaded by the central superstructure and dome. The length of the facade is emphasised by the mainly two-storey construction, and the dome stresses the grandeur of the entire building.

Ships no longer berth opposite the Custom House, but the building links city and docks in a special way. To travellers arriving from the east, it has long announced the eighteenth century character of the city. And even as that character rapidly diminishes, the Custom House still stands as a reminder to citizens who pass on the quays or on the bridges above and below it that, in an age of air and space travel, Dublin is still a seaport and owes its existence to the river. The docks have moved eastward and the Portland stone front of the Custom House has weathered — some of its sharp corners have been more than simply dimmed — but one is a case of evolution and the other growing old gracefully. This building contains the essence of Dublin in that it is classical, it is eighteenth-century and it is portal. As for the masterly James Gandon, it represents him more than any other building in the city.

Custom House

79

The view from the front of the Custom House is not inspiring. On the right, just below Butt Bridge, a ponderous viaduct, disused iron lamp brackets on its parapet, carries the railway from Connolly station in Amiens St to Pearse station in Westland Row. Straight ahead is a ridge-and-furrow warehouse, and as we look across and down the Liffey we see the simple Gothic church of the Immaculate Heart of Mary on City Quay, with its low, triangle-topped spire. Beyond that the big gasometer dominates the South Wall, the same one seen when looking in the unfashionable direction along Fitzwilliam St. The bridge immediately to the left is Talbot Memorial bridge, opened in 1978. The name is a compromise between those members of Dublin Corporation who wished to commemorate Irish merchant seamen killed during World War II and those who wanted to honour Matt Talbot, the saintly Dublin labourer who worked in a timber yard in the port. The railway bridge above us was opened to traffic on 1 May 1891 as part of the City of Dublin Junction Railway, and is now part of the network of CIE, the national transport undertaking. Below the Custom House, and running back from the river towards Connolly station, are the Custom House docks, two basins connected by a lifting bridge, known as George's Dock and Inner Dock. Below them, Commons St, formerly Council St, and Guild St run up off the quay, and below Guild St is Spencer Dock, where the Royal canal enters the Liffey.

A little above the corner of Guild St is North Wall House, the offices of the British and Irish Steampacket Co, former departure point for passenger ships to Liverpool. Here cattle are regularly seen crossing the road from the lairs near the offices to ships. Looking across the river from near the corner of Guild St, we see to the right of the gasometer the tower of St Mary's church in Haddington Road in the distance, rising beyond Sir Patrick Dun's hospital. In the foreground is the building of the Tropical Fruit Co., adorned with two carved stone heads.

Edward Smyth These heads are by Irish sculptor Edward Smyth, and were the central arch keystones in the old Carlisle Bridge, which was designed by Gandon in 1791, finished in 1794 and later replaced by the wider bridge now called O'Connell Bridge.

Below Guild St is Dublin's least known defunct railway passenger terminus, now British Rail offices. A glance at the upriver side of the dark brick building shows the low rear part which housed the platforms, the awning still in place. Below it, in brighter redbrick, is another British Rail office block, surprisingly exuberant, with copper dome, dormer windows, arches, bay windows and wrought iron balcony rails. This, connected by overbridge to the station until 1977, was a hotel for passengers transferring from provincial trains to Holyhead ships, which left from here until 1922. The overbridge and an underground passage to the ship, now blocked up, allowed transit through Dublin without using a public thoroughfare. The station and its short connecting line to the Great Southern and Western system were, like the hotel and boats, owned by the London North Western Railway, (the company that owned Euston, London), and the passenger link existed from 1877 until 1922, the only case of an English railway having a line and station in Dublin.

Part of the design of Dublin port is the work of Capt William Bligh, of *Bounty* fame.

Back at the Custom House, the railway bridge, with its four great iron feet resting on two huge pontoons in the river, obscures the view from upstream. So the building is often looked at from across the water, much detail being missed. It is 375 feet long and 205 feet deep, and its sides almost directly face the four principal compass points. The front, facing the river, is of Portland stone, the other three sides of mountain granite. A central pile 100 feet wide separates two interior courts. The central front projection has eight Tuscan columns, four of them in the portico, and is joined to the end pavilions by arcades, each with seven arches. Each pavilion has two Tuscan columns. All these columns have harps in the capitals. The building has a heavy projecting cornice and is crowned by a large copper dome on a pillared drum, with four pedimented clocks, bringing the height to 120 feet. Above this rises a sixteen-foot statue of Hope, resting on her anchor. There are symbolic stone figures in high relief in the tympanum, and the balustrade over the pavilions is broken by very large stone carvings of the royal arms, emphasising the Custom House's Palladian style. These arms are repeated at the back of the building, where we see a quatrastyle portico, with no pediment, instead of which are four statues representing Europe, Asia, Africa and America. Surmounting the east and west sides are four great urns, each bearing a lion's head. Under each of these, and under each carving of the royal arms, are three smaller lions' heads.

The large lions which, with the unicorns, form part of the royal arms will be noticed, incidentally, to have rows of large stone teeth. Below the building's dividing frieze are thirteen heads of riverine gods, corresponding to thirteen Irish rivers. These form the keystones of various arches. Reproductions of some of them are found on the backs of the older Irish banknotes. Granite steps lead us to the central part of the south front, where we see a fourteenth head, a female representation of the Atlantic ocean, high over the door. Immediately over the door are Neptune's trident and two sea serpents. Above us, on the front and sides of the entablature over the central pillars, are six carved bulls' heads, serving to remind us that beef is one of the main exports through this port. The four bovine heads facing the river are interspersed with carvings of encircled harps.

In the garden behind the Custom House is a memorial by Yann Renaed Goulet to Edward Dorrens, Sean Doyle, Daniel Head, Patrick O'Reilly and Stephen O'Reilly, members of the Dublin brigade of the IRA killed during fighting here on 25 May 1921. During this fighting the Custom House was burned to a shell. It was rebuilt in as near a form as feasible to the original, but a walk around it will show that it is not perfectly symmetrical. The flat east side, with those long windows, should have a two-storey projection, as the west side, facing the line of cherry trees, has.

The old Custom House, designed by Thomas Burgh, had stood on the present Wellington Quay, roughly where the Clarence hotel is now. Rt Hon. John Beresford, second son of the earl of Tyrone, was chief commissioner of Irish revenue, and a member of the Wide Streets

Commission, when he formed his plan to build a new one. The old one was too far upstream for ships of deep draught. This was costing the port revenue, and such large ships as were induced to use the port and unload at Ringsend were causing traffic problems through horse transport of goods between there and the upper quays. Beresford invited

James Gandon   James Gandon, to whom he had been introduced by Lord Carlow, to come to Dublin and plan the new edifice. Gandon, whose paternal grandfather was a Huguenot and whose mother was Welsh, had been a pupil of Sir William Chambers, who was only 16 years his senior; Gandon's English buildings included the New Bethlehem hospital in London and Nottingham county hall and jail. In 1768 he had submitted a design for a royal exchange in Dublin, but the city's bankers and merchants chose Thomas Cooley's plan for the building, now the city hall, placing Gandon's submission in second place.

Before receiving Beresford's invitation, he had been asked by Catherine the Great, through her friend Princess Dashkoff, director of the St Petersburg academy of arts and sciences, to design public buildings in that city. He chose to come to Dublin instead, arriving in 1781.

Residents of fashionable streets near the site proposed for the Custom House believed that it would turn the area into a slum. Mabbot St was one of the oldest of these streets, running along what is now Corporation St and across Talbot St to the site of the present bus station. As early as 1774 they had petitioned parliament to have the rumoured development stopped. Luke Gardiner does not appear to have shared their misgivings, or Mountjoy Square would not have been built. And Mabbot St was still a fashionable address 50 years after the furore. Gandon himself took a house in Mecklenburgh St, near Tyrone House, thus expressing his confidence in the social outcome of his work.

The foundation stone of the Custom House was laid on 18 August 1781. Trenches were built to keep tides from inundating the site, which had formerly been known as Angel's Ground. Sea water was discovered less than a yard below the surface, and a raft foundation, of timber and mortar strapped together by iron chains, was laid. In the meantime, the lord lieutenant was petitioned by the merchants who opposed the venture to have the building stopped.

When this was supported by official hostility from Dublin Corporation, mobs broke down site fences and tried to pull up piles. Gandon received threatening letters, and took to wearing a sword on the site, letting it be known that he had been a good swordsman in his student days, and would 'defend himself to the last'. The entire building took ten years, and cost over £546,000.

Henry Darley, the general contractor, suggested to Gandon that Edward Smyth could work on the building's sculptures. Smyth was a pupil of the sculptor Simon Virpile, who had been brought to Dublin by Lord Charlemont to sculpt the ornaments on the Casino in Marino. Smyth executed the statue for the top of Gandon's beautiful dome, the riverine heads, the figures in the tympanum and the royal arms. Gandon was so pleased that he extravagantly likened Smyth's work to that of Michelangelo.

A pamphlet circulated in Dublin during the construction repeated the old fear that it would introduce to the heart of the city 'a low and vulgar crowd with the manners of Billingsgate'. Mr and Mrs S. C. Hall, in *Ireland, its Scenery and Character*, written 50 years after the Custom House opened, said: 'Unhappily, the paucity of Dublin's commerce is such that a cottage might suffice to transact its 'business', in lieu of a palace.'

Visitors may notice a variation in stone colour in this magnificent building, especially in the darkness of those in the dome's drum. This dates from the rebuilding that followed the 1921 burning.

At the back of the Custom House and also designed by Gandon is a curved row of Georgian houses running from Lower Gardiner St to Store St. This is part of Beresford Place named after John Beresford. The house on the extreme left, formerly the Granville Hotel, has broad steps following the curve of the corner. It is also noticeable that the railway crossing the bottom of Gardiner St here impedes the view of the distant hill rising towards Mountjoy Square. It also hides an employment exchange. Gardiner St runs approximately from the middle of the custom house, though it is not at a right angle to the building. Very approximately, it traces the course of a former thoroughfare called Old Rope Walk. Gandon's Beresford Place terrace has a unified facade, without the usual individual variations found in rows of Georgian houses.

Beresford Place

Gardiner St

The bus station, Busaras, was completed in 1953 to the design of Michael Scott, and its juxtaposition with the Custom House was bitterly criticised. Its central feature is the lowest part of the building, a single-storey quarter circle under a cockleshell roof, filling in the angle of the L-shaped construction. The predominance of glass and the illusion of freedom from the ground were novelties here when the station was built. It its use of an L shape with an extra enclosure in the inner angle, in the illusion of the building 'floating' on pillars and in the idea

Busaras

of isolated glassless areas high up, it resembles the Centrosoyus in Moscow, now the Ministry of Light Industries, designed by Le Corbusier (Charles Jeanneret) in 1928.

With the trees and railings of the Custom House on the left, go back around part of the station and turn into Store St, noting the filled-in arch on the bakery which occupies the former Custom House stores.

Store St

Talbot Place cuts between the orange bricks of Store St garda station – formerly the Red Lamp police station — with its new extension, and the darker Victorian ones of the coroner's court and city morgue. Emerging into shop-lined Talbot St, formerly Moland St, we see the granite Italianate Connolly railway station in Amiens St to the right. Now that Nelson Pillar has gone, this station commands the view along Talbot St, Earl St, Henry St and Mary St, and can be seen from as far away as Capel St. It was begun in 1844, having been designed by Irish architect William Deane Butler. The Italianate style was a mannerism in railway stations which had been popularised in England by the prolific Sir

Connolly station

William Tite. Connolly station is a handsome example of the style, with a striking central tower, and eight pillars and clusters of pilasters in the Composite order. Butler's station front has been spoiled by dissimilar additions to each side, but the overall effect is still impressive, and the brick buildings connected to the station by the great enclosed bridge of Sheriff St continue the Italianate motif with a square tower.

While Earl de Grey, the lord lieutenant, was laying the foundation stone of Amiens St station on 24 May 1844, Queen Victoria's birthday, its owners, the Dublin and Drogheda Railway, were just commencing

Dublin and Drogheda Railway

their service. The company had been incorporated by an act of 1836, and track-laying had begun in 1840. It was seemingly ludicrous for the owners of a railway thirty-two miles long to be erecting a grandiose terminus, but the D. and D. was merely one part of a projected line from Dublin to Belfast. This had been mooted in 1825, when it had been proposed that the Leinster and Ulster Railway Co be set up, but the idea was premature. The act of 1836 establishing the D. and D. was accompanied by one setting up the Ulster Railway which would run from Belfast to Armagh. The Dublin and Belfast Junction Railway Act, to authorise the link over the intervening 65 miles, was passed in 1845, but no viaduct was built over the Boyne at Drogheda until 1855. (The present viaduct is a replacement of 1932.)

The three railways mentioned, and four others, were amalgamated in 1876 to form the Great Northern Railway. The City of Dublin

Great Northern Railway

Junction Railway, already referred to, was opened in 1891 to give the Dublin, Wicklow and Wexford Railway, with headquarters at Westland Row, interchange facilities with the rest of the Irish rail system. Its link with Amiens St was by means of bridges which we have already seen at Westland Row, Pearse St, the Liffey and Gardiner St, and here at Talbot St and Amiens St.

Not everyone, incidentally, appreciated Butler's lofty facade. Those who had to carry heavy luggage up the long flight of steps to the trains in the days before escalators would have preferred another design.

Sheriff St

Going under the bridge at Sheriff St, we pass the postal sorting

Connolly Station, Amiens St

office on our right, turn right and then left, until we pass the church of St Laurence O'Toole and the Spencer Dock canal bridge, beyond which other railway lines pass under us towards the North Wall goods depot. These were distinct from the Amiens St line, and originally belonged to the Midland Great Western Railway, who had bought the Royal Canal Co. in 1844 for £289,000, primarily so that they could build their railway on canal company property, beside the waterway, as far as Mullingar. As Royal Canal tonnage at the time was about two-fifths of that of the rival Grand, the shareholders had been happy to accept the offer. The next left turn is Abercorn Rd, where Sean O'Casey lived for a while as a young man, his family having rented a flat in the two-storey number 18. O'Casey also lived in Hawthorn Terrace, a pleasant street of single-storey houses with gardens, not far from here, which we could reach by taking the next turn on the left, East Road.

Seville Place

Returning to the church, we find it occupying the angle that divides Sheriff St and Seville Place. The smallish spiky Gothic church has a prominent spire, and is totally unlike the classical Gardiner St church, though designed by the same man, J. B. Keane. The influx of people into this area after the opening of the Custom House had been swollen by the immigration that attended the laying and imminent opening of the Dublin and Drogheda railway. Furthermore the Midland–Royal canal deal was rumoured at the time and was expected to bring even more people, and so it was decided to build this church.

The Catholic archbishop, Dr Murray, deciding that a new church was needed to serve about 3,500 Catholics who had moved into the district with the wharves, warehouses and shops that had been established, received a gift of the land, a triangle of 20,000 square feet, and £1,000 from Mr Charles Kennedy. The area had been known as North Lotts, after an old custom among Corporation members of drawing lots for the distribution of land reclaimed from the bay, and there is still vestigial evidence of this custom in such names as 'Mayor', 'Sheriff', 'Commons' and 'Guild' on streets in the district. The first stone of the new church was laid on 3 June 1844, but the church was not opened until 1850, as lack of funds repeatedly halted building.

The best feature of the church is the high altar, in Carrara marble, the work of Kirwan brothers of Bolton St, although somebody in later years covered some of its panels in green paint.

Five Lamps

Walking up Seville Place, note the naming of four short streets of artisan housing on the right, First, Second, Third and Fourth Avenues. We pass under a wide railway bridge, in an area of fortress-like stonework, where the footpath has its individual arch, beyond which are some large houses. At the junction of North Strand Rd, on an island, five lamps sprout from an ornate standard, whose stout base, we see, once accommodated fountains, the water gushing from the mouths of iron lions which are still there. The landmark has given the name Five Lamps to the intersection, and formerly to a tavern there, and is a monument to General Henry Hall of the Indian army.

The road to the right goes to Newcomen Bridge, named after Sir William Newcomen, one of the canal company's original subscribers. Between us and the canal, a street called Synnott St was entirely

Aldborough House and the Five Lamps

destroyed, and never rebuilt, when four German bombs struck Dublin
on the night of 31 May 1941, killing 37 people.

At the bottom of Portland Row is Aldborough House, a brick
mansion with a granite facade and great bulging curves in the back and
the side facing us. It was the last great town house built in Dublin in the
eighteenth century, and carved roman numerals over the top windows
tell us that it was finished in 1796. The earl of Aldborough, Edward
Stratford, had it built from plans sent to Ireland by Sir William
Chambers, who died the year this house was completed. With its two
curving screen walls, Aldborough House reminds us somewhat of
Chambers's Charlemont House, but it is seven bays wide instead of five,
and, with a wide Tuscan portico and pedimented central projection,
lacks the simplicity of the Parnell Square building. Notice the
inscription *otium com dignitate* engraved in gold letters over the portico,
and the words *sic siti laetantur* cut in the facade behind and above it,
under the cornice. The lions on the gateposts are corroded, reminding us
of the nearness of salt water. The bay came nearer to this spot when the
house was built than it does now. Over the pavilion below the mansion,
however, is a fine free-standing stone lion. He is guarding not only the
house but a contemplative sphinx which shares the roof with him.

Aldborough, who was also the viscount Amiens after whom
Amiens St is named, and whose family had links with building the

Portland Row

Aldborough House

87

village of Stratford-on-Slaney in Wicklow, built the house for £40,000, but did not live long there to enjoy his 'otium' or dignified relaxation. He died in 1801. In 1813, and for 17 years subsequently, it housed the Feinaglin Institute, a school run by Prof. Gregor Feinagle, from Luxembourg, using a unique system of memory training. He also called the place Luxembourg College. It later became a barrack, and is now offices and stores of the post office.

Turning right off Portland Row into Dunne St, we cross the top of Clarence St, where Walter Cox, publisher of the pungently anti-government magazine *Watty Cox's*, died in 1837 at number 12. Cox, who called his house Cox's Cot, voluntarily ceased his virulent journalism, which had begun in 1807, on receipt of a government pension. Continuing, we come to the church of St Agatha on the corner **North William St** of North William St and Dunne St. A simple, pleasant building, it was completed in 1908 after an extraordinary lawsuit involving the parish priest and the archbishop of Dublin, which was still unresolved when the priest was drowned in a boating accident at the North Wall in 1904.

The church, begun in 1878, had stopped at the string-course through lack of money. In 1902 an anonymous parishioner left £8,000 towards the building of a church in William St, and the parish priest, Fr John O'Malley, used part of this to acquire a detached Georgian house on the North Circular Road, which faces Great Charles St and was for some years later the St Agatha presbytery. He intended to build the church there, and when the archbishop reminded him that the terms of the bequest specified North William St, and insisted that these terms be carried out, the priest replied that a 'back street' was no place for a parish church, and sued the archbishop. After Fr O'Malley's fatal boat trip the building proceeded without interruption.

North William St contains a Victorian convent building which incorporates a school. An orphanage run by Trinitarian nuns stood here in the eighteenth century, and Mary Aikenhead took it over to establish the Irish Sisters of Charity in 1815. When this was moved to Upper Gardiner St in 1827, Carmelite nuns took over the William St convent, passing it over to the French Sisters of St Vincent de Paul, who are still there, in 1857.

This area had been the extreme eastern end of the monastic lands of St Mary's Abbey for some years before 1539, and a Cistercian chapel had stood about where William St convent is now. Passing on, we come to Summerhill Parade, and on the right is Clarke's Bridge, leading to Ballybough Rd, to which Georgian building eventually spread. Further **Fairview Strand** on, beyond the Tolka in Fairview Strand, is a small house with the legend: 'Built in the year 5618', a Mosaic reckoning. The nineteenth century house has a Jewish cemetery at the back, a reminder that many Jews once lived in the Ballybough–Fairview district. Many of the bigger headstones disappeared from the cemetery, and in 1824 a Jew who called to a Gentile friend's house on Ballybough Road found the man installing a new hearthstone. On being invited to read its Hebrew inscription, he replied: 'It indicates that my father is buried in your chimney.'

Clonliffe Road and Richmond Road both lead to Drumcondra

from the Tolka bridge at Ballybough, and between them stands the erstwhile home of DWD whisky. This began as the Dublin Whisky Distillery Co. in 1873, and two of the original subscribers were W. G. Craig and R. Gardner, accountants. It ended the era of the family distilling business in Dublin. Within ten years, though its older competitors had given it no chance of survival, its annual output was 500,000 proof gallons.

In 1889 DWD merged with Roe's distillery of Thomas St, the firm which had restored Christ Church cathedral, and William Jameson's of Marrowbone Lane, but this was actually a takeover by the newcomer. DWD boldly advertised its product as the 'finest whisky in the world' — some of the advertising mirrors are still found in bars — but it went out of production in the late 1920s. The road leading to its premises from Clonliffe Road is still called Distillery Road, though the former name of the works was 'Jones's Road distillery', since the original entrance had been there.

Back in Summerhill Parade, we go up Richmond Cottages, passing Hutton's small shop on our right, a survival from before supermarket days, which still carries the legend 'regd. dairy'. At the top is North Richmond St, with the main block of the O'Connell schools facing us. Opposite the lower end of the school, number 17 is another former home of James Joyce. He was also a pupil of the school, as we

Summerhill Parade

O'Connell schools

Bella St

have seen, as was his brother, Stanislaus. The school and the street are both briefly referred to in 'Araby', one of the short stories in *Dubliners*. The school takes its name from Daniel O'Connell, who laid its foundation stone on 9 June 1828, but it was then officially called the Catholic Model School, as the Catholic Association had granted £1,500 towards its erection, Catholic parents having withdrawn their children from schools run by the Kildare Place Society. This society had been entrusted by parliament in 1811 with the education of the country's poor, and had annual grants to that end, but was suspected by many Catholics of proselytising. The school in Richmond St became the headquarters of the Irish Christian Brothers when it was completed in 1831. The present main block is not the original, but its site and dimensions are exactly the same.

Oliver St John Gogarty was also a pupil here, as was Sean T. O'Kelly, a former President of Ireland. Others were John Devoy, the Fenian leader, and John A. Costello, eminent barrister and coalition government leader.

The last terrace of the North Circular Road curves down from here, again to Summerhill Parade. Across the road, the top of Portland Row is dominated by St Joseph's home for old ladies, whose harsher former title was 'asylum for aged females', run by nuns called the Poor Servants of the Mother of God. This was founded in 1836 by Bishop Blake of Dromore. The top of its long brick front is adorned by three statues in niches, but sadly these have to be protected by wire meshes.

Summerhill   Turning right up Summerhill, we find footpaths higher than the road level, with intervening stone walls. Blocks of municipal flats replace older houses. Terraced Georgian Dublin can be said to have ended here, as Ballybough Rd, which turns gently north-east, was still the coast road in the eighteenth century, until the building of Annesley Bridge at Fairview in 1797, and the area between Ballybough and North Strand Road — now intensively built up — with whatever area of the present East Wall had been reclaimed from the bay, was known as Mud Island, and was a clearing ground for smuggled goods, with the criminal encampments such activity attracts. Going left into Buckingham St and right into Bella St, we find the street level dropping sharply. In Bella St there is a quaint housing arrangement on the right, a three-storey terrace with a brick balcony running along the first floor. The first and second storeys are reached by going up steps from the street, the ground floor by going down and behind the arches of the balcony. Further on, steps lead up to another terrace, and we eventually climb steps to reach the level of Lower Rutland St. Up to our right is the tall pro-Cathedral national school, in bright red and yellow Victorian style, though the date is 1910, and off the street, opposite to it, is a quaint square of tiny single-storey houses. **Bella St**

At the bottom of the street we come to Sean MacDermott St, formerly Gloucester St. Across the road is the monastery of Our Lady of Charity of Refuge, the name in a gold-lettered horseshoe, whose nuns run an enterprise still called the Gloucester St Laundry, despite the change of street name. Beyond the glazed yellow brick gateposts at its far end is a church, used as a grain store since 1910, with a Doric portico and Greek inscription, and doorways with slanted Egyptianesque surrounds, an architectural rarity. **Sean MacDermott St**

This was erected as a Presbyterian church in 1835 and closed, because of population movement, in 1896. Across the road is a fine brown-painted Regency house, Doric pillars in the doorway and Ionic pilasters at the ends of the facade. This is a trade union headquarters and was previously called the Carpenters' Hall. Going up the street we pass the modern church of Our Lady of Lourdes, with the tomb of Matt Talbot, and come to a road junction formerly called the Gloucester Diamond. The street plan was arranged so that the intersection formed a diamond, and we see that three of the four corners follow the original plan. To our left Corporation St, formerly Mabbot St, runs towards Talbot St, and is crossed by Railway St, with Foley St meeting it further down. Railway St was formerly Lower Tyrone St, and before that again it was part of Mecklenburgh St, named after Princess Charlotte of Mecklenburgh. Foley St was formerly Montgomery St and gave the area the nickname of 'Monto'. Gandon, as we have noted, lived at number 7 Mecklenburgh St and later moved to number 39 Upper Gloucester St. Patrick Heeney, who wrote the music of the Irish national anthem, lived at 101 Mecklenburgh St. The sculptor Edward Smyth lived at number 36 Montgomery St, though he may have been born elsewhere in Dublin. The sculptor John H. Foley was born at number 6 Montgomery St, and it was renamed after him. Cardinal Cullen ran a school called St Patrick's in Mecklenburgh St, and this street contained a botanic garden from 1735 to 1795, when it was called Great Martin's Lane. **Gloucester Diamond**

'Monto'

Having deteriorated into tenements, the area was a noted red-light district in the early part of this century, possibly a belated fulfilment of the fears of those who had opposed the building of the Custom House. The 'Mabbot St entrance to nighttown' in *Ulysses* is the Talbot St end of Corporation St now; but Joyce's uncobbled tramsiding set with skeleton tracks is no longer there. The railway bridge, Cormack's corner (with pub of the same name) and Olhausen's, the German pork butcher shop are all still there. But the nighttown referred to has totally disappeared, all the houses demolished and replaced by municipal housing, and all the streets renamed. Upper Tyrone St, earlier the other part of Mecklenburgh St, which ran from Lower Gardiner St to Marlborough St, is now Waterford St, not too drastic a change of name, since Lord Tyrone, after whom it was named, became marquess of Waterford, and engaged Gandon to design a courthouse in that city. Foley St is still cobbled, but shows no other signs of the past.

This red light district was referred to by *Encyclopaedia Britannica* as having brothels carried on more openly than in southern Europe 'or even Algiers'. It was also noted that they were permitted by the police to operate openly, but were confined to one area. This leniency was thought to be unique in the United Kingdom. After the establishment of the Irish Free State the liberal attitude was changed, and the police were instructed to 'clean up Monto', so that by the middle 1920s the institution with which Joyce and Oliver St John Gogarty had been familiar was no more. As well as the police action, the Legion of Mary, a missionary society of lay Catholics, frequently visited the area, weaning girls away from whoring and bringing them to live in hostels. The convent or 'monastery' in Sean MacDermott St, which we have already seen, with another entrance in Railway St, then Lower Tyrone St, had even earlier been similarly engaged, girls who had given up prostitution going to live there and being employed in the laundry. In *Ulysses*, Bloom, horrified at having been found in Monto, tells Mrs Breen: 'Interesting quarter. Rescue of fallen women. Magdalen asylum. I am the secretary . . .'. The convent and laundry were then known as St Mary Magdalen's Asylum. Some Dubliners still miscall the institution the 'Mag Dillon'.

Monto's literary patrons were less than complimentary to the madames of the area. Gogarty in *As I Was Going Down Sackville Street* says that one of them, Mrs Mack, had a 'brick red face on which avarice was written like a hieroglyphic', while Joyce describes another, Bella Cohen, as 'a massive whore–mistress, with eyes deeply carboned, a sprouting moustache and orange-tainted nostrils'.

Monto was an area of brothels rather than of streetwalkers, though the latter engaged in a peripheral trade. The further east one went in it, the cheaper the services of the girls became, the risk of disease rising in **Mrs Meg Arnot** inverse proportion. One of the better-known madames, Mrs Meg Arnot, paraded her girls around the more fashionable streets in an open carriage as an advertisement. Professional people frequented the area surreptitiously, and in the closing days of Monto, after the establishment of the Irish Free State, a much-quoted calumny was: 'When the Senate is in session Monto is full'.

Going up Gloucester Place, we ascend by what are locally called the twenty-seven steps to emerge under an arch into Summerhill again. This arch was retained in the curious mock-Georgian rebuilding of the street as municipal flats. Across the road, a little right of us, the bus garage was once the works of the most famous Dublin coachbuilding firm, Hutton's, one of the European leaders in the field. It first became a bus garage under the Dublin United Tramway Co, now defunct, whose initials are still on the wall.

Hutton's

The Irish (or Glass) Coach, still used by Queen Elizabeth on State occasions in Britain, was built here by the firm of John Hutton, and was bought by Queen Victoria at the great Leinster Lawn exhibition in 1853. It was designed to have a driver in a central position in front, with an outrider on each horse, but the queen had this arrangement altered so that the driver's box was placed at the back. Otherwise, she said, her subjects would be unable to see her. The coach was partly rebuilt by Barker's of London after fire damage in 1911, but is still referred to as the Irish coach. Hutton's had begun business in the eighteenth century in Great Britain (Parnell) St. and the move east was made through lack of space. They specialised in large ornate coaches, but before they went out of business in 1923 were building automobile bodies, on Rolls-Royce, Benz and Daimler chassis. Annie Hutton, sweetheart of Thomas Davis, commemorated in his ballad 'Annie Dear', was one of this family.

Crossing Gardiner St we pass shops and stalls in Parnell St and turn left down Marlborough St. On our right, in the island between Cathal Brugha St and Findlater's Place, is St Thomas's Church, a nice brick neo-Byzantine building designed by Mr F. G. Hicks to replace one that had been badly damaged in the fighting of 1922 and 1923.

St Thomas's Church

Further down Marlborough St on the same side is the pro-Cathedral which was originally intended to be built where the GPO stands. The second choice was the mansion of Lord Annesley, which stood in Marlborough St facing Tyrone House, with Drogheda House roughly at its back. This was bought in 1803 by the customary middle man, a Mr Val O'Connor, for £5,100, and to swell the building fund it was rented to the barrack board for the accommodation of troops until 1814. The pro-cathedral's designer was an amateur architect, John Sweetman of Raheny, Dublin, who had lived in Paris. He made the facade of the church, with its six-pillared Doric portico, a copy of the Temple of Theseus in Athens, and modelled the renaissance interior on the church of St Philip de Reule in Paris. The first stone of the church was laid on 28 March 1815, and it was finished in 1825. Its style is more suitable to the original site, as one has to go into the grounds of the Department of Education, across the road, and walk back some distance, to appreciate the great spread of the facade, and to see the dome. In the apse of the church are two altars with lovely mosaics, and a memorial window to Sir James Power, chairman of Power's distillery.

Marlborough St pro-Cathedral

The square granite house facing us on the right, as we look over from the church, is Tyrone House, built for Sir Marcus Beresford, earl of Tyrone, in 1740 by Richard Cassels. Three storeys over a rough stone basement, it is a sombre building, unrelieved by the six square pillars in its portico. A similar building, though not a replica, stands a little away

Tyrone House

on its left. Tyrone House originally had a Venetian window above the portico, and still has Francini plasterwork and a fine rear staircase. The would-be replica is a nineteenth century construction. A white marble pieta occupies a grass area between the houses, a little way back. Unsuitably kept outdoors, it was presented to Ireland by the Italian government in 1948, in gratitude for post-war Irish aid to Italy, and is the 1930 work of Ermenegildo Luppi of Rome. The cost of transporting it to Dublin was borne by the Italian community here.

Lower Abbey St

Abbey theatre

Down at the corner of Lower Abbey St stands the Abbey theatre, a simple modern block incorporating the Peacock, designed by Michael Scott and opened on 17 July 1966, the fifteenth anniversary of the fire that destroyed the old Abbey. The first Abbey had opened in 1904 and almost immediately produced a playwright of genius in John Synge. His *Playboy of the Western World* opened in 1907 and so offended the delicate sensibilities of the audience — Catholic and nationalist in the main — that they rioted. There was more rioting, again by irate and offended nationalists, when O'Casey's *The Plough and the Stars* was first presented in 1926. It was regarded as being too unsentimental a view of the 1916 Rising. Before being bought and equipped as a theatre in 1904 by Miss Annie Horniman, who had previously managed the Gaiety in Manchester, it had been the Mechanics' Institute and before that again it had been, in turn, a morgue, an opera house and a music hall.

The Abbey achieved a world reputation, particularly for poetic drama, but by the 1940s, with Yeats dead, the original spirit had been dissipated and there were some unkind souls who suggested that it was rapidly reverting to its former status of morgue. During this decade, the Fianna Fail government endorsed a proposal for a 'Shamrock theatre', which would have entailed demolition of the old Abbey and its replacement by three theatres in a single building stretching from Abbey St to Eden Quay. One theatre would have continued the Abbey tradition, one would have devoted its energies to plays in Irish and the third would have presented 'world masterpieces'. The change of government which followed the general election of 1948 put paid to that idea and nothing has been heard of it since.

The Plough bar, across the road from the theatre, stands on the site of an old synagogue. Abbey St itself is a hotch-potch of architectural styles. On the left going back towards Beresford Place, there is the Metropolitan Christian Union building, its Venetian touch lost somewhat in the heavy brickwork, the small classical Dublin Savings Bank, and the very modern Irish Life centre, one of the more successful developments of recent years. All these stand on the site of an old bowling green. On the right-hand side of the street the main building of interest is the asymmetrical Gothic Scots' church. The right turn into Beresford Place leaves us in the shadow of Liberty Hall, a 200-foot concrete and glass tower, the headquarters of the Irish Transport and General Workers' Union. Its construction in 1965, on the site of the original Liberty Hall, destroyed in the fighting of 1916, was a case of tradition overruling intelligent town planning.

Irish Life centre

Liberty Hall

Butt Bridge

Butt Bridge, overshadowed by Liberty Hall, is named for Isaac Butt, the founder of the Irish Home Rule party in 1870. It was opened in 1879 and was the last bridge over the river until the Talbot Memorial Bridge opened in 1978. Eden Quay, running between Liberty Hall and O'Connell Bridge, commemorates William Eden, first Lord Auckland, and was formerly Iron Quay, as Burgh Quay, facing it, was the Stone Quay.

Eden Quay

6   Legal Men and Rebels

Four Courts — Mary's Abbey — City Markets —
new St Michan's — Green St — Henrietta St—
King's Inns — Broadstone — Richmond penitentiary — Richmond hospital — old St Michan's.

The Four Courts, Inns Quay

*In Inisfail the fair there lies the land of holy Michan.
There rises a watchtower beheld of men afar.*

— James Joyce, *Ulysses.*

The Four Courts, standing on Inns Quay, on the north bank of the **The Four** Liffey between Father Mathew bridge and Winetavern St bridge, is **Courts** considered by some to be the most beautiful building in Dublin, surpassing even the Custom House in magnificence. Like its rival, it was built in the late eighteenth century when classicism was at its peak, and both buildings were designed by James Gandon, though in the case of the Four Courts he took over the design from another Englishman, Thomas Cooley. The Four Courts dominates the upper stretch of the Liffey's course within the city as the Custom House does the lower. The Four Courts was commissioned by the government to replace law courts near Christ Church which had fallen into decay. Cooley, designer of the Royal Exchange, which is now the City Hall, had begun work on plans for the new courts when he died, and Gandon took over while the Custom House was still being built, in October 1785.

The entire frontage of the Four Courts on the Liffey is 440 feet, with a depth of 170 feet to the rear. The central pile is 140 feet square, and is flanked by two courtyards, each fronted by a handsome screen wall perforated by arches. This central pile was built to contain the courts which originally gave the structure its name, though possibly 'Five Courts' would have been equally appropriate, as they were listed as the Courts of Judicature, Chancery, King's Bench, Exchequer and Common Pleas. The portico contains six Corinthian columns, and over the centre of the pediment stands a statue of Moses, flanked by those of Justice and Mercy over the ends of the pediment. Out on the corners of the central pile, over the coupled pilasters, are seated figures of Authority and Wisdom. During the Irish civil war the Four Courts was largely destroyed by a bombardment in 1922. Its restoration was completed nine years later, the exterior regaining its original form, though the saucer dome is not a replica of its predecessor, and purists complain that it rises too high.

The Four Courts was originally built for about £200,000, and at times Gandon had trouble in securing the necessary finance, once having to plead his case in parliament. His original estimates having been overtaken by inflation, the rising cost was constantly questioned by the government. So was the delay in building, but this was partly due to the war with France which broke out in 1793. The Four Courts is often stated to have been completed in 1796, but was not actually finished until 1802. Gandon's decision to leave Ireland in 1797 had possibly been misinterpreted to mean that the work was over, but he was simply moving his books and his papers to Liverpool, in anticipation of a revolution. This came in 1798, by which time Gandon had rented a furnished house in Great Portland St, London. But in 1799, the rebellion being over, he came back to Dublin 'to complete the public works he had in hand', including, of course, the Four Courts.

The Four Courts stands on the former site of the great Abbey of St Saviour, a 1224 foundation of the Dominicans or 'black friars'. This had been suppressed by Henry VIII but was reoccupied by the friars in 1685, when a new tolerance of Catholics accompanied the accession of James II. Ironically the Dominicans were ousted again by this same king, who required their building for sessions of parliament. But long before that, the abbey had been already demolished and rebuilt, if not totally, then at least significantly. About 1317 Edward de Bruce, brother of Robert, had landed in Ulster and marched towards the city of Dublin, stirring the citizens to action only when he camped at Castleknock, about a mile beyond the furthest extremity of the present Phoenix Park. The mayor, Robert Nottingham, and the city commons decided on a 'scorched earth' policy as the best defence, burning down many houses so as to deny the invader accommodation. Most of the city was on the south side, but it did not escape the mayor's attention that de Bruce might camp in the monastery of the 'friar preachers', as the Dominicans were also known, across the river, and attack the town from there.

So he ordered the demolition of the abbey, then stones from it were taken across the river to build St Audoen's and Winetavern St gates. These stones still form part of the city wall in St Audoen's Arch in Cook St, and are now the only physical remains of the great abbey which once occupied the Four Courts site, apart from a tunnel which is said to run under the Liffey from the site of one of the abbey's outbuildings in North Anne St to Christ Church.

A story popular among residents and workers in North Anne St in the late nineteenth century concerns an army officer who had attended a funeral in Christ Church. He strayed through the vaults and into the cathedral end of this tunnel through a door which had been left open, but which was unwittingly locked while he was inside. He was posted as missing, and his fate was discovered only when the door was reopened on the occasion of another funeral. (Seemingly the tunnel end was used as a store for furniture used only in funerals of a certain solemnity.) His skeleton lay on the ground, grasping his sword in bony fingers, and around it lay the skeletal remains of more than 200 rats, showing the tremendous struggle he had put up before the rodents overpowered him by sheer weight of numbers.

At the eastern end of the Four Courts, partly on the site and partly just outside it, facing Chancery Place, once called Mass Lane, there had stood in the eighteenth century another religious establishment, a Jesuit school and chapel. These priests had continued to function, without the title 'Jesuit', during the Papal suppression of that order from 1773 to 1814, but it is uncertain at what date this Chancery Place building disappeared. It is unlikely to have been still there when work began on the Four Courts.

Father Mathew, or Church St bridge, just above the courts, is the oldest bridge in Dublin, and this was the site of the old ford of hurdles from which the city's Irish name, Baile Atha Cliath, derives. This was also the Liffey crossing point of Sligh Cualann, one of the early five great roads of Ireland, which ran from Tara to Glendalough. A bridge built in 1210 here was called the Old Bridge, but this collapsed in 1385. On 9 January 1386, the 'men of Dublin' were granted the right to maintain a ferry for four years. A little after that two masons named Nicholas Mason and John More were commissioned to build a new bridge. Their work was obviously satisfactory, because their fourteenth century bridge lasted until 1818, when it was replaced by a new

structure called Whitworth Bridge, later renamed after Father **Father Mathew**
Mathew, noted campaigner against drunkenness. Until 1670 no other
bridge had existed across the Liffey, and in that year the Old Bridge was
joined by Bloody Bridge, at the foot of Watling St, now called Rory
O'More Bridge.

Going east along Chancery St, at the back of the Four Courts, one **Chancery St**
passes St Michan's St on the left, formerly known as Fisher's Lane,
whose cobbled roadway runs between the Corporation fish market on
its left and the fruit and vegetable market on the right. The latter is a
solid Victorian redbrick structure of 1892 which replaced a street and
lane market system which had become uncontrollable and unhygienic.

The market is decorated with appealing stone carvings of the food
available within, and its main entrance in Mary's Lane is an impressive,
but rather gloomy, classical archway surmounted by the city arms.
Almost adjoining this market is the Daisy market, a rather informal
array of stalls which sell secondhand clothes and what are loosely
grouped as 'nicknacks'.

Going east towards Capel St, one passes through Mary's Abbey, **Mary's Abbey**
where number 12 was the first premises of the Bank of Ireland, which
opened there in 1783, the year after the first board was convened. The
Rt Hon. David la Touche was the first chairman, and the bank was
colloquially known as la Touche's bank, though la Touche's own
banking business was in Castle St. The Mary's Abbey bank premises
were abandoned in favour of the disused parliament house in College
Green after the Act of Union, and were then occupied by a sect called
the anti-burghers, who used the house as a meeting house after the
building of the Four Courts forced them to move from Mass Lane;
hence the name Meetinghouse Lane on the side thoroughfare off
Mary's Abbey. When the anti-burghers moved to larger premises in
Lower Abbey St, the Mary's Abbey building was sold to the Jewish
community in 1836 for £300, as a synagogue 'to cater for Dublin's 16
Jewish families'. The Jews remained there until 1892, when they moved
to their new place of worship in Adelaide Road.

In Meetinghouse Lane, running off to the left behind Capel St, the
chapter house of St Mary's Abbey is preserved. It is surrounded on all **St Mary's**
sides by warehouses, one even being on top of it, and the six feet drop to **Abbey**
its floor shows how the level of the city hereabouts has risen over the
centuries. The chapter house was built in about 1180. It is forty-five feet
long and twenty-four feet wide, and has a vaulted roof with groin and
cross ribs. The mouldings of these ribs give a clue to the date, as they are
very similar to those in the chapter house of Buildwas Abbey, in
Shropshire, which dates from around that time. Mary's Abbey
chapterhouse is the scene of the defiance of Lord Thomas Fitzgerald,
called 'Silken Thomas' because of his love of fine clothes, who, while **'Silken**
acting as Lord Deputy and chairing a meeting there of the Supreme **Thomas'**
Council in 1534, heard a false rumour that his father had been executed
by Henry VIII.

He drew his sword and flung it onto the council table, renouncing
his allegiance, and began a rebellion, supposing it his duty to avenge his
father. He surrendered in August 1536, and was executed at Tyburn on

the following 3 February.

This great Cistercian abbey had been the largest building on the north side before the Reformation, and was founded in 1156, and dissolved in 1539. It had exercised a huge influence on life in the city, and its lands stretched as far east as what is now Ballybough, though the monastic buildings themselves were bounded by what are now Capel St to the east, Little Mary St to the north, East Arran St to the west and Mary's Abbey to the south. The chapter house is now all that remains of the abbey, but the cemetery of the foundation lies under parts of Green St and North King St. The latter street was once known as Abbey Green. The Cistercian abbey had been predated by more than a century by a Benedictine monastery, which was probably founded in 1038, although 948 has been suggested as its date of building.

George's Hill

Going back to the markets, if we walk up St Michan's St and go straight on we come into George's Hill, where on our right we meet Dublin's oldest convent. Incorporating a school, it is run by the Presentation nuns, and has an oddly cluttered look, rising behind its railings to a serrated skyline untypical of Dublin. It was opened in 1794 by Mary Teresa Mullally, and was the first legally permitted Catholic school of its era, a provision in the Foreign Education Act prohibiting 'Papish' schools having been repealed. An unofficial school had been in operation intermittently here since 1787, replacing one run by the same woman since 1766. Some Jesuits, during the time of their order's suppression by the Vatican, lived in number 3 George's Hill, then beside the convent, now part of it. Going on up the street past the junction with Cuckoo Lane, we come into North Anne St. On our right is St Michan's Catholic church, and on our left are buildings now belonging to the distillery of John Jameson and Sons, part of Irish Distillers, but formerly part of the brewery of Jameson and Pim. A lease of 1715 shows that a brewery stood here then, but part of the site, embracing an earlier brewery called Hassard's, is said to go back to the late 1600s. The yard opening on North Anne St is not worth more than a glance, but behind this is a fine five-storey granite building, erected in the late 1880s. This overlooks Beresford St and was designed by Joseph B. Pim as a malthouse and barley store.

John Jameson and Sons

Today, walking along Cuckoo Lane below it, one can still get the strong smell of maturing whiskey. Standing in front of Jameson's premises here, looking down towards George's Hill, we see on the far corner of Cuckoo Lane, opposite the convent, a gate leading to a yard. This is the former Bailey's timber yard, from under which the tunnel to Christ Church is said to begin. Workers in the brewery and the timber yard in the late nineteenth century were familiar with two vaults near the tunnel end, one being 100 feet long, 50 feet wide and 15 feet high, another 150 feet long and 50 feet wide. The vaults contained two wells, one appropriately called the well of St Anne.

St Michan's Catholic church

St Michan's Catholic church replaces an earlier one in Mary's Lane, in whose administration Jesuits were also involved, and it stands on the site of a mansion which was a haunt of merchants doing business in the linen hall, off Bolton St. The church is nearly always referred to as 'Halston St', as its castellated cut stone tower overlooks that street, and

it was finished in 1893. The opening of each new law term is marked in this church with a Mass attended by the legal profession. On completion of the church, the arms of a family from Jenkinstown called Bryan were incorporated in the porch, as a Captain Bryan of this family had contributed many hundreds of pounds towards its construction. Going through the church from North Anne St, and coming out into Halston St, we see a public park and handball alley, laid out on the site of Dublin's 'new' Newgate prison. In its heyday this prison was notorious for indecent assaults among the prisoners crammed into tiny cells, and a government commission of investigation even had to admit that murders had been committed there. Lord Edward Fitzgerald and Oliver Bond, leaders of the rebellion of 1798, died in Newgate that year, the former from wounds. The jail was opened in 1780, completed in 1781, and demolished in 1893, but the sheriff's prison, erected in 1794 above it, beyond Green St courthouse, survives. In the park, in front of a water pump, is a monument to Newgate's political prisoners, comprising a stone female figure of Ireland, with a wolfhound and Celtic cross.

Halston St

Newgate

Green St courthouse, lately used to house the special criminal court, was built in 1790 to the design of Thomas Cooley, and runs from Green St to Halston St. Here were held the trials of Henry and John Sheares in 1798, Robert Emmet in 1803, the Young Irelanders in 1848, the Fenians in 1867 and the 'Invincibles' in 1883. On the Halston St side of the courthouse, part of the sheriff's prison is visible through a gateway. It was opened as a debtors' prison to eliminate abuses carried on towards the end of the eighteenth century in private debtors' prisons, which were called 'spinginghouses'. One could be committed to it by

Green St courthouse

the Lord Mayor and Court of Conscience for debts of £2. It was afterwards converted to a police barrack.

At the far end of the park from the courthouse, and running from there to Capel St, is Little Britain St, where Arthur Griffith, founder of Sinn Fein and the *United Irishman* newspaper, and signatory of the 1921 Treaty, was born in 1871. In this street also was Barney Kiernan's pub, where the Cyclops episode of *Ulysses* was set.

Barney Kiernan's pub

Going down the east side of the fruit market and continuing along East Arran St, we reach Little Strand St on the left. Shaped like a half swastika, it connects with Capel St. In one of its bends is the brown and redbrick Holy Faith convent school, established in 1891 when the area was crowded with the poor children whom these nuns sought to educate. Teaching in poor districts by day, they would return in the evening to their convent at the top of Glasnevin Hill, which had been established in 1865 by Mrs Margaret Aylward in the former residence and grounds of the Protestant bishop of Kildare, Dr Lindsay, then in a rural setting.

Yarnhall St

Going back to North King St, and along it into Bolton St, one comes to Yarnhall St on the left, at the top of which the handsome gateway of the linen hall is still standing, though the hall itself, built in 1716, was later turned into a military barrack and was destroyed, with other buildings, in 1916. Its memory survives not only in the gate, but in the nearby street names of Coleraine, Lurgan and Lisburn, as the linen industry was a northern one, and nearly all the merchants who came to sell here were Ulstermen, though many of the buyers were English. The linen hall occupied $2\frac{3}{4}$ acres and was built around four courtyards. An Act of Parliament of 1711 had granted £20,000 a year for the development and encouragement of the linen trade. But this grant was reduced early in the nineteenth century, and in the meantime Belfast had become the centre of the trade. The Dublin linen hall failed to survive the dual setback. Nevertheless the recorded value of linen sold here for the 1812–1816 period is £5,254,988.

Bolton St

Bolton St itself now has only the handsome college of technology to make the passerby pause, but it has had some minor claims to attention. In the pre-railway era the stage coaches to Drogheda and Newry set off from numbers 1 and 2 respectively. Number 55, now demolished, housed the manor or seneschal court for the area known as Glasmanogue.

Henrietta St

A turn off Bolton St leads up a hill towards Broadstone. This hill, with the King's Inns crossing the top, is Henrietta St, a place of magnificent Georgian houses. Much of it is now decayed. It is not typical of Dublin's great Georgian streets, as it was the first of them, building having been commenced in 1720, and the houses are made on a grander scale than that usual elsewhere. Some are really staggering in size, and the variety of doorway styles alone is worth the journey up the hill. Number 11 has been beautifully restored, and has a big fanlight of delicate tracery, but mostly the appeal of the street is not in delicacy, but in sheer bulking magnificence. St Brigid's Hostel, at number 9, has a massively decorated, pedimented doorway and numbers 3 and 4 are really huge houses, the high granite front steps of the latter adding to the

The King's Inns, Henrietta St entrance

impression of towering height. Number 14, across the street, declares its
individuality by having a great semi-elliptical pediment instead of a
triangular one. This street remained the most fashionable in Dublin
well into the nineteenth century and its popularity with archbishops
and bishops, as well as earls, led to its being called Primate's Hill.

The street was laid out by the first Luke Gardiner, and the
Gardiners' own house was number 10 at the top on the right-hand side.
It is now a convent. That decorated doorway of number 9 and the
whole facade, were designed by Edward Lovett Pearce about 1730.
Cassels also designed houses in Henrietta St about 1730, and Gandon's
King's Inns at the head of the street means that three outstanding
architects in Classical Dublin are represented here.

The King's Inns library, a granite-faced latecomer in Henrietta
St, built in 1827, faces the convent. Near it we pass under an arch and
enter the courtyard of King's Inns, Gandon's last great public building.

**King's Inns
library**

Overhead are ten great circular windows in two facing rows. We
emerge onto a vast lawn, now a public park, separated by railings from
Constitution Hill. The foundation stone of King's Inns was laid by the
earl of Clare, lord chancellor of Ireland, on 1 August 1795. But the main
construction was not begun until 1802. We have already seen that
Gandon was in England while the 1798 rebellion was in progress, and

King's Inns

his own remark on his return to Dublin suggests that a backlog of work faced him. By 1802 he was 60 years old and suffered badly from gout. He left much of the work on the King's Inns to his pupil, Henry Aaron Baker, and some say that Baker should be entirely credited with this beautiful building's design. Yet when Lord Chancellor Redesdale decided, sometime between 1802 and 1806, to complain about the delay in finishing the building, it was to Gandon that he did so. Some post-1802 drawings were jointly signed by Gandon and Baker. A drawing of an elevation of 1815 is signed by Francis Johnston, but his contribution was minimal, probably only a few flourishes of decoration. The building was completed in 1817. Gandon had retired to his house, Cannon Brook in Lucan, in 1808, and left the King's Inns to Baker, then master of the Dublin Society's architectural school, to finish.

The entire building can be seen only from the lawn, and here four figures are visible, two flanking the doorway to the dining hall, and two the doorway to the prerogative court. They were executed by Irish sculptor Edward Smyth. The female figures on either side of the diningroom door are Cares, goddess of food, and a follower of Bacchus, god of wine, who holds a goblet. The male figures on the other door are Law, with a book and quill, and Security, with a key and scroll. King's Inns has long been referred to locally as 'the temple', not because it occupies the site of a former temple, but because its London counterpart does.

Broadstone station

Across Constitution Hill, a small side road takes us to Prebend St, which ends in front of Broadstone station, built, as an engraved date proclaims, in 1850, as the headquarters of the Midland Great Western railway, and now a Coras Iompair Eireann road freight depot. The bus depot below it stands on the old site of Royal Canal warehouses. Victorian railway architecture in Dublin tended to be extravagant, and also solid, partly to inspire public confidence in a relatively new form of transport. Broadstone, built of smooth granite, is a beautiful example, designed by John Skipton Mulvany, whose father, Thomas James, wrote a biography of Gandon.

Broadstone is the only large Graeco–Egyptianesque building in Dublin, the Egyptianesque features being the massive projecting entrance block and ground floor window surrounds. Along the side of a former platform, overlooking Phibsborough Road, is a highly pleasing Ionic colonnade. Like some other granite buildings, Broadstone looks best after a rain shower. There are two splendid Victorian iron lamp standards on granite bases at either side of the entrance, but the lamps have been removed. The symmetry of the facade has also been impaired by the erection of a low extra storey on the side nearer Grangegorman, with a green felt roof, and a tall radio mast over the central block does not improve the appearance, but these are minor defects. Mulvany also designed Dun Laoghaire railway station, and some provincial ones. The Midland Great Western became part of the Great Southern railway in 1925 and Broadstone closed to traffic in January 1937.

Below the station there is a T-shaped road junction, overlooked by a statue of the Virgin Mary, and visitors will notice a sharp drop in the road level. The road from Western Way to the station formerly crossed

Broadstone Station

the top of Constitution Hill here by a bridge called Foster Aqueduct, half of whose width once carried the waters of an arm of the Royal Canal over to the top of Prebend St. This arm, now filled in, ran parallel to Phibsborough Road and entered the mainstream above Mountjoy prison. The origin of the name Broadstone is in doubt. An underground river called the Bradogue flows down Phibsborough Road and Constitution Hill, and a 'broad stone' may have formed a crude bridge across it at this point before it was culverted. Alternatively, Broadstone may be a corruption of 'Bradogestown'.

Broadstone was the starting point of trips on the Royal Canal before the railways came. In 1812 the boats were advertised as travelling at $3\frac{1}{2}$ miles an hour. There were first and second class cabins, a rule of the director-general of inland navigation stating that liveried servants could never set foot in the first class part, but that dogs could do so, if paid for as passengers.

Royal Canal

As we go up Phibsborough Road from Broadstone, the styles of domestic architecture move backward and forward in time. Close to the station is Royal Canal Terrace, built in 1826, whose houses retain flights of steps and classical fanlights, but the smallness and pillarless simplicity of their halldoors contrast with the grandeur of Henrietta St. The footpath in front of the gardens here is several feet higher than another outer one that flanks the roadway, and the paths are separated by a stone wall, matched on the far side of the road, so that this really is a terrace. The word 'terrace' frequently appears in Dublin street names,

Phibsborough Road
Royal Canal Terrace

but is seldom literally accurate. The slightly younger houses across the road, four of them, in Foster Buildings, have consoles flanking the halldoors, but the Georgian grandeur has disappeared. It is even missing from the rectory of All Saints, the Protestant parish church for Grangegorman, further up, though this is a solid stone house among trees in its own ground, fronted by a black stone wall, with an incongruous rural aspect that makes one think of the Brontes. Its old school and simple Gothic church stand above it; the church was damaged by fire some years ago, and it contains in its renovated form an unusual and rather beautiful cruciform stained glass window, well worth a pause. Further up the road again, on the far side from the church, numbers 193 and 194 Phibsborough Road are three-storey high-roofed houses of some former eminence. Again we see very simple doorways here. Beyond this, number 182, four storeys and including a shop, with an ornate curved top, is a vivid redbrick announcement of the arrival of Victoriana. Around here a quaintness enters the scene. A cobbled laneway runs down to Royal Canal Bank (an obsolete name), bisecting Phibsborough Place, and its tiny cottages are protected from the vibrations of motor traffic by a fluted cast iron bollard; it is simply called Kelly's Lane.

Royal Canal Bank

At the end of it is the linear park which has replaced the former arm of the Royal Canal. Entering the nearest section of the park, we see a door in a wall, opposite a raised round flowerbed which covers a disused stone dais. Going through the door, we find a large rectangle of water, surrounded by bushes. This is a former filter bed, once part of a north-side water supply, and the squat granite tower beside the island in the centre of the basin is part of the former works, more remains of which will be seen at the far end, which adjoins the top of Blessington St. The water is nearly always inhabited by a pair of swans, with a year-round population of mallard supplemented in winter by tufted duck, goldeneye and sometimes Arctic terns, and an occasional heron. Great black-backed gulls are often seen using the central tower as a vantage point. Turn to the left, past the old pump, and walk around the perimeter. The place, naturally, is known locally as 'the Basin'. Notice the pleasant gate lodge at the far end, with its small wooden-railed patio. Turn right here, around the end of the water, until a side gate leads out to Primrose St. A right turn a short way along this street brings us into Primrose Avenue. We walk between neat terraces of yellow-brown brick houses, with rough granite lintels over doors and windows. Notice the bollards at the top of the avenue, preventing access to motor traffic. From here we go back to Phibsborough Road through Kelly's Lane.

'the Basin'

Nearby Lynch's Place was formerly named for its narrowness with the Dickensian title of Pinchgut Lane. A cul-de-sac called Weaver Lane is evidence that not all the weavers in Dublin remained in the Liberties, and there is more evidence of this on the far side of the road, where a small street simply called Phibsborough runs off. At its junction with Phibsborough Avenue, this street sports an amazing little fortress of a house, with heavy window architraves, steps, railings and a seeming watchtower of a slate-walled attic. Behind it, in Phibsborough Avenue,

Gate Lodge beside 'the Basin', Blessington St

we find a wide front-gabled house of great antiquity, with an oval attic window, probably dating from Queen Anne times, and a surprise on the north side. Back to Phibsborough Road and we continue to Doyle's Corner, another puzzling name to strangers. On two of the intersection's four angles stand public houses, neither now called Doyle's, though Mooney's upper brickwork is ornately inscribed 'J.D. 1906'. The intertwined letters J.D. stand for John Doyle, who indelibly stamped his name on the corner by owning both pubs.

Before Doyle's time it was Dunphy's Corner, by which it is referred to in *Ulysses*, as Paddy Dignam's funeral passes on its way to Glasnevin cemetery: 'Dunphy's corner. Mourning coaches drawn up drowning their grief. A pause by the wayside. Tiptop position for a pub.' Looking now at the pub facing us on the right, we see it inscribed 'Murphy's Corner'. It ceased officially to be Doyle's corner on 19 October 1963, when Doyle sold out, but in popular parlance Murphy has never replaced Doyle. Down to the right is Blaquiere Bridge, another name from the days of the canal branch. The name survives, though it bridges nothing now, and a kneeling statue of a volunteer on the right, and 1934

Doyle's Corner

public library on the left, with its trees, occupy the old waterway space. Coming back up to Doyle's Corner, we seen an ornamental pediment in the centre of the block between the library and Murphy's, with terracotta tiles in the tympanum. The mixture of red and brown bricks in the block is a common late Victorian style.

Just around Doyle's Corner is a pub called the Hut, where the passerby will see a distorted reflection of himself in trick mirrors on the outside, and the interior is worth visiting for lovers of mahogany, marble, mysterious small drawers, carved wood screens and Victorian bar fittings. At the end of Phibsborough Road, where the main artery of the Royal Canal is spanned, there stood until late 1978 a fine Egyptianesque stone arch, part of the property of the Ranks milling company, once an entrance to a mill and erected in 1848. This is Cross Guns Bridge, named after a village that once stood beyond it.

Cross Guns Bridge

St Peter's

Going back to Doyle's Corner and up the North Circular Road, we find the view dominated by the Catholic church of St Peter, with a redbrick Baptist church on the left. St Peter's is a Vincentian foundation, designed by George C. Ashlin, once a partner of Pugin. This is a quite magnificent pile, with a lovely limestone-pillared interior and fine rose windows in the transepts. It was finished in 1911, but might have been completed much earlier had not a lawsuit forced its builders to demolish a huge central tower.

Great Western Square

Its spire is now a landmark separating North Circular Road from Cabra Road. We go to the left, where roadside plane trees begin to appear, and a side road brings us into Great Western Square, where a pleasant gated park containing 'monkey puzzler' trees is surrounded by solid redbrick houses with heavy eaves. These, as the name indicates, were built for employees of the Midland Great Western railway, which ran up from Broadstone immediately behind the square's west side. Consistent with the thoroughness of railway builders, redbrick is used throughout, whereas the sides and backs of many of their contemporaries were filled with cheaper materials. Return to the main road, turn left, then left again down Rathdown Road, and come to Grangegorman, once the grange of Gormond, the Dane. A grim stone building looms up on our left, with prison-like qualities. This is now an administrative unit for St Brendan's mental hospital across the road, but when it was erected in 1816, a date confirmed on the weathercock over the cupola, it was the Richmond penitentiary, or Grangegorman prison. It was designed by the ubiquitous Francis Johnston, and served sometimes as a debtors' prison, sometimes as a jail for women about to be transported, and at times as a cholera hospital. Outside the first part of the building is a rare cobbled footpath, now defaced by a weighbridge. Further down, in the lowest of the three storeys are three narrow slits, for all the world like archery slits, in place of windows.

Grangegorman

The main entrance of the mental hospital, where older buildings were also designed by Johnston, is directly facing that of the former jail. The hospital gates were brought from the Compton Domville estate at Santry Court over 20 years ago. In the centre of each ornate gate is an 'X', replacing the Domville arms. Continuing down Grangegorman, we pass tiny Stanhope St on our right. A 'house of refuge for industrious females' was opened here in 1811. The convent that is here now is usually entered from its other side in Manor St. It stands on part of the old lands of Gormond, later owned by Sir Thomas Stanley, after whom Stanley St, leading to the nearby municipal incinerator, is named. Further down we turn left into North Brunswick St, and find, again on our left, a splendid redbrick palace with seven copper domes, verandahs, a lawn and an Elizabethan or possibly Jacobean air. But it is Victorian, and barely qualifies even for that title, dating only from 1900. This is the Richmond hospital, one of a group of three known as the St Laurence hospitals. The other two, the Whitworth and Hardwicke, stand roughly behind it. Two Benedictine convents stood in this street in the seventeenth century, when the thoroughfare was called Channel Row.

Richmond hospital

That name referred to a channel running along the middle of the road, connected with the Bradoge river. One convent stood a little behind the present Richmond hospital, the other on the site of the Christian Brothers' school across the road. That on the hospital site was known as King James's monastery, and had been put up on the orders of King James II. While in Dublin Castle in 1688 he told his lord lieutenant, the Duke of Tyrconnell, to write to Dame Mary Butler, abbess of an Irish monastery in Ypres, asking her to establish a convent in Dublin, and the king personally attended the opening of this in 1689. But after the Battle of the Boyne, when the convent was ransacked by Williamite troops who took away the church plate as 'souvenirs', Dame Mary closed the establishment and returned to the comparative quiet of Ypres.

In 1772 the corporation for the relief of the poor was founded in Dublin, and opened a workhouse called the house of industry, part of which survives as the Legion of Mary's Morning Star hostel, behind the group of hospitals. The workhouse was 'to rid the streets of sturdy beggars and idle, strolling and disorderly women'. The Hardwicke fever hospital was built in 1803, the Richmond surgical hospital in 1811 and the Whitworth medical hospital in 1817. The names are those of the viceroys in office at the times of building, the earls of Hardwicke and Whitworth and the duke of Richmond. The buildings were designed by Francis Johnston, and though his Richmond hospital has been replaced, his Hardwicke and Whitworth buildings are still with us, and are reached from Morning Star Avenue, off Brunswick St. The subdued portico of each of these stone buildings, typical of the institutional style of the day, was in the 1970s further subdued by a concrete extension, necessary to the running of the hospitals but architecturally disastrous. In the Hardwicke, to the right of the avenue, this incongruous extension was added simply to house a lift shaft. The florid new Richmond hospital, on a site nearer to Brunswick St than its predecessor, which was hidden behind a dairy farm, is a near copy of the Jacobean Hatfield House. But whereas Hatfield, seat of the Marquess of Salisbury and built between 1603 and 1611, is perfectly shaped like the letter 'E' in memory of the queen who spent much of her early life in the palace it replaced, the central section of the pleasantly rambling Richmond does not protrude to form the middle bar of the letter.

With the passing of Sir Robert Peel's Poor Law Act in 1838, giving the three hospitals autonomy, they came under the direction of the poor law commissioners, who retained the office of salaried governor, set up in 1820.

The workhouse section of the house of industry complex became a separate responsibility. In 1856 the hospital buildings were vested in the commissioners of public works, and the lord lieutenant was empowered to nominate a board of governors.

'Billy in the Bowl'

An early inmate of the house of industry was 'Billy in the Bowl', a beggar who had been born without legs and who propelled himself along the streets in a large bowl reinforced with iron bands, which had been made for him by a compassionate blacksmith. A pair of powerful arms and hands compensated for his affliction, and he gravitated from begging to robbery and murder, killing several people before he was apprehended in 1786.

On the far side of Morning Star Avenue from the Richmond is the Carmichael school of medicine, behind railings, now a residence of medical students. It was designed by Rogers in the Victorian Venetian style, strongly reminiscent of Woodward's Kildare St Club and Trinity museum, and opened in 1864. The Carmichael school is small, but architecturally pleasing.

Church St

Going down Church St, we pass the Fr Mathew hall, lately painted in yellow and pink and looking a bit unreal, and come to the Catholic church of St Mary of the Angels, with a fine rose window in its east front and two elegant timbered ceilings, rare in Dublin. The Capuchin friars of this neo-Gothic church once had a chapel in St Stephen's hall in Bridge St, directly across the Liffey, but were ousted from it in 1634 or 1635. The friary is behind the church, and here people with drink problems come to 'take the pledge', a figure of speech which reverses what actually happens, giving a pledge.

'old' St Michan's

Further down the street is the Protestant or 'old' St Michan's. Michan, a Danish bishop, built his church here in 1095, and it was the only parish church on the north side until 1697, when it was joined by St Paul's and St Mary's. There was considerable rebuilding of St Michan's in 1686. The battlemented west tower looks ancient, but the date 1686 over the west door suggests that the rebuilding involved at least part of the tower, so it is doubtful whether any of the Danish bishop's church is still there.

A highlight of the church's woodwork is an elaborate carving of a group of fourteen or more musical instruments in high relief on the front of the organ loft, a really beautiful piece of work whose author is unknown, but which is believed to have been executed by an apprentice woodcarver. The organ was made by Cuvillie in 1724, and Handel is believed to have played on this instrument in 1742, the year of the first public performance of his *Messiah*, which also took place in Dublin, in Fishamble St. The large window in the east wall of St Michan's is a replacement of one that was shattered during the shelling of the Four Courts in 1922.

St Michan's is renowned for the preservative properties of its vaults, which are said to be almost unique. Here lie corpses in a state akin to natural mummification, the skin brown and leathery. They include members of the Osborne, Gill and Beard families. Coffined remains are reputed to be those of the brothers John and Henry Sheares. In the cemetery adjoining the church a large tomb belonging to an Emmet family gave rise many years ago to the theory that Robert Emmet was buried here, but this theory exists concerning several other burial places.

A few explanations of the vaults' preservative properties have been suggested. One claims that the secret is in the magnesium lime from which they are cut, another that their dryness and almost complete freedom from dust is responsible, and a third that preservation is due to the tannic acid that impregnates their earthen floor. This substance, once called tannin and used in tanning leather, comes from the barks of oak trees, and the area of the church was once on the edge of the great oak forest of Oxmantown.

7   Oxmantown — the Viking Refuge

St Paul's churches — Jameson's — Smithfield —
Bluecoat School — Stoneybatter — Stanhope St
convent — McKee barracks — Oxmantown
houses — Arbour Hill — Collins barracks.

*There had been a great how-do-you-do about this Bluecoat
School for Johnny. Ella and Archie had fed him with the
grandeur of the boys' lovely blue uniform.*

— Sean O'Casey, *I Knock at the Door.*

Oxmantown is a corruption of Ostmantown, meaning 'town of the man from the east', and the forms 'Oestmantown', 'Oxmanby', 'Oxtmanton' and 'Austmannaby' have all been used. The easterners referred to are, of course, the Vikings, colloquially called the Danes in Dublin, though they included Norwegians. An early general distinction was to call the Norwegian a 'Fionngall' (blond foreigner), and a Dane a Dubhgall (dark foreigner), and these Gaelic names remain, here and in Britain, in the forms of Finglas, Douglas, Fingal, Dougal and Doyle. The Vikings were also called Lochlannaig, from Criocha Lochlainn, the Norwegian mountains, and an anglicised form is found, for instance, in Loughlinstown, near Bray, Co. Wicklow, and in the name Macloughlin.

It was the Vikings' custom, having decided to colonise an existing coastal settlement, to establish their own dormitory town outside it, if possible across a deep and broad river. This could be used as a base from which to attack the natives, and as a retreat if the natives proved too strong.

When the Danes and Norwegians arrived at the end of the eighth century to attack the small south side settlement of Dublin, an oak forest came east as far as modern Church St, and the Liffey was broader than it is now. Taking advantage of this double protection, the newcomers established their base, digging ditches and erecting stone walls. As we shall see when we come to deal with Christ Church, their years of ascendancy on the Liffey were busy, as they used Dublin as a base for attacks on various places in Ireland and Britain. As regards their stronghold in Oxmantown, they had many occasions to seek its refuge before the eventual arrival of the Normans. In 890, Gregory, king of Scotland, occupied Dublin. In 916 many Vikings were slaughtered by a son of Niall, the Irish king. Congelach MacMelith, king of Ireland, drove them out of the city south of the river in 944, and burned down the buildings they had evacuated. Under Blacar, Danish king of Dublin, they recrossed the river and reoccupied the city the following year. But they were routed by Congelach in 947, and again in 948. This is also the earliest year suggested for the foundation, by christianised Ostmen, of the Benedictine abbey that was St Mary's forerunner.

In 980 the Danes of Dublin, as all Scandinavians here from about that time are usually called, were badly beaten in a battle at Tara by Maolseachlann, or Melaghlin, king of Ireland, a defeat that considerably curtailed their future influence. The following year Maolseachlann ravaged their lands in Fingal, burning homes and crops, making Oxmantown again important as a retreat. The Danes had mixed fortunes after that. A group of them from Dublin ravaged Derry in 985, but the same fate befell their walled city of Dublin — still distinct from Oxmantown — at the hands of Brian Boru, king of Munster, in 999. In 1014 Brian defeated the forces of King Sigtryggr of the Silken Beard, afterwards more conveniently referred to as Sitric, at the celebrated battle of Clontarf; this probably centred, as we have noted earlier, around what later became Mountjoy Fields and then Mountjoy Square.

Clontarf did not end the usefulness, or need, of Oxmantown as a stockade. Brian Boru died and Silkenbeard Sitric reigned on. In 1066 Godfred Crovan, Danish king of the Isle of Man, conquered much of Leinster and established himself as king of Dublin. His later expansionist policy undid him; in 1088 his Dublin Danes attacked two old-established Danish settlements, Waterford, which they plundered, and Cork, where they were repulsed. The Irish king, Murtagh O'Brien, displeased at this treatment of Munster, drove Godfred out of Dublin in 1095, and held the city until his death in 1120. Oddly, we find his son Donald, now called king of the Dublin Danes, battling against the Irish of Leinster in 1115. The last serious attempt by the Danes to hold Dublin was made in 1171 by Hasculf. Having been driven out the previous year by Dermot MacMurrough and the Anglo-Normans, he returned with a fleet of 60 ships, and warriors protected by round red iron-bound shields, but now wearing Norman-type shirts of mail. His bid failed and he was executed.

The Viking era may be said to have officially ended in 1172, when Henry II received the homage of Irish kings and chieftains in Dublin. But the Anglo-Normans under Milo de Cogan and Raymond le Gros in the walled city had had to withstand three sieges the previous year, including that of Hasculf; it has been said that if the Danes and native Irish had had a concerted plan to besiege the city they would certainly have dispossessed the invaders.

Meanwhile on the north side of the Liffey Michan had built his church and the Cistercians had built St Mary's Abbey. Oxmantown forest is said to have supplied the roof timbers for Westminster Hall to William II (Rufus, the Red) in 1098, an early example of export initiative, but there is some doubt. Rufus began building Westminster Hall in 1097 as a royal palace, but he died in a hunting accident in 1100. The palace's magnificent oak roof was not erected until sometime after 1394 by Richard II. This may have come from Oxmantown's oak trees, or may have replaced an earlier one brought by Rufus from Dublin.

After 1172 Oxmantown probably became a ghetto. The Ostmen had made the south side city a permanent trading post and exploration base in 852, and had freely intermarried with the Irish since then, though Scandinavian was the predominant language of Dublin until it was replaced by Norman French. It is unlikely that all of the Danes would have relished having to withdraw into a ghetto and spend the rest of their lives as siege-expectant neurotics, but some of them at least preferred to live in this place of restricted autonomy than to be subjects of a new regime. (Some others took refuge in Howth.) A Danish historian, Professor J. J. Worsaae, noted in 1852 that Vicus Ostmanorum, or Oxmantown, continued 'through the whole of the Middle Ages' to form an entirely separate part of Dublin, and that the gates of the strong fortification that surrounded it were carefully closed each day at sunset.

There are no physical remains of the Viking settlement above ground, though future archaeologists may dig out many artefacts. If the lack of standing ruins seems strange, since Roman ruins of far greater antiquity are found elsewhere, it should be remembered that the Vikings are likely to have built mainly in wood at Oxmantown, because

Oxmantown Road

of their familiarity with this as a construction material in their own countries, and the plenitude of it here.

Our approach to Oxmantown takes us west along Arran Quay from Father Mathew bridge. We meet St Paul's Catholic church, with its Greek Ionic tetrastyle portico, its tall clock tower and green copper cupola, giving this part of the riverfront a vaguely Mediterranean appearance. Over the portico are statues of SS. Peter, Paul and John, in dramatic poses. The church was erected in 1835–37 and is the work of Patrick Byrne, also the designer of the Catholic St Audoen's in High St, St Andrew's (All Hallows) in Westland Row and the church of SS. Mary and Peter in Lower Rathmines Road whose great dome is inspired by St Peter's basilica in Rome. Inside St Paul's, the classical altar screen clearly shows its affinity with those in High St and Westland Row. Outside, a Lourdes grotto has been built onto a side wall, and this sometimes puzzles onlookers from across the river; if they are directly in front of the church, the figures are invisible, and the passer-by sees only what appears to be a sudden outcrop of rock.

Arran Quay
St Paul's Catholic church

At this point we become aware of a disparity between the north and south riverfronts. This classical church, along with Gandon's giants, Four Courts and Custom House, below it, cannot be called overbearing, yet they make the facing quays, which have nothing of similar quality to complement them, look drab by comparison. The southern side has churches at City Quay, at Exchange St (a little back from where Essex Quay and Wood Quay meet) and at Merchant's Quay, but none presents a memorable facade to the river, and the first

115

noteworthy building met is Heuston (Kingsbridge) station, where the road leaves the river. The quay in front of the Four Courts is balustraded and has trees, but Arran Quay is treeless and walled, the contrast made less harsh by a gentle bend in the river. Between the church and the Four Courts, number 12, now gone, was Edmund Burke's birthplace.

Going up Lincoln Lane beside the church, we come to a crossing, with Bow St ahead, Hammond Lane to the right and Phoenix St to the left. In the eighteenth century Lincoln Lane, then called Pudding Lane, contained a Carmelite convent. Hammond Lane, now with its match factory, was originally Hangman's Lane, and the new name is a corruption of the unpopular old one. Phoenix St leads us out onto the wide cobbled thoroughfare of Smithfield, sometimes referred to as a square, though scarcely that. Despite appearances, it is not as wide as O'Connell St.

Smithfield

Smithfield was laid out at the end of the seventeenth century as a great enclosed cattle market. Before that it had been an open space adjoining the east side of Oxmantown Green. It continued to serve as Dublin's cattle market until 1886, when this trade was removed to a Corporation market at the North Circular Road. Bective House, home of the earl of Bective, stood in Smithfield in the eighteenth century. In 1775 it was reported that while foundations were being laid for buildings in this thoroughfare 'many parts of the pavement gave way, leaving an aperture into a cavern many feet in depth'. This was supposed to be part of a warren of caves existing under the district, with a former entrance in Arbour Hill. A sixteenth century bandit named Scaldbrother, whose habit was to ambush and rob the people of Oxmantown, was said to live in these caves with his gang, and store his booty there. It was also believed that some houses later built in Queen St stood over vaults formed from these caves.

Haymarket

Looking up Smithfield, a short wide street on our left has the self-explanatory name of Haymarket, also dating from cattle market days. Further up the same side is the quaintly named Thundercut Alley, and facing Smithfield across North King St is Red Cow Lane, named after an inn. On our right as we look up is a great slab of redbrick wall, and a tall circular brick chimney stack, dated 1895 and mounted on a massive octagonal base. This is Bow St distillery, always so called, as its main front is in Bow St, at the other side. New Church St, at the lower end of the redbrick, leads through walls of grey limestone to Bow St, the view pleasantly closed by the tower of old St Michan's, rising above its trees.

Bow St

In Bow St there are more sombre grey stone walls, relieved by a vivid redbrick office block with a fine brown sandstone porch.

Bow St's owners, the Jamesons, stated in 1878, when the distillery had achieved world renown, that its origins could not be traced, that the foundation date of 1780 was guesswork as there was no documentary evidence of it, and that it was not even known at what date before 1802 the Jamesons came to own the firm. Tradition said that three men founded it, one a baronet and another a retired general, and that they had lost their capital in the venture.

In 1783 there were several distilleries in Smithfield. John Swan

In Smithfield

had one at number 52, and Edmond Grange had two. John Stein had
one in Bow St and one across the river in Marrowbone Lane, and these
two firms were later owned by Jameson brothers. In 1784 the original
Jameson came to Dublin from Alloa in Clackmannanshire, and one of
his sons married Isabella, a daughter of John Stein. This son was the
John Jameson later celebrated as the originator of 'John Jameson and
Sons' of Bow St, for he took over the ownership of the stills there from
Stein, while his brother William took over the south side Stein distillery.
A younger brother of John and William took over a distillery in
Fairfield, near Enniscorthy, Co. Wexford. His daughter Anne became
the wife of one Signor Giuseppe Marconi, and their son pioneered
wireless telegraphy.

Bow St distillery became part of United Distillers of Ireland in

1966, by merging with two other distilleries, with a view to improving American sales. The name of the consortium was later changed to Irish Distillers. Though all distilling for the group is now done in Midleton, Co. Cork, the name Jameson is retained, as is the flavour, on the product formerly made between Bow St and Smithfield.

North King St

Across the top of Smithfield runs North King St, which, as we have noted, was once called Abbey Green. (The subdivisions of St Mary's Abbey land were at one time named individually, Ash Park, for instance, being where Upper O'Connell St is.) However, the name 'King St, Oxmantown' dates at least from 1552, and there was a King's Lane in Oxmantown in the early fifteenth century, possibly the same thoroughfare. Going west along it we come to Queen St, which probably commemorates Catharine of Braganza, Charles II's queen.

Queen Maev Bridge

Spanning the river at the bottom of the street is Queen Maev Bridge, now named after a pre-Christian queen of Connaught, but formerly known as the 'Queen's bridge'. Since this was built in 1776, the queen referred to is probably the wife of George III, Princess Charlotte of Mecklenburg. The present bridge is the oldest existing span on the Liffey in Dublin. It replaces a 1683 structure which was known in turn as Arran Bridge, Bridewell Bridge and Ellis's Bridge. From Queen Maev Bridge, looking upstream, we see an iron structure now called Rory O'More Bridge after the leader of the 1641 rebellion. Formerly named after Queen Victoria, it was built in 1863 and crosses the river at an angle to link Ellis St and Watling St. In terms of commemoration, neither Victoria nor Rory O'More can compete with the legend which is grossly embossed along both of the bridge's iron sides. It reads: 'Robert Daglish Jnr, St Helen's Foundry, Lancashire, 1858.'

Going back up Queen St we see the gaps left by fairly ruthless demolition. An isolated gate, with black and white arch, leads to the former stableyard of an hotel, now the stableyard of Cooper's, horsedealers, probably the only such firm remaining in the city.

Blackhall St

Turning left into Blackhall St, short and wide and with municipal flats, the remaining three Georgian houses on our left indicate its former elegance. Directly ahead, across Blackhall Place, is the former King's Hospital, or Bluecoat school, now occupied by the Incorporated Law Society. This was founded as a school in the lower part of Queen St, then the south-east corner of Oxmantown Green, in 1669 by Dublin Corporation, and granted a royal charter by Charles II in 1670. The Irish parliament met in the Queen St building during 1729, attracted by its convenience and comfort.

But the Queen St building became ruinous after a century of use, and the new school in Blackhall Place was begun in 1773, Lord Harcourt laying the foundation stone, and completed in 1783. From then until the school moved out of it in 1970 it was variously called the

Bluecoat school

Bluecoat school, King's Hospital school and Bluecoat boys' hospital, but its correct title was the Hospital and Free School of King Charles II. It was designed by Thomas Ivory, a Corkman who began his career as a carpenter. It is a splendid Palladian building, with an Ionic tetrastyle portico, and curving balustraded screen walls, with niches, terminating in three-storey pavilions. Both the central green copper cupola and its

The Bluecoat School, Blackhall Place

drum are octagonal, and we notice ornamental consoles on the angles of the drum. Ivory originally submitted another design for the school, but this proved too costly, and the present building is a compromise, but a highly pleasing one. The central cupola had not been erected when building finished in 1783, and the present one, differing from the original plan, was added in 1904. The school's boardroom is noted for its fine plaster ceiling, executed by Charles Thorp between 1778 and 1780, for which his bill was £72. Parts of the present ceiling are reproductions of those parts damaged in an accidental fire earlier this century.

The 'blue coat' reference is to the uniform worn by the pupils until 1923. This originally consisted of a dark blue, brass-buttoned, cutaway coat and dark blue knee breeches, yellow waistcoats and long yellow stockings, and silver shoe buckles. This ensemble, with various modifications, was *de rigeur* for the pupils until 1923, when it was considered an inconvenience and discarded. The choirboys of the school continued to wear scarlet cassocks as a reminder that their school was a royal foundation. The school uniform, now of conventional cut, retains the colour blue.

Oxmantown Green

The playing field at the back of the Bluecoat school was the last surviving part of Oxmantown Green. In September 1956 the school absorbed Morgan's school for boys, which had been founded on the Navan Road near Castleknock in 1813. In 1966 the Bluecoat school also took over the running of Mercer's school for girls, the successor of Mary Mercer's establishment in the street named after her. Morgan's and Mercer's had had a close affinity, and in 1879 it had been agreed between their trustees 'that the girls in Mercer's school should make shirts for the boys in Morgan's school'. Even before that, the affinity existed between pupils as well as managements, girls in Mercer's having been flogged in the 1840s for entertaining boys from the neighbouring school to a pancake party in their kitchen. An eight-foot wall between the schools failed to prevent the exchange of letters.

The takeover of Mercer's school gave the King's Hospital its first female students. When the Bluecoat establishment moved to Palmerston in December 1970, the tradition of occupying Ostman ground was not lost, as the Palmerston school stands on land once owned by the twelfth century Ailred the Dane (Ailred Palmer).

The name Blackhall commemorates Sir Thomas Blackhall, who was lord mayor in 1769, and the street was laid out in 1789. In the last century this area was regarded as having the mildest climate in Dublin, it being reported that grapes and figs ripened in the open air in its gardens. Going up Paul St, which runs parallel to Blackhall Place, and turning to the right in North King St at the top, we meet St Paul's Protestant church on our right, a dull grey building with a square tower. St Paul's was established here in 1697 as the church of a new parish formed from the western end of St Michan's area of jurisdiction, but the church we see now is a replacement of the original, which fell into disrepair. The existing granite building, despite its Elizabethan appearance, was built in 1824. Inside the railings we notice two brick houses with console keystones over the halldoors. The houses are

St Paul's Protestant church

considerably older than the church. The vaults of this church are another rumoured burial place of Robert Emmet, but searches for his remains here have been unsuccessful.

The buildings on the northern side of King St, running towards where it meets Stoneybatter, now have the mundane role of a livestock food store, but the site is that of the duke of Tyrconnell's house, where his widow founded a convent of Poor Clare nuns. She had begun life simply as Fanny Jennings, sister of Sarah, who later married John **Fanny Jennings** Churchill. In due course Sarah became the duchess of Marlborough who for a time manipulated Queen Anne to the point where it was said that the duchess, not the queen, was ruling England. Fanny, who was said to be remarkably beautiful, married a Count Hamilton, and on his death she found herself much sought after, being a 'highly eligible widow'. She married again, her new husband being Richard Talbot earl of Tyrconnell, a close friend of James II. James, on his arrival in Ireland in 1689, created Talbot a duke, so Fanny became duchess of Tyrconnell.

It may be said that she became a duchess through her husband's friendship with King James, in the same way as her sister's friendship with Queen Anne later made Churchill a duke. In 1723 the duchess of Tyrconnell went as a boarder to the convent that stood a little behind the present Richmond hospital, the old King James's monastery, but since 1717 run by Dominican nuns. She stayed there two years, then returned to her husband's house at the north-western end of North King St, to establish the Poor Clares convent referred to above. She was seventy-seven years old then, and died five years later in the newly-established convent. After the duchess died, the nuns remained there for a further twenty-two years, then moved to the house off Drumcondra Lane that later became the Hardwicke St forerunner of both Belvedere college and the classical church in Upper Gardiner St.

We turn right into Stoneybatter, a name which began as an Anglo- **Stoneybatter** Gaelic hybrid, Stony Bothar (stony road). The name was a compliment, as it distinguished this, as a paved highway, from the less important tracks of bare or straw-covered earth. The main roads in ancient Ireland were paved with large stone blocks, somewhat as Roman roads were. Stoneybatter formed part of Sligh Cualann, one of the five great roads of Ireland, running from Tara in Co. Meath to Glendalough in Co. Wicklow, and deriving the name from the Cuala district around the present town of Bray, through which it passed. It was also known as Bealach Duibhlinn (road by way of the dark river pool), because it crossed the Liffey at the Ford of Hurdles (Father Mathew Bridge). A continuation of the line of Stoneybatter today would reach the river at this point. As the five great roads were laid down in the second century, Stoneybatter must have been running through this area when the Vikings set up Oxmantown.

A maypole festival was held regularly in Stoneybatter, possibly connected with a legend which claims that Little John, companion of Robin Hood, fleeing from the justice of the sheriff of Nottingham, hid in this area, or in the nearby wood of Arbour Hill.

Little John, according to the legend, entertained the residents with feats of archery, but was eventually hanged at 'Gibbet's Glade' or 'Gibbet's Shade', a name for part of Arbour Hill where a gallows stood. The legend may have grown out of the maypole festival, as in England Robin Hood was the hero of folk plays performed on May Day, and was closely associated with the May King.

A riot at Stoneybatter in 1771 led to the abandonment of the mayday festival. A few soldiers from the Royal Barracks, now Collins Barracks, which we shall pass shortly, attempted while drunk to pull down the maypole, and were attacked by the revellers, who drove them back into their barracks, then stoned the windows. An hour later the soldiers reappeared, now armed with muskets, and fired into the crowd at the maypole. Frederick 'Buck' Jones, who was then city sheriff, commandeered seven soldiers and went to the barracks, satisfied that the provocation had originated there. A Major Digby imprisoned three soldiers whom he took to be the ringleaders, and the riot was suppressed, leaving many windows broken in the neighbourhood. A vote of thanks to Mr Jones and two army officers was, said the newspapers, passed by 'the inhabitants of Prussia St etc.'

Manor St

Going up the right hand side of Stoneybatter towards Manor St, we pass the corner of Brunswick St and come to the long black Victorian facade of a bar whose gold chunky lettering reads 'L. Mulligan. Grocer.' Unfortunately the interior of the bar does not match the front in period. Further up this side of the street a Gothic stone arch leads to the convent and school of the Irish Sisters of Charity, usually known as 'Stanhope St'. This convent was established on 2 February 1819, before Mary Aikenhead had moved the order's original convent from North William St to Gardiner St. The Stanhope St convent, as we have noted, replaced an 1811 'house of refuge for industrious females'. The different shades of the buildings here, grey, brown and red, show how the establishment has grown. A Victorian chapel in redbrick Gothic overlooks the entrance, and is flanked by a brick tower, but is not out of tone with the older part.

Beyond the northern wall of the convent enclosure, Kirwan St runs from Manor St to Grangegorman, and Kirwan St Cottages, off it, occupy an unusual, almost triangular, retreat.

The upper part of Stoneybatter was named Manor St in 1780 after Grangegorman Manor House, which overlooked it, — and still does — and behind which were the lands formerly owned by Gormond and by Sir Thomas Stanley. In the mid-nineteenth century most of the dairy cattle in the north city were kept in yards around Stoneybatter. We notice that Manor St widens at the top into a triangle, one side of which terminates the street and separates its junctions with Prussia St and Aughrim St, formerly the lower ends of Cabragh Lane and Blackhorse Lane respectively. This triangle once contained a village green. On our

Prussia St

right, before we go up Prussia St, an arch that led to dairy yards is followed by a terrace of houses with high steps and an interesting form of modified, pillarless Georgian doorway. These are numbers 32, 33, 34, 35, 36 and 37. Notice the small window over the arch, below the terrace. At the top end of the street on this side, the tall number 42, four storeys over a basement, is the former manor house, and was also a police barrack earlier this century. Observe that the window proportions are not those usually found in Georgian houses, those in the second being as short as the top row.

Prussia St is named after Frederick the Great, Hohenzollern king of Prussia, but was part of Cabragh Lane until 1765. Its eighteenth-century suburban character, more rural than urban, is still apparent in some of the houses, as in number 11, with its sideways flight of steps to the halldoor. Notice the wide fronts of numbers 28 and 29, and of number 38, with its console keystone over the halldoor, but the house facing number 38 is what dominates the street. This is the City Arms hotel, a splendid Georgian specimen seven bays wide, flanked by pillared gates on either side, though on the lower side a bar intervenes, with a quaint Gothic doorway between bar and hotel. The house stands three storeys over a basement, with a broad flight of steps sweeping outward on each side onto the path, the curved ends of the railings surmounted by two big hexagonal lamps, which must have looked beautiful when lit by gas. **City Arms hotel**

The upward curves of the walls and railings of the basement areas at the City Arms do not extend to the last bay on either side, and these flanking bays are set some inches back from the rest of the house, suggesting that they are later additions. Though the halldoor has been replaced, the pediment remains, and the place still has a noble character. This house was owned by the Jamesons, whose distillery we have seen, and was also once the residence of Henry Stevens Reilly, after whom the 1792 Ratoath Road bridge on the Royal Canal, at the top of the old Cabragh Lane, is named.

Looking down Prussia St, one can see Christ Church cathedral across the Liffey, a reminder that both parts of the city in Viking times were considerably west of the present centre. Making a detour along St Joseph's Road brings us to St Gabriel's church at its junction with Aughrim St, a fine neo-Gothic building of 1880, with three pleasing stained glass windows in the apse and a large timber organ gallery. Going back to Prussia St and up to its junction with the North Circular Road, we are facing the pub that gives this place its name of Hanlon's Corner. **Hanlon's Corner**

From Hanlon's Corner, go up the North Circular Road, past Blackhorse Avenue on the right, formerly a continuation of Blackhorse Lane, which was named after the Black Horse Inn, still there as the Hole in the Wall. Further up the main road turn right into Marlborough Road, and look across the railway line to McKee barracks, an adventure in high Victoriana, dating from 1889, with bricks and roof tiles all in vivid red, turrets and sometimes double rows of dormer windows in the high steep roofs. This was built as Marlborough cavalry barracks. There is nothing else quite like it in Dublin. Buildings eminently unsuited to their surroundings have given rise to the story that they were originally planned for India, that the plans were transposed, the Indian building was erected 'at home' and vice versa. This tale is also told concerning Nash's pavilion in Brighton, the courthouse in Ennis, Co. Clare, and a large hospital in Enniscorthy, Co. Wexford, and while picturesque, is quite untrue. **McKee barracks**

123

Oxmantown Road

Straight across the North Circular Road from here is Oxmantown Road, and at its lower end are streets whose names contain the words 'Ostman', 'Norseman', 'Olaf', 'Sitric' and 'Viking', whose derivation is obvious.

The houses in these streets, in Oxmantown Road itself, and in the other streets and roads off it were mostly built in the 1890s as artisans' dwellings. They comprise two styles; a two-storey brown brick unit with one front upstairs window, the door and window surrounds being in redbrick; and the grey single-storey terraces such as Arklow St, on the west side of Oxmantown Road. The two-storey streets resemble those built during the second phase of the industrial revolution in, say, Lancashire and Belfast for working-class tenants. In Ringsend, however, between Dock St and Gordon St, is a housing scheme which far more closely matches the Belfast type than do these Oxmantown streets. In the Oxmantown scheme one can feel isolated in an enclosure of brick lines and elevations, a feeling that a modern council housing estate does not give because of its gardens. The sameness of the Oxmantown streets is striking. The 1895 St Gabriel's schools in Cowper St have the same materials and colours as the houses, relieved by some Gothic arches. A 1953 extension to the schools stands out as an intruder. In Carnew St the use of redbrick, still sparing, is varied slightly, but elsewhere the discipline is stricter than in any Georgian square, and even the two corner shops in Sitric Road must conform, their diagonal doors matching and their iron cornerposts cast from the same mould. Here and there the residents have escaped from uniformity by individual use of colour on wood and brick.

Swing left at the bottom of Oxmantown Road, then bear right through Mount Temple road and Ard Ri Road. The feeling still persists, of walking in the middle of an enclosed community. This disappears as soon as we arrive at Arbour Hill, where we turn right.

Arbour Hill

Collins barracks

On our left as we go up Arbour Hill is Collins barracks, which we will soon see again from the Liffey. It was erected between 1704 and 1706 to the design of Thomas Burgh, as the Royal Barracks, but is considerably altered since then. It is said to be the oldest inhabited barracks in the world, and to have the largest barrack square in Europe, Royal Square, the oldest of its four. On the right is the old military detention barracks, now known simply as Arbour Hill and including a civilian jail. In the cemetery behind Arbour Hill are buried the leaders of the 1916 Rising.

Passing this complex, we see a row of barrack stables running up to the right. Turning left, descend the hill for a moment and go right, into

Montpelier Hill

Montpelier Hill. Many of its old houses are demolished, but three remaining on the left may be of late seventeenth century construction, and are certainly not much younger. They are numbers 52 and 50, with windows immediately below the eaves, and number 48, a front-gabled house whose windows are on staggered levels. Across the road is a long-fronted Georgian house called Cambridge House, once occupied by Prince George of Cambridge, first cousin of Queen Victoria and grandson of George III. He later became duke of Cambridge and commander-in-chief of the British army. While stationed in the Royal

Barracks as an officer, he eschewed barrack quarters for awhile to live on here. In the church on Arbour Hill he married an actress named Louisa Farebrother, but as he failed to seek his cousin's royal assent to this, the marriage was regarded as morganatic, and his eldest son, a Colonel Fitzgeorge, did not succeed to the dukedom.

At the end of Montpelier Hill turn left and go down Infirmary Road and left again along Parkgate St, passing Ryan's bar with its fine Victorian interior and facade, and the Royal Oak further on, with mural of the 'tree of Boscobel' incident from the life of Charles II. Further on, as we come towards our second look at Collins barracks, is a triangle of grass called Croppies Acre. Some of the rebels of 1798 are buried here, including Wolfe Tone's brother Matthew.

Croppies Acre

McKee Barracks, Blackhorse Avenue

8 The Phoenix Park

People's Gardens — zoo — Garda depot — Aras an Uachtarain — Papal nunciature — US ambassador's residence — ordnance survey office — St Mary's hospital — polo grounds — magazine fort — Wellington monument.

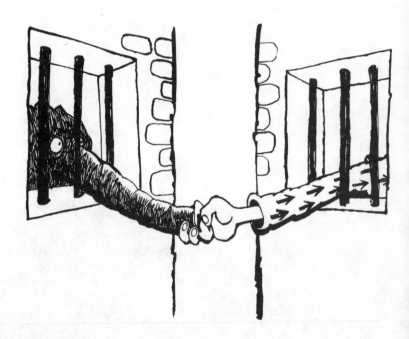

Had Mr Gladstone shown firmness in dealing with the Irish rebels, Lord Frederick Cavendish and Mr Burke would not have died.

— Queen Victoria

Going up Parkgate St, past a handsome limestone arch of what used to be a munitions factory on the left, the road ahead divides and the section on the right rises as it enters the Phoenix Park. Although only a mile-and-a-half from Butt Bridge, we are at the entrance to the most splendid public park immediately adjacent to a European capital. This park has a circumference of about seven miles, and the total area is 1,752 acres. In London terms, this is the combined area of Hyde Park, Regent's Park, St James's Park, Green Park, Kensington Gardens, Hampstead Heath, Parliament Hill and Primrose Hill.

Most of the land in the park was in the estate of the Knights Hospitallers of Kilmainham, which also included the area now occupied by the Royal Hospital on the south bank of the Liffey, and which reverted to the crown on Henry VIII's dissolution of the monasteries. The Phoenix Park was designed and walled by the Duke of Ormonde in 1671, and opened to the public by Lord Chesterfield, the lord lieutenant, in 1747. The name 'Phoenix' is a corruption of the two Irish words '*fionn uisce*', meaning pale or clear water, derived from a chalybeate or iron spring, once noted as a spa, now in the grounds of the zoological gardens. On the site of the Magazine Fort stood Phoenix House, built in or about 1611. It has been suggested that this was so named because of its solitary and desirable position on a hill, making it a 'phoenix' or paragon among houses. (According to legend, only one phoenix existed at a time.) It is more likely that the house was named after the spa, and the corruption followed.

People's Gardens Going up the main road, we pass on our right the People's Gardens, with their lake, laid out in 1864. This attractive plot includes what was formerly called Bishop's Wood. Bordering the gardens is the headquarters of the Department of Defence, whose main building, formerly a military infirmary, was designed by James Gandon, and whose office, with vivid red bricks and tiles, is called the 'Red House'. A statue in the gardens of the seventh earl of Carlisle, through whose influence the gardens were laid out, was blown up several years ago. The gardens contain a bust of Sean Heuston, the 1916 rebel after whom Kingsbridge station was renamed, by Laurence Campbell.

Past the gardens we reach an intersection where an equestrian statue of Lord Hugh Gough, a distinguished Irish general, formerly stood. Executed by John Henry Foley, it was erected in 1880. In 1944 the head was sawn off the statue and the sword removed; the head was found in the Liffey at Islandbridge and put back in place. The entire statue was blown up in 1957.

the Hollow We next pass, on the right, the aptly-named Hollow, with its bandstand, and turn right to visit the zoological gardens, whose entrance lies ahead on the left. Facing us beyond that is a long, two-storey building, with a parade ground in front, flanked by other buildings. This is now the headquarters of the Garda Siochana, or Irish police force. It was built between 1839 and 1842. A simple monument to members of the Garda Siochana who died in the service of the state stands in front of this rather monotonous building, whose series of mean entrances, without an imposing central one, do not help its appearance. **Garda depot** The road to the left of the Garda depot leads to the fish pond, formerly

127

popular with skaters. Inside the zoo, we will see a lake of which the fish pond is a natural continuation, though they are not joined.

The society now known as the Royal Zoological Society of Ireland came into being as the Zoological Society of Dublin on 10 May 1830, at a meeting in the Rotunda. Its formation was proposed by the earl of Longford and seconded by Mr Philip Crampton, the surgeon-general. At the meeting, which was public, it was mentioned that the lord lieutenant, the duke of Northumberland, was willing to give land in the Phoenix Park for the laying out of a zoological garden. The following year the society acquired this land, five-and-a-half acres, little more than a sixth of the zoo's present area. The first animal the society owned was a wild boar, and through the winter of 1830 this lonely creature was the sole justification of the society's name.

Dublin zoo

It has been claimed that the Dublin zoo is the second-oldest privately-owned zoo in the world, the oldest being that in Regent's Park, London (1826). Whatever the value of this claim, there were certainly close links between London and Dublin. A Major Vigors, who had an important part in establishing the London zoo, also helped to initiate the Dublin one, and the Phoenix Park layout was designed by Decimus Burton, architect to the Zoological Society of London.

Dublin zoo opened to the public on 1 September 1831. A gatehouse, built in 1833 in mock-Tudor style with overhanging thatched roof, and rough timbers supporting the eaves on one side, was formerly used as a ticket office, but is now simply preserved inside the granite-pillared railing, having been restored to its original condition by a building society. The title 'Royal Zoological Society of Ireland' was not adopted until 1837, when Victoria became the society's patroness.

In the zoo, however, at the top of steps leading down to the lake, is an arch supporting a crown, and also bearing the 1830 date of the initial Rotunda meeting. While perhaps historically important to the society, this arch is grossly unworthy of its lovely surroundings, being a piece of that iron 'sewerpipe' architecture which still gives the Victorian era a bad name.

The zoological society is a non-profit making organisation, the maintenance of the large collection of animals being paid for by admission fees, subscriptions and sponsorship by commercial firms. It is administered by a council which meets regularly, a feature of some of their meetings being that they are held immediately after a breakfast which is eaten in the zoo.

H. V. Morton, describing a zoo breakfast he attended, in *In Search of Ireland* in 1930, told how he was conducted from the zoo gates to a room decorated with dead animals, where 'a dozen grave professional men were standing about eating porridge in little bowls. It is a tradition with the zoologists of Dublin that porridge is never consumed from a sitting position'. He was invited to inspect an elephant's foot, preserved in the room, which had the inscription: 'Sita, who killed her keeper and was shot, 11 June 1903.'

Dublin zoo contains no such rarities as the white tigers of Bristol; what tigers it owns are conventionally coloured and probably its most

Gate Lodge, Dublin Zoo

famous individual inmate has been a tuatera lizard, with a socket for a third eye under the skin of its forehead. But the Phoenix Park enclosure has achieved world fame for successfully breeding many lions, and for their worldwide export. It is one of the few places in the world where lions will breed in captivity. In its early years the zoo was forced to sell lions to raise money, but in 1855 a government grant was obtained, and experimental breeding began with a pair of lions bought for £285.

The first recorded births of cubs were in 1857, and nearly 700 of them have been bred since then, going to many parts of the world. 'Maire', a Dublin lioness, probably set a world record by producing 75 cubs in 16 litters in 12 years. Many Dublin zoo litters have numbered five, and some seven, cubs. Edward VII gave the zoo a lioness named 'Nigeria' which produced 26 cubs, all of which lived. One lion lived in the zoo until he was 27 years old, about ten years more than a normal span. Perhaps the best-known of all the Dublin lions was the celebrated 'MGM lion', whose roar was familiar to millions of cinema-goers.

For many years the lions were mostly kept in the Roberts House, a pleasant 1902 redbrick building with animal head keystones in its

entrance arches and wrought iron leaves on the internal pillars. Though some big cats are still kept there, the lions have been moved to the Craigie enclosure across the lake, and tigers to a similar enclosure nearby.

The general view of the zoo is extremely pleasant, especially when its roses and other flowers are in bloom, and a flock of pink flamingoes can be seen in the shallow part of the lake near the footbridge. Modernisation has changed the zoo's appearance, and there are now fewer iron bars and more glass, but its character has not so far been destroyed. An octagonal aviary has lost its shape, the 1898 Haughton House's mock-Tudor walls have nearly all been demolished in catering enlargements, and a concrete cantilever ape house hangs over the lakeside near the polar bears' grotto. But the superintendent's house is solidly unchanged, and the zoo's predominantly outdoor aspect quietly absorbs the changes.

An eye-catching woodcarving is a Haida Indian totem pole, presented to Ireland in August 1970 by the Canadian government to mark Canada's participation in a meeting in Dublin of the World Craft Council. The Irish government pondered the problem of selecting a public place for it, one both suitable to its character and beyond the reach of vandals who might wish to add to its carvings. Its present location meets both requirements. It is in the zoo's American black bear enclosure.

If we follow the perimeter of the zoo past the end of the sealions' pool, we see on our right an enclosure of crowned cranes. In this, a wooden arrow marks the site of the chalybeate spring which in 1611, through Phoenix House, gave the name Phoenix to the park.

Leaving the zoo and turning right, we follow its perimeter until we see on our left a large flat area with parallel fences, overlooked by an **Polo Grounds** attractive pavilion with seats on its roof. This is the Polo Grounds, once known as Nine Acres, administered by the All-Ireland Polo Club. In summer, crowds line the rails here to watch this highly entertaining equestrian sport, regarded by some as the best free outdoor spectacle in Dublin. The playing area or 'course' is 300 yards long, and about 170 yards wide.

This area was formerly used by cricketers, and the first polo match was played here in the 1870s. It had been first played in Ireland a short time earlier in Carlow, introduced there by Mr Horace Rochfort, also one of the organisers of the first match in the Phoenix Park.

If we take the road from the pavilion, away from the direction of the zoo, we come again to the park's main road. Turning right, we are struck by the seeming endlessness of the broad road ahead. From this point it continues dead straight between its elm trees to Castleknock gate for about 1.6 miles. Going up it towards the Phoenix monument, we pass on our right the grounds of Aras an Uachtarain, official **Aras an** residence of Ireland's president, and formerly of lords lieutenant or **Uachtarain** viceroys, hence the name vice-regal lodge, which still has some colloquial currency. This was built in 1751 as the home of Rt Hon. Nathaniel Clements, chief park ranger and deputy Irish vice-treasurer, and was a relatively small three-bay house. But is was considerably enlarged in 1782, having been bought by the English government as a residence for the lord lieutenant. The house we see from the park's main road has an Ionic portico, wings have been added to the ends and an Edwardian block has been added to the west wing. All these additions were made after the house changed hands. The main additions were made by Francis Johnston, who added the wings between 1801 and 1806, a portico on the north front between 1807 and 1813 and the portico facing the main road between 1813 and 1817. It was a gallant attempt to turn a fairly ordinary house into a stately mansion, but it did not quite succeed. Aras an Uachtarain still looks like a rambling rustic house with classical trimmings.

George IV in 1821, Victoria in 1849, 1853, 1861 and 1900, Edward VII in 1903, 1904 and 1907 and George V in 1911 all stayed in

Aras an Uachtarain

the vice-regal lodge. George IV drove there from Howth, which then was a passenger terminal. It is said that on this visit the king, while staying at Powerscourt House near Enniskerry, Co. Wicklow, escaped death by having a hangover. It had been arranged for him to view the famous Powerscourt waterfall, but this was found to have dwindled to a trickle. A boulder dam was erected, with a mechanism which would breach it at the viewing time, giving a spectacular flow. By viewing time the king, having drunk copiously the night before, was in no mood for waterfalls, and sent his apologies. Nevertheless, the dam mechanism was released as arranged, and the boulders came down with the water, sweeping away the platform on which the monarch should have been standing.

Queen Victoria's first journey to Dublin was made aboard her luxurious *Victoria and Albert* yacht. Her feelings about Ireland were mixed. She sympathised with Irish Catholics on the grounds that, as a majority, they could not be called dissenters. Earlier in life she is said to have disliked the Irish as a race. Yet when the *Victoria and Albert* was leaving Kingstown (Dun Laoghaire) at the end of the 1849 visit, its royal standard was lowered and raised again, a salute to the citizens of Dublin in appreciation of the reception they had given the queen. This salute had, until then, been reserved for royalty. Later Victoria was simplistically to contrast the disloyalty of Ireland with the loyalty of Scotland.

In *King Edward and His Times*, André Maurois relates how the king, before his first visit to Dublin as sovereign, was told of the Irish desire for education and for 'security in their land' and declared: 'I shall come to Ireland with an Education Bill in one hand and a Land Bill in the other.' A Land Act that satisfied Irish nationalists was later passed, and the king was greeted on arrival in Dublin with 'unexpected enthusiasm'. Driving from the vice-regal lodge to Maynooth college, he was welcomed by young priests in front of a picture of his Derby winner, Persimmon. They had decorated the frame with ribbons in his racing colours, and 'the blend of loyalty, sporting spirit and religion amused and pleased the king'.

The Anglo-Irish political issue of sovereignty over Northern Ireland precludes a state visit and stay at Aras an Uachtarain by Queen Elizabeth II, but the house, since it was upgraded to the residence of a head of state, has been visited by European royalty and by other heads of state.

On the establishment of the Irish Free State the vice-regal lodge became the residence of the governor-general. Mr Timothy Healy, Mr James MacNeill and Mr Domhnall O Buachalla in turn occupied this office, until, in 1938, Dr Douglas Hyde moved into the lodge, renamed Aras an Uachtarain, as first Irish president under a new constitution.

The most dramatic incident in the history of the Phoenix Park occurred on the evening of Saturday, 6 May 1882, when Lord Frederick Cavendish, chief secretary for Ireland, and his under-secretary T. H. Burke, were murdered at a spot on the main road almost directly opposite the vice-regal lodge by members of a secret society called the National Invincibles. Cavendish was a new appointment, just arrived

The Phoenix Park murders

Lamp standard, Phoenix Park

from London, as was earl Spencer, the lord lieutenant. Spencer went straight to the vice-regal lodge. Cavendish spent most of the day in Dublin Castle, and about 7 p.m. went by carriage to the Phoenix Park. Ahead of him along the main road lay the Phoenix monument, from which a road to the left led to his residence, now that of the United States ambassador. Burke's house, which became the Apostolic Nunciature after independence and had formerly been Ashtown Castle, lay to the right. Cavendish, driving through the park, met Burke in another car, and they apparently both dismounted to walk towards the monument. This means that they were both walking towards their residences, and some accounts say they were going to these, while others claim that they were both going to dine with the lord lieutenant in the vice-regal lodge, and that Spencer saw what happened to them from a window, but was unaware of the murder victims' identities. Cavendish and Burke were surrounded by seven men and stabbed to death by Joseph Brady and Timothy Kelly, who used surgeons' amputating knives which had been bought in London. It was generally believed afterwards that the intention had been to kill Burke only, and the point was made that the Invincibles would not have known the newly-arrived

133

Cavendish by sight. The informer James Carey later said that the decision to murder Burke had been taken on 3 May and that the successful attempt was the fourth one, the Invincibles having been in the park on the Friday morning and afternoon, and on the Saturday morning. Burke, he said, had escaped on one of these occasions by walking across the polo grounds instead of along the road. Carey told how he had heard Brady's account of the crime, from which it appeared that Cavendish, seeing Burke attacked, struck Brady in defence of Burke, whereupon Brady stabbed Cavendish to death, while Kelly completed the murder of Burke.

Carey told how Joseph Smith, a workman at Dublin Castle, pointed out Burke to him, and how he himself passed on the signal, pointing out which of the two pedestrians was Burke. Immediately before that Carey had passed the time by watching a game of polo. After the crime, the Invincibles left the park in two vehicles, an open car driven by Michael Kavanagh and a cab driven by James Fitzharris, known as 'Skin the Goat'. Kavanagh, who gave information leading to the arrest of 'Skin the Goat', told how he himself drove his passengers across a large open space to our left, now used as football and hurling pitches, called the 'Fifteen Acres', an area where they could easily see whether they were being pursued, and act accordingly. They left the park by Chapelizod gate, almost knocking down a pedestrian, later a witness against them, who shouted after them that they were in danger of prosecution for 'furious driving'. They drove rapidly over a long circuitous route through the south-west, south and south-east of Dublin, re-entering the city over Leeson St bridge, so as to look as if they were coming from the direction of Kingstown (Dun Laoghaire). Kavanagh later drove a police officer over the route, pointing out the place, now Walkinstown Road, where Brady and Kelly got down and wiped the blood from their knives on long roadside grass.

The Phoenix Park murders, which had stunned the country, might have remained unsolved, had it not been for two more murder attempts later that year. On 11 November Patrick Delany, armed with a revolver, attempted to kill the unpopular Judge Lawson outside the Kildare St Club, and was arrested and later convicted. On 27 November Denis Field, a stationer who had served on a jury which had convicted Michael Walsh of the murder of a policeman in Galway, was stabbed by two men with long knives outside his house in North Frederick St. A few days after this, fearing an ongoing pattern, the authorities set up a secret police inquiry. Robert Farrell, summoned before it, and erroneously believing that he was not the first informer, named Kavanagh as the carman who accompanied the attackers of Field. Kavanagh was arrested and told police that he drove Kelly, Brady and two other men to and from the attack on Field, and that the knives used had been thrown into the Grand Canal dock in Ringsend. He later told of driving Brady, Kelly, Delany and Thomas Caffrey from the Phoenix Park murders.

Later Carey gave his comprehensive Queen's evidence. Three other informers were Carey's brother, Peter, Joseph Smith, who had pointed out Burke, and Joseph Hanlon, one of those who left the park in

'Skin the Goat's' cab. Brady, Kelly, Caffrey, Daniel Curley and Michael Fagan were hanged. James Carey was kept in Kilmainham jail for a few weeks for his protection, then sent by the authorities under the assumed name of Power to Natal with his wife and family. A few miles off Port Elizabeth he was shot dead by another Irish passenger named Patrick O'Donnell, later hanged in London for this murder. O'Donnell had not, as is popularly supposed, been 'sent after' Carey by the Invincibles. An English passenger named Robert Cubitt had merely shown him a picture of Carey in a newspaper and pointed out its resemblance to 'Mr Power'.

It is hard nowadays to reconcile these events with the serenity usually found in this part of the Phoenix Park, with its quiet classicism and expansive greenery. This classicism is exemplified by the Phoenix **Phoenix** monument; the fabulous Arabian bird spreads its wings atop a slender **monument** Corinthian column, whose flutes are filleted in the lower part of the shaft, the column standing on a tall pedestal over an elaborate spreading base. The monument was erected in 1747 by Lord Chesterfield, then viceroy. The Portland stone column is 30 feet high, and the monument originally stood in the middle of the main road, then called Chesterfield Road.

Of the roads leading to our right, we notice that the short wide one nearer to the city terminates in the gates of Aras an Uachtarain, and this did not exist when the monument was erected. Chesterfield was a lover of the classics, and perpetuated here the legend of the phoenix, said to burn itself to death when it had lived 500 years, a new bird arising from the ashes. The name of the bird denoted that its bright plumage was coloured like the famed Phoenician purple dye. The monument, which was once surrounded by a stone circle, bears the Chesterfield coat of arms and Latin inscriptions denoting that he erected it, and beautified the park, for the delight of Dublin's citizens. The Phoenix monument is usually referred to in Dublin as the Eagle monument, as the bird has a somewhat aquiline appearance; the flames are the distinguishing feature, but these lack impact in the sculpture.

In 1747 Chesterfield opened the Phoenix Park to the public, planted the magnificent main avenue of elm trees and many of the other woods and copses in the park. At the Phoenix monument we are in the part of the park where it is most common to glimpse the herd of fallow deer which roams wild here. The turn to our left leads across the most open area of the park, the Fifteen Acres, to Chapelizod gate. As there **Fifteen Acres** are in fact about 200 acres here under playing fields, the name is ludicrous. A branch off the 'Acres' road near the main road leads to the American ambassador's house, beyond which, running towards the ordnance survey office, is Oldtown Wood, a name rarely used. If we **Oldtown Wood** turn for a moment and look back in the direction of Parkgate St, the wood to our right in the middle distance, across the main road from Aras an Uachtarain, has the old name of Black Wood, containing blackthorn trees. Turning towards Castleknock gate again, go a little more than two-thirds of a mile and come to a crossroads. Either side road will bring us almost to the perimeter of the park, then sweep back in the direction in which we have travelled, the roads meeting the main road again two miles behind us, where, as we noted, the Gough monument formerly stood. The road ahead from our crossroads goes only to Castleknock gate, with woods north and south of it, Butcher's Wood on the left and Oak Wood on the right, to give them their old names. The road to the right of the crossroad is the secluded 'back road', and we traversed part of it, at its other end, when we visited the zoo. It passes the back of Aras an Uachtarain, and is probably the best place within the city limits for a long contemplative stroll.

As this purely personal exercise can be undertaken any time the weather and mood are suitable, and as there is little of noteworthy interest along the way until one again reaches the shores of the fish pond, we will turn instead to the road on our left. But before leaving the right hand turn, it is worth mentioning that it leads also, by way of the Ashtown gate, to the Phoenix Park racecourse, which is just outside the park. This is the nearest racecourse to the city centre, and was founded in 1902. It retains much of its original Edwardian atmosphere.

Phoenix Park racecourse

White's Road

Taking the road to the left at our crossroads, we pass a turn on the right, which leads out through White's gate and along White's Road to Castleknock college, founded in 1835, in whose grounds is the ruin of Castleknock castle. The White commemorated here is the same Luke White whom we have already encountered as the vendor of the original Shelbourne hotel site. Luttrellstown Castle, which he also owned, is further along White's Road, beyond the college. Between us and the college, to the left of the road just outside the park wall, is Farmleigh, residence of Lord Iveagh, where the foreign ministers of the European Economic Community countries held talks in April 1975. Continuing south past the White's Road turn, we pass the attractive Quarry Lake on the left, with its island, and a little further on, to the right, a path runs up to the ordnance survey office, the original building of which was erected about 1728 by the ubiquitous Luke Gardiner, who had been appointed a park keeper. The position and house later passed to his son Charles and to his grandson Luke, first Lord Mountjoy, who, as we noted, was killed in 1798. The house in 1812 became Mountjoy cavalry barracks, and the ordnance survey was established there in 1825. The buildings have been considerably added to since then, but before his death Lord Mountjoy had already built a private theatre at the house.

Farmleigh

ordnance survey office

Passing on, we reach another crossroads. The road to the right goes to Knockmaroon gate, in a corner of the park, just outside of which is Mount Sackville convent, with its school, established there by the Sisters of St Joseph of Cluny in 1864. The name probably commemorates Lord George Sackville, son of Lionel Sackville, duke of Dorset, after whom Sackville St and Dorset St were named. The angled road to the left of the cross roads goes back to the main road through Oldtown Wood, but we go straight ahead along a winding road, passing the Glen Pond over on our right, and skirt the Furry Glen, one of the most attractive parts of the park. One is forgiven for feeling that this epitomises the *rus in urbe* concept, for we are still inside the city limits. Continuing along the road, which now meanders freely, we go through another wooded area with Chapelizod village away to our right. A little further on, a path on our left through the trees goes to a Cheshire home,

Mount Sackville convent

a refuge for the incurably sick. Some way beyond the turn for the home, two more turns on the left go to St Mary's hospital, and the second, broader, one is also the road across the big plain of the Fifteen Acres to the Phoenix monument. On the right this road continues to Chapelizod gate. St Mary's hospital occupies some former buildings of the Royal Hibernian Military School, which was granted a royal charter in 1769 by George III, and which was devoted to the maintenance, education and apprenticing of children of soldiers in Ireland, especially orphans. It was built in 1766 and Thomas Cooley added the chapel between 1771 and 1773. The school catered for children of both sexes and included an eighteen-acre farm on which the boys worked. The main building was enlarged by Francis Johnston between 1808 and 1813.

St Mary's hospital

Passing on, the winding road overlooks the Chapelizod road outside the park wall on our right, with the Liffey and the Dublin hills in the distance. Through another wood the road zig-zags along Corkscrew Hill, straightening out to bring us to our next landmark, a grim and lonely fort above us on the left. This is the Magazine Fort, standing on Thomas's Hill. Sir Edward Fisher built Phoenix House on this hill in or about 1611, having been assigned 400 acres of land by Sir Richard Sutton. It was a summer residence of the viceroys from 1617, Lord Grandison, Lord Falkland and the earl of Strafford being among its occupants, and Henry Cromwell, a fourth son of Oliver, occupied it between 1655 and 1659, adding a new wing. A further wing was added by the duke of Ormonde in 1662. In 1735 the building of the magazine fort began on the site, the duke of Wharton, then viceroy, feeling that it was needed 'as a retreat from disturbances'. It was finished in 1801, with barracks, magazines for ammunition and gunpowder, a moat and a drawbridge.

Magazine Fort

On Easter Monday 1916, a group of insurgents stole rifles from the fort, and these were used in fighting in Dublin in the following few days. The fort was again raided by the IRA on 23 December 1939, when rifles, ammunition and machineguns were stolen, most of the haul being recovered in a few days.

Crossing the Islandbridge gate road in front of the fort, a winding road brings us back to the erstwhile site of the Gough monument. As we near it, with the cricket ground on our left, a narrow straight path leads across the grass on our right to the Wellington monument, a huge granite obelisk which stands on a plinth over a flight of eleven sloping steps, the plinth and steps being of the same stone. The steps go around the four sides of the monument, the bottom one being 480 feet square. The steps and plinth have a combined height of fifty-five feet, and the obelisk, which is twenty feet square at its base, is 150 feet high, diminishing in the proportion of an inch to the foot. Its pyramidal cap comes to a point 205 feet from the ground. Down along the four sides of the obelisk are inscribed the locations of all the victories of the duke of Wellington, and on three sides of the plinth are panels cast from captured cannon, depicting in relief two battle scenes and a political scene from his life. On the remaining side, facing Parkgate St a bronze commemorative panel bears the verse, in English and Latin:

Wellington monument

Asia and Europe, saved by thee, proclaim,

Invincible in war thy deathless name,
Now round thy brow the civic oak we twine,
That every earthly honour may be thine.

A plaque below this somewhat devalues the words by telling us that they were written by Richard Wellesley, the duke's brother.

The £21,000 which the monument cost was raised by subscription, the design was by Robert Smirke and construction went on from 1817 until 1861. Facing the side which bears the verse an empty plinth stood for some years, a few yards from the monument, on which it was intended to erect an equestrian statue of the Iron Duke 'after his decease'. Dublin's Wellington testimonial thus shares with Edinburgh's, on Calton Hill, the distinction of not having been finished, probably for the same reason, lack of funds.

An eccentric German prince, Hermann Von Pueckler-Muskau, described the obelisk in 1828 as ill-proportioned, and it became

The Wellington Monument, a detail

fashionable to agree with him. (He also denigrated the Nelson Pillar, the George IV monument in Dun Laoghaire, Howth castle and Malahide castle, and said Dublin's streets were dirty.) The Wellington obelisk would, indeed, be better proportioned if taller, but it would have attracted less criticism had it been smaller. It dominates the view along the upper North Circular Road and can be seen from the quays and from many parts of the park.

The Phoenix Cricket Club was located near the monument when it moved to the park from Baggot St about 1840, and about five years later it crossed the road to its present location. Founded in 1830 for 'officers and gentlemen', it is the second-oldest surviving cricket club in Ireland, that in Trinity College being the oldest. Two other clubs founded before Phoenix, in Ballinasloe and Kilkenny, then 'garrison' towns, have vanished. The name 'Phoenix' was used by the club while it still had no connection with the park, and is purely coincidental.

Phoenix Cricket Club

Church of SS. Michael and John — Wood Quay — Adam and Eve church — Brazen Head inn — city walls — St Audoen's churches — Christ Church cathedral — St Nicholas Within — St Werburgh's — Dublin Castle — City Hall — south city markets.

I reached the Ting where stand our fathers' tombs,
And round its grassy side shield crowding shield,
And sword in hand the Northland's sons arrayed.

— Frithiof's Saga.

Going upriver along Essex Quay from Grattan Bridge, we find the narrow path giving way to an open space, and see the facade of a smallish church on our left. This is the church of SS Michael and John, founded in 1811 and completed in 1815, though it had been partly opened in 1813. It was built as a replacement of the four pre-Reformation parish churches of St Michael, St John, St Werburgh and St Nicholas Within the Walls, and was opened simply as St Michael's but as it stood in the ancient parish of St John, that saint's name was later added. It occupies the site of the seventeenth-century Smock Alley theatre, Smock Alley being the old name of West Essex St, behind the church. The land bought by the parish priest, Dr Michael Blake, for the church was described on a lease dating from 1773 as 'the piece or parcel of ground whereon the old theatre and other tenements adjoining thereto lately stood, with the messuage, house or tenement now called the theatre or play house on the north side of Smock Alley, containing in front to Smock Alley 63¼ feet, and in depth backward to the blind quay (Exchange St) 139 feet'. The church, while seeming to occupy a quay site, actually faces out onto Lower Exchange St. Standing outside it facing the river, we see how Exchange St curves away on our right in a south-easterly direction; it is following the line of the mediaeval city wall. The building on our right between this street and the river occupies the site of Isolde's Tower, part of the former fortification, a round tower forty feet high.

Continuing west along the river, we enter Wood Quay and arrive at the bottom of Fishamble St. On the left is Kennan's ironworks, the site of the 'musick hall', where on 13 April 1742, Handel first performed his *Messiah* in public. Fishamble St was a fish market in the fourteenth century, 'fish shamble' meaning a fish stall. Still going west, the splendid spectacle of Christ Church Cathedral dominates the ridge to the left. We have just passed through the site of Fyan's Castle, a four-storey square tower of the old fortifications, and between us and the cathedral is the former site of the Norse St Olaf's church, which lasted until the time of Henry VIII. Continue west, passing O'Donovan Rossa Bridge on the right, and the eloquently named Winetavern St on the left, curving to the right at the top into St Michael's Hill.

St Michael's Hill is gracefully crossed by the enclosed bridge that links Christ Church with its synod house. Looking right, O'Donovan Rossa Bridge was formerly Richmond Bridge, built in 1813 to replace the 1683 Ormond Bridge which was swept away in 1806.

Ahead is the Franciscan Church of the Immaculate Conception, almost universally called 'Adam and Eve's'. Fronting on Merchants' Quay, it backs into Cook St, where these friars had a former foundation. The original Adam and Eve was a tavern at the corner of Cook St and Rosemary Lane, the lane running from the street to the quay past where the church's side door now is. From the time of Henry III to that of Henry VIII the Franciscans occupied the site of the present St Nicholas of Myra church in Francis St. There they had a large monastery, and were known as conventual friars. After they were dispossessed they dispersed, and later rented the back part of the Adam and Eve tavern for Divine worship, Cook St, once known as Via Cocorum, was noted

Essex Quay

SS Michael and John

Smock Alley theatre

Isolde's Tower

Wood Quay

Fishamble St

St Michael's Hill

'Adam and Eve's'

Cook St

141

for its taverns as well as for religious establishments. Religious services were held surreptitiously in the inn until the arrival of Catholic Emancipation. As the law dictated that taverns be closed during the hours of divine worship in Protestant parochial churches on Sundays, and as Catholics attended divine service in the Adam and Eve on the pretext of going for a drink, the friars had to time their services so as not to coincide with those of the Protestants. A sign with a full-length picture of Adam and Eve swung from the corner, and below it the door was guarded by a doorman who scrutinised all would-be worshippers, and asked for the password, which was: 'I am going to the Adam and Eve'. The erection of the present church began in 1832. From the quayside it has a totally non-ecclesiastical appearance, especially for such a large church, and it presents a far more pleasing impression from behind. Its big olive-green dome, ribbed like a giant sea urchin, has a distinctly mid-eastern look. The church has an airy interior and a fine high altar.

Brazen Head hotel

Continuing along Merchants' Quay turn left into Bridge St and a little way up on the right enter an opening in a building and pass into the little courtyard of the four-storey Brazen Head hotel, established about 1666, but said to have been built on the site of a much older inn. Certainly the foundations of the building predate the seventeenth century. In *Ulysses* Corley tells Stephen Dedalus that 'you get a decent enough do in the Brazen Head over in Winetavern Street for a bob', the expatriate Joyce, writing from faulty memory, placing the inn in the wrong street. Notice how the level of the ground drops in the courtyard, the drop itself an indication of antiquity.

Robert Emmet, Daniel O'Connell, Wolfe Tone, Henry Grattan and William Smith O'Brien all patronised the Brazen Head, and it was a regular meeting place of the revolutionary United Irishmen, some of whose leaders were arrested there in 1797. A desk used by Emmet, who stayed there, stood in a corner of the bar until recently, usually surmounted by a copper ewer, but has now been moved to an upstairs room.

Going up the hilly street, we turn left into Cook St, and see a section of the city wall preserved on the right. Near the Bridge St end of it a post called Fagan's Castle survived at least until the end of the eighteenth century. It is somewhat confusing to find that city walls existed on the quays, in Cook St and again much further south, but in fact the Cook St wall was an inner line of defence.

St Audoen's Arch

'old' St Audoen's

Passing along, on the right is St Audoen's Arch, the last remaining city gate. Going under the arch, we mount steps that turn to the right, then turn left around the west tower of the Protestant or 'old' St Audoen's church. These are locally called the Forty Steps. Old St Audoen's is now roofless except for a small section, about a quarter of the whole. Mr Alex E. Donovan of Wicklow, who devoted much time to a study of this church's history, says that the part of the church still roofed was built in 650, with the Normans adding the west tower and belfry in 1169, and the larger, roofless, part of the church being an addition of 1431. But Sir Thomas Drew, architect of the graduates' memorial building in Trinity, and sometime president of the Royal

Hibernian Academy, attributed the entire church to Anglo-Norman sources, saying that the west doorway of 1169 was its oldest part. The church, dedicated to a seventh-century bishop of Rouen, Normandy, contains fifteenth-century stained glass, and the tower contains Ireland's oldest bells, three in number, dating from 1423. There are also bells from 1658 and 1694, the most recent one having been recast in 1732, as it sounded like a cowbell and offended fastidious ears. The guilds of butchers, bakers, smiths and bricklayers once had chapels in the church, all of which was roofed until 1820.

As St Audoen's arch — or gate — was not built until 1240, there is no clue here to the church's true age, but a church called St Columcille's existed here as part of a pre-Norse settlement, and it is probable that some of this structure is incorporated in St Audoen's.

Coming out onto High St from the steps, we are in what was the   **High St**

The Ancient City Wall

143

Catholic St Audoen's

main street of the walled mediaeval city. This ran along a high curved ridge, roughly parallelling the Liffey, with Christ Church as its focal point, and now definable as High St, Christchurch Place and Castle St. We emerge beside a lone redbrick commercial building, ennobled by a long stained glass window. Turning left, we see the side of the Tailors' Hall, to be visited in another chapter, over on the right, and down to the left the railings and yard of the classical Catholic St Audoen's church, with its yellowbrick presbytery. Patrick Byrne designed St Audoen's, which was opened in 1846, though the great Corinthian portico which is the church's best feature, giving an illusion of extra height, was not added until 1899. The church's organ, in its mustard-coloured case, is a rarity, being an early work by Walker's of London, and the only earlier example of this firm's work of any significant size being in Antigua cathedral. There is also in High St a richly-carved wooden pulpit, a thing of considerable beauty. This church has traditional links with the Italian community in Dublin and was visited by Giovanni Montini, the future Pope Paul VI when he was attached to the Vatican secretariat of state.

High St leads past Schoolhouse Lane to St Michael's close on the left. The corner ahead is dominated by the tower of the synod house of Christ Church. The tower predates the rest of the synod house, being all that remains of the mediaeval church of St Michael and All Angels,

Christ Church Cathedral

whose parish area was five acres. St Michael's church was open until 1868, and was demolished to provide a site for the synod house, the tower being spared and incorporated in the new building. Looking at the side of the tower facing the quays, marks of where it was joined by the rest of the former building can be seen. The narrow John's Lane East passes below the cathedral's north wall, still leaning outward, with its flying buttresses. Passing the north transept, notice a tall building straight ahead, whose redbrick and terracotta are in such ridiculous contrast to the sombre grey stones of the cathedral that it almost halts us in our tracks. This vivid building was erected in the 1880s to the design of W. G. Murray as the 'Dublin working boys' home and Harding technical school', popularly shortened to Harding boys' home. It forms one side of the top of Lord Edward St, and in that street we will shortly see on the home's long side a terracotta panel bearing the full name and a figure in relief of one of the 'working boys'.

Concentrating on Christ Church again, we go around its east end to its south side. Entering the grounds, there are ruins in a low-lying central position. These are the remains of the chapter house of an Augustinian priory which was attached to the cathedral until the Reformation. What is left of the priory's sleeping quarters, refectory and other buildings is probably buried under Christchurch Place, outside the railings. The mass of the cathedral's south door draws the eye immediately as one considers the building. Notice its great arch, with clear chevron carving, typically late twelfth-century Norman, the name given to Romanesque architecture in Ireland and Britain.

Christ Church Cathedral

The south transept is clearly older in style than the rest of this side of Christ Church. The curved arches here, with the zig-zag carving, give way elsewhere to the pointed Gothic style, a reminder that the ecclesiastical style changed while the cathedral was being built. Christ Church is related in style to English cathedrals at Wells and Glastonbury. Its large groin-vaulted crypt, its transepts and crossing are the earliest parts, the crypt dating from 1172. The nave was begun in 1213, its most westerly bay, differing from the rest, being built about 1234. Look up at the tower, with its splendid weathercock. This was built in 1330, to replace one blown down fourteen years earlier. The cathedral's earlier choir, now replaced, was built about 1350. The carved stone-work of Christ Church, English oolite stone, a granulated limestone, was imported. In 1534 the south wall of the cathedral collapsed, and was poorly rebuilt, as was discovered over 300 years later. By 1871 the building was in a state of considerable disrepair, and the chapter accepted the offer of Henry Roe, distiller, of Thomas St, to restore it. Roe engaged architect G. E. Street for the work, which took seven years and cost £250,000, involving extensive rebuilding. This rebuilding, of course, included the addition of the new synod house across the road, and the neo-Gothic bridge over the top of the hill, which is now so essential to the striking views of Christ Church from both north and south that it is hard to visualise the cathedral in the days when it was separated from St Michael's church at this point.

In view of the outcry and accusations of desecration that greeted Street's work, opinions on the cathedral before it was restored are relevant. Mr and Mrs S. C. Hall said of it in the 1840s that 'its architectural beauties are even less than those of its rival (St Patrick's), although it contains some good examples of Saxon ornaments'. Sir Richard Colt Hoare said savagely that 'the choir presents a sad medley of Gothic and Italian architecture, combined in the most unnatural manner'. Later Street was to be accused of 'destroying a fourteenth-century choir of unique interest', and the entire restoration was to be dismissed by its critics as an ill-conceived amusement. But Street had found that the walls of the nave, including the rebuild of 1534, were too thin to support the vaulted stone roof. He rebuilt the south wall again, jacked up the north one, replacing the piers, and added the flying buttresses. Even then he was unable fully to remove the bulge from the north nave wall. Street also defended his removal of the old choir on the grounds that the replacement, which we see now, more closely resembled a pre-1350 one which he believed to be the original.

In the nave of Christ Church are three prominent sarcophagi. One is that of the Bishop Lindsay who died in 1846, on whose land in Glasnevin the Holy Faith convent and schools were later built, but the two facing it across the church are the subject of controversy. Said by some to contain the remains of Strongbow, the Anglo–Norman coloniser of Dublin, and his son, whom Strongbow is said to have killed over the boy's alleged cowardice, and by others to be the tombs of Strongbow and his consort Eva, daughter of Dermot MacMurrough, they are held by a third school to have no connection with Strongbow whatever. The tombs are side by side, one considerably shorter than the other, and are surmounted by effigies hewn from black stone. The smaller effigy, whose clasped hands below the abdomen may indicate visceral remains alone, is apparently a female figure, and the larger, with hands joined and legs crossed, a knight dressed for battle. The arms on the knight's shield differ from some which have been attributed to

Strongbow

Strongbow, who was really Richard de Clare, earl of Pembroke, and assumed the title of king of Leinster in 1171. He died in Dublin in 1177, 'about the kalends of June', of 'mortification of the foot'. Strongbow's tomb, generally admitted to be in Christ Church, is believed to have been damaged in a roof fall in 1562, and restored in 1570. Perhaps his effigy was irreparably damaged in the mishap, and the one which appears to bear the wrong arms, not being identified, was later mistakenly assumed to be that of Strongbow. The bishop's tomb across the church was obviously made to resemble the 'Strongbow' one for purely cosmetic reasons, through somebody's misguided sense of symmetry. One cynical theory regarding the Strongbow tomb is that Sir Henry Sidney, lord deputy of Ireland, as the viceroy was then called, at the time of the roof fall, having to repair the damage, brought a sarcophagus with a knight's effigy, of about the right age, from Drogheda, and had its inscription chipped off and erected it over the spot where Strongbow was buried, so that the location, at least, is correct.

Lambert Simnel, the boy pretender, was crowned in the title of King Edward VI of England in Christ Church 1487. The crown used in this ceremony was borrowed from a statue of the Blessed Virgin. The

statue is variously said to have been in St Mary's Abbey, in a niche over
Dame's Gate at the top of Dame St and in the church of St Mary del
Dame, which stood beside that gate, roughly on the site of the present
city hall. Certainly such a statue had stood over the gate — it was there
until the Reformation — but it is generally believed that the statue in
the abbey was used. The abbey statue still exists, in the Carmelite
church in Whitefriar St.

The official name of Christ Church is the Cathedral of the Holy
Trinity, and it replaces a wooden church founded by King Sitric in
1038, on the same commanding site. Donat, bishop of Dublin, who took
possession of the building from the king, also founded St Michael's
chapel about this time. This later became the parish church whose
tower, which we have examined, is incorporated in the synod house.
Christianity had given a new dimension to the activities of the Vikings.
The tenth century, despite many setbacks, had seen them as warlike as
ever. From Dublin in 911 they had invaded South Wales, in 916 they
ravaged Anglesea, in 937 they unsuccessfully attacked
Northumberland, in 946 they ravaged Meath and in 985 Derry. The
new experience of churchbuilding, of which Christ Church was to be
the most important facet, provided the Norse overlords with a further
way in which to express their dominance. But seemingly it in no way
diminished their appetite for strife.

Laurence O'Toole became archbishop of Dublin in 1162, and was
still in this position at the time of the Anglo–Norman invasion, the
arrival of Strongbow and Henry II, and the decision to build a new
Christ Church.

The crowning of Lambert Simnel was not the only strange event to
take place in the cathedral. In 1539 Archbishop Browne, appointed by
Henry VIII to see through the Reformation, publicly burned relics

147

there, said to include the staff of St Patrick, which had been brought from Armagh. In 1559 a parliament was held in a room in the cathedral, and by 1582, the year Edmund Spenser visited the master of the guild of the Holy Trinity in Christ Church, the nave had become a place of business, and there were taverns in the crypt.

the Tholsel

At the corner of Christchurch Place and Nicholas St, across the road from the cathedral, the erstwhile site of the Tholsel, or ancient city hall, is now derelict. The first Tholsel was built here early in the fourteenth century, and it was a meeting place of citizens, with lord mayors being elected on St Michaelmas Day. The Tholsel also housed a merchants' exchange and the court of conscience. The word is derived from toll booth, the place of payment of market tolls. Just beyond the site the remains of the walls of the church of St Nicholas Within can be seen in Nicholas St. This parish church was built in 1707, the successor to a Norse establishment. Lacking a congregation in a declining area, it was closed and unroofed in 1840, after its tower had been removed.

Skinner's Row
St Werburgh's
church

The street on the south side of Christchurch Place, formerly called Skinner's Row, because of the trade practised here, leads to the top of Werburgh St, with the lovely classical facade of St Werburgh's church, built in 1759. There had been a church of St Martin of Tours here before the Anglo–Norman invasion. Shortly after the invasion the first St Werburgh's was built, and this was rebuilt in 1662; after further modifications, the church was badly damaged by fire in 1754, necessitating the 1759 reconstruction. The fine interior gallery, designed by John Smith, was built in 1767, and a tower and spire were added in 1768. This 160-foot spire, which appears in Malton prints of Dublin Castle, gave the church considerable stature, but it was taken down in 1810, probably because the authorities, remembering Emmet's 1803 rising, feared that it could be used as a vantage point for spying on Dublin Castle, or as a launching site for a ballistic attack thereon. Later the tower was also demolished. The vaults of St Werburgh's contain the remains of Lord Edward Fitzgerald. The porch contains ancient firefighting equipment. Before the days of organised fire brigades parish churches were mustering points for voluntary firemen.

Beyond the church in Werburgh St, on the same side, is Hoey's Court, where Jonathan Swift was born in 1667. The employment exchange now stands on the site of the house. An entrance across the street is inscribed 'Derby Square', but the little square itself has disappeared. Here the poet James Clarence Mangan studied at a school named Courtney's Academy. Further along Werburgh St, the cobbles of Little Ship St lead off to the left, with a long fragment of the original city wall on the left hand side, embellished by the remains of Stanihurst's Tower, the five sides of which on the street side of the wall have been refaced in cut stone. This tower was named after James Stanihurst, recorder of Dublin, who owned the adjoining land. His son Richard produced a *History of Ireland* in 1577, and it contained a woodcut of Lord Thomas Fitzgerald, 'Silken Thomas', attacking Dublin Castle from Ship St in 1534.

Ship St

The eastward view from here is dominated by the Bermingham Tower of Dublin Castle. Before leaving Ship St, take a glance at the modern redbrick office block on the right. The car park behind the offices, formerly a timber yard, covers the remains of the church of St Michael le Pole, a pre-Norse church whose Celtic origin was obvious from its round tower, one of the only such towers in the city, and 90 feet high. The 'le Pole' part of the name derived from the Pole gate in the city wall. The fragment of wall on the left ran up to connect with this gate, which stood behind us, almost at the corner of Werburgh St and Ship St, named in turn from a 'pole' or pool, part of the River Poddle, which had formed here. The church and its tower stood until late in the eighteenth century. Back past St Werburgh's church is the corner of Castle St, along which the mediaeval high ridge of the city continues eastward. Castle St had housed the early Anglo–Norman settlers in the thirteenth century, comforted by the proximity of the castle, and the 'men of Bristol', to whom Henry II had granted the city of Dublin, are recalled by the name of a block of tenements on the right, looking eastward, called Bristol Buildings. This block is a reconstruction of older tenements which had become ruinous and were taken down in 1890. Through number 8 is an entrance to St Werburgh's church.

Instead of going down Castle St, however, walk in the direction of Christ Church again and turn right, beyond the inn, into broad Lord Edward St. At the turn, glance across at the top of Fishamble St, noting that on its left, just beyond the north side of Christ Church, once stood St John's twelfth-century church, which lasted until 1884, and whose carved Gothic pulpit is now in St Werburgh's. Going down Lord Edward St, the long side of the Harding home is on the left, with the terracotta panel mentioned earlier. Soon in a wall on the right we see a disused drinking fountain in a niche, with a great elliptical red marble basin. This is in the side of the municipal buildings, formerly Newcomen's bank, completed in 1781 to the design of Thomas Ivory. The entrance, with portico and curved steps, is around the corner in the short leg of the L-shaped Cork Hill.

Cork Hill
Dublin Castle

Going around, with city hall on the left, we enter Dublin Castle. There is very little in its present architecture to suggest a castle, as it was largely rebuilt in the eighteenth century. The old main entrance, a little westward of the present one, incorporated a drawbridge and portcullis, and two D-shaped towers, the curved part of each tower facing towards the Liffey. This was demolished in 1750. Between the present outer and inner gates, a brown brick building on the left, with a very obvious crack running down it, beside a drainpipe, straddles the base of the old castle wall, which is under the cracked part. Subsidence of the ground on each side of the old base has caused the brick wall to split.

Meiler FitzHenry, on the orders of King John, began building Dublin Castle in 1204. Most of the building was carried out by Henry de Londres, archbishop of Dublin, and the castle seems to have had a fairly comprehensive array of buildings by 1224. It was threatened by Edward de Bruce in 1317, and besieged, as we have noted, by Silken Thomas in 1534. The only damage caused by Silken Thomas's men appears to have been one hole bored in the gate by a pellet, which lodged harmlessly in the mouth of a cannon. By the middle of the sixteenth century the castle had fallen into disrepair, and was described

as 'foule, filthie and greatlie decaied' before Sir Henry Sidney, viceroy, renovated it between 1566 and 1570, building a new viceroy's residence on the site of the present state apartments, facing us across the upper yard. In 1591 and 1592 Red Hugh O'Donnell, son of a powerful Donegal chieftain, made his celebrated escapes from the castle. These were made from what is now the record tower, which we shall see presently at close quarters. In 1803 Robert Emmet's plan to capture the castle went wrong, as did his entire rebellion. In 1916 a party of volunteers and members of the Citizen Army scaled the gates into the upper yard of the castle and occupied the roof of the city hall on Easter Monday. In a day-long skirmish, one policeman was shot dead. That was the last attack made on the castle, and on 16 January 1922, it was handed over by the viceroy, Lord Fitzalan, to members of the Irish provisional government.

Over the inner gate stands a statue of Justice by John Van Nost. Note that she is facing into the yard, which has caused cynics to remark that Justice has turned her back on the city.

The scales of justice at one stage hung unevenly, so that the extended arm of the statue would shelter the outer pan and prevent the accumulation of rainwater, but criticism of the implied symbolism led the authorities to straighten them out and solve the rain problem by boring holes.

Going into the yard and turning right, we find the genealogical office on the right, between the gate we have passed through and another, blind, gate, over which is a statue of Fortitude, also by Van Nost. The genealogical office, formerly the office of arms and designed by Thomas Ivory, is surmounted by the Bedford Tower, a domed octagonal clock tower named after the duke of Bedford, a former viceroy. This tower stands on the base of the castle's original western gate tower. The genealogical office, containing the heraldic museum, was built between 1750 and 1760. It was from here that the regalia known as the Irish crown jewels was stolen in 1907. The yard in which we are standing coincides approximately with the extent of the original castle. The buildings forming it were mostly built between 1685 and 1760. Originally they were two-storey, with dormer windows, but these upper windows were replaced by an attic storey in the last century. A 1792 print by James Malton shows them with the dormers. In the print, the fine spire of St Werburgh's is seen rising behind the western range, just to the right of the pediment. Across the yard is the entrance of the state apartments, with a hexastyle Tuscan portico, and hexagonal sentry boxes set into the wall, one on either side of the door. Notice the phoenixes over the four hexagonal lamps. In the outer hall, there are four chandeliers, each also surmounted by a phoenix. The state apartments occupy the entire first floor of the southern range of upper yard buildings. They provided living accommodation for viceroys, but after the establishment of the viceregal lodge in the Phoenix Park were rarely occupied. There has been much rebuilding of these apartments, the latest, in the eastern section, being finished as recently as 1968.

At the top of the grand staircase, past an incongruous painting of Hannibal crossing the Alps, is the Battleaxe Landing, named after the

genealogical office

state apartments

weapons carried by the viceroys' ceremonial bodyguard. Here, amid Waterford glass chandeliers and eighteenth-century French tapestries, one first has the feeling of the opulence which permeated this place through so many years, despite the strife and famine outside.

The carpets on the landing, stairway and in the hall below are in Robert Adam style, incorporate the arms of the four Irish provinces and feature, on the landing, the swans into which, according to legend, the children of Lir were turned. Designed by Raymond McGrath, these carpets were made in Killybegs, Co. Donegal. Over the landing's central doorway are the arms of Ireland, a reminder that the official national colour is blue, not green. To the sides of the doorway are the personal arms of Ireland's presidents. Through a lobby to the left is the

St Patrick's Hall

splendid St Patrick's Hall, with its ceiling paintings, and gilt Corinthian pillars fronting the galleries at either end. One gallery is for musicians, the other for spectators. The hall, built some time after 1746, was first used as a ballroom. Its name derives from the Order of St Patrick, created by George III in 1783. The ceremonial meetings of the knights of the order took place here, and their names are on stallplates around the walls. Over the plates are some crests, and hanging above these are the royal standard and the colourful standards of 21 of the knights. The ceiling paintings are by the Italian Vincenzo Valdré, who was brought to Ireland in 1787 by the then viceroy, George Grenville. The centre painting is of George III seated between Britannia and Hibernia, with harp. Note that Britannia holds the flag of 'Greater Britain', not the Union flag, nowadays misnamed the Union Jack. The painting was executed before the 1801 Act of Union.

Bermingham Tower

From St Patrick's Hall we pass into a room of the Bermingham Tower, called the supper room. This is the south-west corner of the castle. The Gothic windows of the circular room suggest antiquity, but are only about 200 years old, as the tower, which had been used as a state prison in the sixteenth century, was damaged by a gunpowder explosion in 1775, and demolished, apart from the base. Two years later it was rebuilt, with thinner walls than before. The big chandelier in the supper room is of nineteenth-century brass, made in nearby Fishamble St. Notice the shamrock, rose and thistle in a garland below it, representing the union of Ireland with England and Scotland. The carpet design, which also includes the shamrock, rose and thistle, is a repetition of the ceiling pattern. Off the north side of the Bermingham tower is the beautiful oval Wedgwood room, with its four alcoves. The room is decorated in a silky matt blue finish to resemble Wedgwood pottery. A Waterford glass chandelier hangs over a grey and cream carpet depicting a phoenix arising from its ashes. The room contains an Adam marble fireplace, Chinese-style Chippendale chairs, three paintings by Angelica Kaufmann, circular reproductions of 'Night' and 'Day' by the Danish sculptor Berthel Thorwaldsen, a bust of Voltaire and four black Wedgwood plaques by John Flaxman, a sculptor who worked for the Wedgwood family. The billiard table which occupied this room in the nineteenth century has mercifully been removed.

George's Hall

A door from here leads to the picture gallery, which runs along the north side of St Patrick's Hall, and also to George's Hall, in the western

In Dublin Castle

extremity of the castle, and its anteroom. An aerial picture of Dublin
Castle will clearly show that George's Hall is a late addition, jutting out
to the west as it does. It was built as a supper room for the visit of George
V and Queen Mary in 1911. It contains monochrome chiaroscuro
paintings by eighteenth-century Flemish artist Peter de Gree. These
give a rather extraordinary three-dimensional illusion.

Eastward is the picture gallery; Ionic columns show where it was
once divided into three rooms, a main dining room, small dining room
and drawing room. It contains portraits of viceroys and chandeliers of
Venetian glass, a type of glass often found in the ornate shades of oil
lamps.

East of this room is the throne room, whose heavy throne was
probably presented by William of Orange. Weight, indeed, is the
dominant theme in this rather stuffy apartment. Its brass chandelier
weighs over a ton, and is suspended from a hidden iron beam, inserted
specially in the ceiling. Ovals and roundels by the eighteenth-century
Venetian artist Giambattista Bellucci adorn the walls. Eastward again,
the state drawing room leads into the Apollo room. A fire in 1941 badly
damaged the drawing room, and it was rebuilt and refurnished in
eighteenth-century style, the work being completed in 1968. It is now
an attractive apartment, with French silk upholstery, Waterford glass,
paintings by Giovanni Panini on loan from the National Gallery and a
thirteenth-century Chinese punchbowl adorned with wedding scenes.
The square Apollo room has, as the name indicates, a 1746 plaster
ceiling depicting the sun god. The room is a reproduction of the back

throne room

drawing room (first floor) of Tracton House, which was at the corner of Merrion Row and St Stephen's Green, the mantlepiece and ceiling being the originals. The Apollo room was incorporated in the state apartments in 1968. Behind it and the drawing room is the state corridor, designed by Sir Edward Lovett Pearce, and on the far side of that are five rooms formerly used as bedrooms, now designated as 'supplementary drawing rooms'. The most easterly of these was called the queen's bedroom, and the centre one the king's bedroom. The second and fourth rooms in the row have ceilings from the demolished Mespil House. One of these rooms, the second most westerly, called the Granard room, has a Van Dyck painting of Elizabeth, countess of Southampton, Louis XV furniture and two solid marble Italian vases. In the most westerly room of the row James Connolly, the Citizen Army leader, was held prisoner in 1916. Looking out the windows from these rooms, the castellated stone wall which can be seen across the castle garden is said to have been built on the orders of Queen Victoria to hide the backs of the Stephen St houses.

The state apartments were used as a Red Cross hospital during World War I, and as the headquarters of the Irish Courts while the Four Courts restoration went on in the 1920s.

Passing through the range of buildings that divides the upper and lower castle yards, and turning right, the reconstructed record tower is found in a corner. Its top storey and battlements were added in the early nineteenth century. One of the castle's original corner towers, it is now one of the few fortress-like features remaining. Formerly a prison, it now houses historical documents.

record tower

Red Hugh O'Donnell

Red Hugh O'Donnell, the Donegal chieftain's son who made two dramatic escapes from here, had been taken prisoner in 1587 in an attempt to force his independent father to submit to castle authority. The Lord Justice, Sir John Perrot, had sent a ship to Lough Swilly in Co. Donegal disguised as a Spanish wine carrier, with instructions to the captain, also disguised as Spanish, to lure O'Donnell aboard, ply him with wine, then tie up the intoxicated young man and deliver him to Dublin Castle. In January 1591 O'Donnell and some companions lowered themselves by a rope from the record tower, and escaped as far as the Wicklow Mountains. In the lands of the O'Toole clan Red Hugh was overcome by exhaustion. He and his companions had been forced to leave their outer clothing behind when they squeezed out through a window. Forced to stop, he was found by the O'Tooles and betrayed by them. Brought back to the castle, he again escaped from the tower a year later, on 6 January, with two companions, Arthur and Henry O'Neill.

Church of the Most Holy Trinity

Below the record tower is another example of the work of Francis Johnston, the Church of the Most Holy Trinity, formerly called the Chapel Royal. The church, erected on the site of a smaller 1700 foundation, was begun in 1807 and opened on Christmas Day 1814. Its neo-Gothic style shows the considerable daring of its architect, working long before the revival of Gothic became fashionable. It also shows Johnston's versatility, especially when contrasted with the Greek classicism of St George's in Hardwicke Place. The Chapel Royal has been dismissed by critics as 'gingerbread Gothic', but the adjective is probably an unthinking slur on its decorations, which are considerable. Its exterior bears over ninety heads carved in Tullamore limestone by Edward Smyth and his son John. The plasterwork in the church is by George Stapleton, and notice how he has swept some panels downward to central clusters of four cherubic heads. The carved oak panels in the church are by Richard Stewart. Those in the gallery sides carry the coats of arms of early viceroys. The arms of later viceroys are on carved panels on the chancel walls and in stained glass in the gallery. All viceroys from 1172 to 1922 are represented. The stained glass in the four centre panels of the east window shows scenes from Christ's Passion, and was brought from the continent by Lord Whitworth and presented to the church.

Leaving the castle by the lower gate, we go next down to Dame St. Across the street is the Olympia theatre, formerly the Empire Palace, **Olympia** and once known as 'Dan Lowry's', though its official name when this **theatre** promoter owned it was the Star of Erin. Founded as a music hall, it has staged drama, variety and pantomime. Notice that the roadway just to the left of the theatre is lower than elsewhere, indicating that the River Poddle flows beneath it here, on its way to join the Liffey at Wellington Quay, where it once formed an inlet.

The City Hall, with its hexastyle Corinthian portico, faces down **The City Hall** Parliament St, the first street to be laid out by the Wide Streets Commission. The name of this street derives from the fact that, when Essex Bridge was the lowest bridge on the Liffey, the route from the north side to the parliament house in College Green came through here. The City Hall was designed by Thomas Cooley and built between 1769 and 1779, as the royal exchange, at a cost of £40,000. Its balustrade is decorated with urns and with four black iron trefoils of lamps. A plinth for a statue of Daniel O'Connell stands outside the building, empty. The statue is inside. With its classical facade and dome, the building is a noble termination of the view up Parliament St. But the dome is best viewed from inside. Looking up from the circular hall, its clear glass centre is seen surrounded by an arrangement of hexagonal and diamond-shaped coffers, in pastel shades. In the hall are marble statues of Daniel O'Connell, Dr Charles Lucas, Thomas Davis and Thomas Drummond. Lucas, an eighteenth-century Dublin apothecary, opposed attempts by the English parliament to impose its will on Ireland, and advocated the reform of Dublin Corporation. He was praised by Grattan as a pioneer of Irish liberty. His statue is by Edward Smyth. Drummond, a Scot, was under-secretary at Dublin Castle from 1835, and one of the organisers of the Irish Constabulary. The statues of Drummond and O'Connell are by John Hogan. Out the main door and through a door on the left is a stairwell, in which is a fine marble statue of Henry Grattan, by Sir Francis Chantrey.

The part of Dame St in front of the city hall and turning above it towards the castle's main entrance is called Cork Hill. This is **Dame St** because the first earl of Cork's home stood on the city hall site, with the **South Great** church of St Mary del Dame occupying the position between times. **George's St**

Down Dame St now towards the corner of South Great George's

St. On the right, past an ornate Gothic bank, is the old-established firm of riding outfitters. O'Callaghan's, over whose windows a large white horse's head surveys the passing scene. Behind him is a row of five dragons. Across the road is the top of Eustace St, where the Friends' Meeting House of the Quakers is at number 6. In 1663 the congregation in the old St Audoen's was addressed by Elizabeth Fletcher and Elizabeth Smith, who had just arrived in Dublin, on the principles of Quakerism. For this 'offence' the two women were committed to the old Newgate prison. They were released after a brief spell, and the first meeting of Quakers in Dublin was conducted by them in the home of Richard Fowkes, a tailor, near the Pole gate, which we have already noted.

    To the right is South Great George's St, originally George's Lane, after a mediaeval church of St George. The street's curve indicates its age. It is now filled with shops. Heading south along it, notice that the block between Exchequer St and Fade St, on the left, is filled over the shops by a redbrick Gothic palace. In its centre is the entrance to the **South City Market** enclosed South City Market, and here is a stout marble pillar with Romanesque capital and base. The entrance is flanked by octagonal towers, there are round brick turrets at the ends of the building, and notice the brick ropework effect in the window divisions near the corners. With some modifications, this facade is repeated along Exchequer St to Drury St, and it is faithfully repeated along Fade St to Drury St. At the back of the market, in Drury St, it gives way to a charming line of low buildings over shops, each painted in its own colour. The market was almost entirely destroyed in a fire on 27 August 1892, and what we see is the replacement. It is a coincidence that its outer appearance is so palatial. Henry II built a palace on this site, or very close to it.

10 Brewing, Distilling and the Gothic Revival

Old Newgate — John's Lane church — Power's distillery — D'Arcy's brewery — St Catherine's church — the Onion Tower — the Fountain — Guinness's brewery — Phoenix brewery — Basin Lane — Back of the Pipes.

Short Mass was still the favourite service, and Brian Boru's harp still bloomed on the bottles of beer.

— Sean O'Casey, *Innisfallen Fare thee Well.*

Our road to Europe's biggest brewery, and Dublin's biggest industry, begins at the top of Bridge St, at its junction with Cornmarket. Looking across to the south side of the latter street, we see a section of the original city wall, still at its ancient height and thickness. This is a surviving portion of the stretch of wall which connected the city's Newgate with a watchtower south of here. Newgate straddled the main route from the city. If we look westward, we see a shop on the southwest corner of Cornmarket and Bridge St, approximately occupying the position of the northern part of the gate building, which was an elaborate construction with a circular tower at each corner, cellars and a gate and portcullis in the centre. In the twelfth and thirteenth centuries the building was leased to tenants, until it became the city jail in 1285. This was the forerunner of the Newgate jail which we have already encountered between Halston St and Green St, the name — with the function — eventually being transferred to the north side.

In 1780, on the opening of the new Newgate, the old one, which had been in bad repair for many years, was partly demolished. The demolition was halted to allow the place to be used as a prison for prostitutes, or, to use the euphemism of the day, 'female nocturnal strollers' for two years. In 1782 it was razed.

Visitors will probably wish to cross the road to examine the segment of old city wall. From a point just east of it, looking north, the contours of the Liffey valley can be appreciated. We can see the dome of the Bluecoat school, the top of the tower of Arbour Hill chapel, almost the entire granite front of Broadstone station and the turrets of Berkeley Rd church in the distance.

Go west a little without recrossing the road, look across and down St Augustine St. An almost flat roof is covered by grass. This lawn covers a building of Power's distillery, whose main part we will see shortly.

Between the distillery and the river at Usher's Quay stood D'Arcy's Anchor Brewery, separated from Power's by a street now called Oliver Bond St, but for many years known as Mullinahack, literally translated as 'the filthy mill'. There is no need to go down and examine the site, as nothing recognisable remains, but it was one of Dublin's most flamboyant commercial firms before it closed in 1926. It advertised itself as 'the largest brewery in Ireland (but one)'. Some of the brewery buildings had an ecclesiastical appearance, and skeletons were found on the site, suggesting a connection with the hospital and priory of St John, which we will consider shortly. When workmen digging foundations for an extension in 1866 found these human remains, the proprietor, Matthew Peter D'Arcy MP, an extrovert with a patriarchal beard, decorated his office wall with some of the skulls. D'Arcy claimed that his brewery contained the biggest copper boiler in the world, and widely travelled brewery inspectors would not contradict him. It had a capacity of 1,300 barrels and a modern single-storey house could fit into it. At an 'official opening' reception to display this phenomenon, D'Arcy's entertained thirty guests, not in the capacious boardroom, but inside the boiler.

The area to the right of St Augustine St, as we look down, contained a four-storey tower named Brown's Castle after Sir Richard

Church of SS Augustine and John, Thomas St

St. Augustines, High St. Dublin.
Thomas Ryan

Brown, lord mayor in the early seventeenth century. Near it stood another prison known as the Black Dog. There is no trace of either of these, nor of the 'filthy mill'. John Speed's map of 1610 shows buildings at Mullinahack referred to simply as 'the mills'.

Thomas St

West of St Augustine St is a Victorian bank whose handsome Gothic facade has not been improved by modern signs. Staying on the south side of the street, walk west a little, along Thomas St. Pause opposite the towering Augustinian church of St Augustine and St John, and look upward at its great spire before crossing to inspect the building.

'Ailred le Palmer'

This church has a continuous tradition dating from 1180, when Ailred the Dane returned from a pilgrimage to Jerusalem, carrying a palm which was to earn him the nickname 'Ailred le Palmer'. Ailred's house stood where the church now is, and his lands spread beneath the present Power's distillery. His name is still perpetuated in some of his other holdings, in Palmerstown, beyond Chapelizod. Inspired by the hospital for sick pilgrims and crusaders in Jerusalem, he built its Dublin counterpart on the site of his house, adding a convent and priory, and he and his wife took religious vows under the rule of St Augustine. The priory cemetery was where a builders' provider's yard with an incongruous classical gate, now stands on the far side of the street. Ailred the Dane is buried here. In 1188 Pope Clement III, at Ailred's instigation, assumed direct jurisdiction over the foundation, thus freeing it from local overlordship, and the Liberty of Ailred was established. In about 1260 the priory and hospital, called St John's, were taken over by the Cruciferi, other Augustinian hospitallers who wore a red cross on their white robes, the same cross which to this day is synonymous with the relief of physical suffering.

When the foundation was suppressed in 1539 by Henry VIII, William Brabazon sold most of the effects of the buildings, after the Cruciferi had been dispersed. The denuded buildings were acquired by a Cabra merchant named James Sedgrave, and soon all that remained was a castellated stone tower, similar to that of old St Audoen's. This was a remnant of the St Magdalen's chapel that had been part of the priory. In the centre of the present church site, it remained standing until 1800.

For some years after their suppression Augustinian friars went about their work incognito, with an unmarked headquarters at Arran Quay, and in about 1700 they had 'underground' premises at the backs of houses in Bridge St, Cornmarket, High St and Hammond Lane. One of them, a Fr Edmund Byrne, who masqueraded as Colonel Byrne with sword and uniform, established a chapel in a stable near St Magdalen's tower, and gave it a title which incorporated both a nearby landmark and a description of its conditions — St Audoen's under the Elements.

John's Lane church

This survived into the nineteenth century, but in 1862 the new John's Lane church was begun. Its plans were by Augustus Welby Pugin, leading Gothic revivalist, who designed the Gothic details and decorations of Sir Charles Barry's Houses of Parliament in Westminster. Pugin had died in 1852 and George C. Ashlin took over as consultant architect. The church, which Ruskin described as a 'poem in stone',

St Audoen's Churches, High St

took thirty-three years to build, being halted more than once by lack of money. The great spire can be seen from Butt Bridge, both circular roads and as far away as Drumcondra. In 1874, when the spire and roof were complete, the church was opened for worship, while the rest of the building proceeded.

The contractor was Michael Meade, and the sculptor of the twelve statues of the Apostles which adorn the spire was James Pearse of 22 Great Brunswick Street, the London-born father of Patrick and Willie Pearse. Pearse produced the statues at the rate of one a month. The high altar and side chapels were designed by Ashlin and Coleman of Dawson St, George C. Ashlin's firm. The church, in French decorated Gothic, has one of the most striking ecclesiastical facades in Ireland. With its spire, which rests on a rectangular tower measuring thirty-eight feet by twenty-three feet, it reaches more than 200 feet in height. Its eminence as a landmark is enhanced by the fact that it stands on the western ridge of the hill of Dublin. The nave is 152 feet long and, with the aisles, sixty-two feet wide, and the height of its groining is seventy feet. The nave is divided into five bays, with columns of red Cork marble on Sicilian marble and limestone bases, with richly carved Portland stone capitals. The high altar is of marble and the stained glass in the chancel and side chapels is by Mayer of Munich. The floors of the chancel and side chapels are covered in ceramic mosaics, and elsewhere in the church, gold, Siena and Carrara marble and onyx appear.

Looking down John's Lane, just west of the church, we see some of

**Power's
distillery**

the works of Power's distillery, whose offices are just beyond the lane in Thomas St, giving the corner a pleasant curve. Like Jameson's, this firm is now part of Irish Distillers and the actual manufacture of spirits has been transferred to Midleton, Co. Cork. James Power owned a tavern on this site, where he began to distil, and he founded the firm in 1791. After his death it spread to six acres, and in the 1830s it had access to the Liffey at Usher's Quay, beside D'Arcy's brewery.

**St Catherine's
church**

St Catherine's church is found on the south side of Thomas St, opposite the broad hill of Bridgefoot St. St Catherine's is no longer used as a place of worship, but concerts and other functions are held there, and the building is preserved, and has been restored by Dublin Corporation. It was designed by John Smith and was built between 1760 and 1769. With its Tuscan facade and square tower it is a handsome, but not memorable building. It replaces a church of St Catherine built in the 1180s by the monks of the abbey of St Thomas Becket. Robert Emmet was executed in the roadway opposite St Catherine's on 20 September 1803. A plaque on the western part of the railing indicates the exact location.

Bridgefoot St

Detour down Bridgefoot St for a moment to look at the site of a noted debtors' prison, the Marshalsea. Built soon after 1740, it was used by improvident members of the social elite as a refuge from their creditors. Going down the street, a turn on the left near an open space leads to its site. The Marshalsea, whose inmates included Isaac Butt and 'Buck' Jones, later became a military barracks, then a tenement for those evicted from other municipal housing.

**The
Marshalsea**

James's St

Return to the top of Bridgefoot St, and turn right. The broad street, once the main road into the city from the west, is still inclined slightly towards the river. Soon, when James's St takes over from Thomas St, it will curve in the opposite direction and already it is beginning to lose its 'shopping street' character. We come to the offices of the Irish Agricultural Wholesale Society on our right. In a building which occupied the site of the offices' eastern end Lord Edward Fitzgerald was arrested on 19 May 1798. Looking through a garage a little further up on the right, one can see an old windmill tower, known locally as 'the onion tower'. The site of the windmill is now part of Guinness's brewery, but was formerly the distillery of Roe's, the firm which restored Christ Church cathedral. Before that again, a corn mill occupied this site, having been established about 1700. The onion tower is believed to be the biggest windmill tower ever built in the British Isles, being 150 feet tall and seventy feet in diameter at the base. It is the only surviving building of Roe's, but a pear tree near its base is a more homely survivor. This tree appeared in an 1878 print of the distillery, and still bears fruit. The windmill tower is topped by a copper 'onion' dome, with a figure of St Patrick as a weathervane.

**The onion
tower**

The Roe dynasty began in 1757 when Peter Roe took over an existing distillery on the south side of Thomas St, later moving across to the corn mill site. It became famous for its pot still whiskey and had a large export trade. In 1862 Henry Roe and his brother George took over as owners, and after Henry's retirement the firm became a limited liability company. In 1889 Roe's was taken over by DWD, already mentioned, and the Thomas St distillery went out of business in the late 1920s.

Beyond the Roe site we come to the corner of Watling St. A bank on our right was the assembly place for tours of Guinness's before these were discontinued in 1971, and the building has been leased to the bankers by the brewers, a factor in favour of the leasing decision having been that it would encourage brewery employees to open bank accounts. **Watling St**

As we look down Watling St, which runs from here to Victoria Quay, the left hand side of the street is occupied exclusively by Guinness's, as is Victoria Quay itself. The Rupert Guinness memorial hall is near the top of the street, and is a part of the brewery. This housed the Abbey theatre company for about two months after the fire in that theatre in July 1951. The street and quay do not require a detour. At the beginning of the nineteenth century two breweries, other than the present one, were in Watling St, as was a distillery. These have gone, and so has a Gothic arch that stood on the quay at the bottom of the street. This was erected in 1812 to Francis Johnston's design and spanned the roadway of the quay, but the increased traffic generated by the opening of Kingsbridge railway terminus up the river forced its removal, stone by stone, to Kilmainham, where it now forms a gate of the Royal Hospital, and where it will be seen in due course. Also gone from Victoria Quay is the wooden wharf from which the brewery barges brought cargoes of stout and porter to Dublin port, their funnels specially hinged for dropping as they passed under the eight bridges en route. Nothing remains either of Holmes's hotel, which stood a bit downriver at Usher's Quay, but it yields this curious story. Towards the end of its life it was bought by Joshua Jacob and his 'White Quakers'. Mr **Guinness's**

'White Quakers'

Jacob and his wife, Abigail, had kept a teashop at their home in number 34 Nicholas St, but sold it when Joshua founded his sect and appointed himself its 'apostle'. They acquired a 'convent' in Clondalkin and a 'tabernacle' in South William St, and the sect achieved notoriety by marching stark naked from Clondalkin to Holmes's hotel, led by Joshua and Abigail.

At the top of Watling St we are at the end of Thomas St and beginning of James's St, with Guinness property on our left and right. But the oldest part of the brewery site is directly behind us, and if we turn and look across the street we see St James's Gate, where it all began. The line of brick offices that flanks the gate, running from Crane St on the left and curving gently from Thomas St into James's St, is over 200 yards long. The building immediately left of the gate was once the home of the first Arthur Guinness. **St James's Gate**

Before examining the brewery's history and some of its physical features, let us walk up James's St. The original St James's Gate stood at a right angle to the present one, and was a mediaeval entrance to the outer city. This was the parish of St James, extending in the twelfth century from Newgate to Kilmainham. Nearby was St James's Well, scene of a pilgrimage each year on the saint's feast, 25 July. The pilgrimage was followed by 'a merry fair with much ale drinking'. Well served with a water supply and standing at the beginning of the route to the midland corn-growing areas, it was a natural district for brewing. On the north side of the street we pass the brewery powerhouse with its chimneys, a handsome functional building, and come to the former Protestant church of St James, now used as a confectioner's store-room. Across the street we see the Catholic St James's, with its pleasant little redbrick parochial hall at the corner of Echlin St. Keep going west and in the middle of the road we see a small obelisk. Beyond the obelisk are public toilets, and since the Victorian notion of decency sometimes decreed that these conveniences be camouflaged, eight trees were planted here. (We will see another example of this in the Liberties.) If it is summer, two of the James's St trees will be hiding the top of the Portland stone obelisk, so that we cannot see the date 1790 at the top, or the four sundials which adorn the tops of the sides. At the foot of the obelisk is a disused drinking fountain, and the whole construction is still simply called 'the fountain'. A sign embossed on the ironwork exhorts us to 'keep the pavement dry'. This may be the site of St James's well, which probably stood outside the old St James's Gate. Within living memory it was *de rigeur* for funerals from this neighbourhood to drive three times around the fountain before setting off for the cemetery.

Crossing to the south side of James's St, where a tall business premises is a former cinema and stands on the site of a quarry, we go down a little and head up Echlin St, with tenements on the right. At the top turn left into Grand Canal Place. Approaching the tall brewery buildings ahead, one notices a 22-inch gauge railway running through the cobbled street. These tracks continue in Grand Canal Place, Portland St, Market St, Robert St and Rainsford St, all cobbled thoroughfares and are the overflow of the defunct internal brewery rail system, which was the largest industrial system in Ireland. It began in **Grand Canal Place**

Thomas St, corner of Power's Distillery

1874, and in 1878 an Act of Parliament allowed Guinness to extend it into the streets. It also ran through a tunnel under James's St, had a spiral tunnel, a miniature of that found in Switzerland on the St Gothard line, and had a broad-gauge link from the brewery to Kingsbridge station. The corkscrew tunnel was necessary because the brewery is built on three different levels, going down towards the river. The Guinness railway had nineteen engines, most of them built by the engineering firm of Spence of Cork St, Dublin, and two by T. Lewin of Poole, Dorset.

For about fifty years until 1935 the St James's Gate brewery was the biggest in the world. Yet at the beginning of the last century it was only one of fifty-five Dublin breweries, and these were the survivors of a much bigger field. In the eighteenth century the revenue laws of both Irish and English parliaments favoured English beverages to such an extent that many Irish firms could not survive. The drink known as porter originated in London, not, as is widely imagined, in Dublin. It got its name from the fact that it was drunk mostly by labouring people, especially porters, and from the middle of the eighteenth century shiploads of London-brewed porter arrived regularly in Dublin and in Cork. This trend was accidentally reversed when the Cork ale brewers of Beamish and Crawford, who also acted as import agents for London porter, found that they had no porter stocks due to a shipload being held up by bad weather at sea. To satisfy their customers, they decided to brew some themselves as a stopgap measure. It was acclaimed as better than the English product. Porter had been brewed in Dublin, Cork and elsewhere in Ireland before that, but the Cork firm's success paved the way for popular acceptance of the Irish brew. Then in the nineteenth century the penal taxes on home brews were relaxed and by 1809 Beamish and Crawford had the biggest brewery in Ireland, with Guinness in second place.

To trace the Guinness origin, we must note that the area at the back of the brewery is called the Back of the Pipes. And the older part of the brewery is built on a site once known as The Pipes, as it was where the main water supply for Dublin, coming from the Poddle, passed through to the city. A brewer named Giles Mee was given a lease to water rights here in 1670, and these were taken over by Sir Mark Rainsford, a city alderman. He went out of business in 1715, leasing the premises for 99 years to Paul Espinasse, whose lease mysteriously expired in 1759, when it was transferred to the thirty-four-year-old Arthur Guinness, eldest son of Richard Guinness of Celbridge, Co. Kildare.

Arthur Guinness

Guinness leased St James's Gate for £45 a year, and for 9,000 years. He assumed a position of influence fairly quickly, and in 1762 was master of the Dublin Brewers' Corporation. In 1773 he told a commission set up by the Irish parliament to investigate the discrepancy in revenue rates that he would emigrate to Wales, if he could find a readymade brewery in the Holyhead area, unless he had an assurance that the tax on the Irish product would be reduced. Whether he meant it or not, the tax was cut four years later and it was clear that Mr Guinness was not a man to be pushed about. When, in 1775, Dublin

Corporation decided that he had no right to a water supply from one of the celebrated 'Pipes' that ran through the brewery, and sent a work gang supplemented by the city sheriff to cut off the supply, Guinness stood over the pipe with a pickaxe — 'borrowed' from a Corporation navvy — and defied any of them to touch the water supply. The dispute dragged on for nine years. In 1784 Guinness was granted a lease of the water-course for 8,975 years, giving it the same expiry date as his brewery lease from Rainsford.

Rhymesters were not lacking; the following appears in M. J. McManus's *Dublin Diversions*:

> *The brewery at St James's Gate,*
> *Has made the name of Guinness great;*
> *The publican who passes that*
> *Must genuflect and raise his hat.*

Arthur Guinness died in 1803, aged 78, and the brewery went to his second, fourth and fifth sons, Arthur, Benjamin and William Lunell. The younger Arthur survived his brothers to become sole owner, and when he died in 1855 his third son, Benjamin, afterwards Sir Benjamin Lee Guinness, took control. He is remembered as the restorer of St Patrick's Cathedral. Sir Benjamin died in 1868, leaving the brewery to his eldest and third sons, Arthur and Edward Cecil, afterwards Lords Ardilaun and Iveagh. At that time the brewery used the Grand Canal, which had a harbour nearby, at the top of a specially-made extension running in through the Back of the Pipes, to convey stout in barges down to Limerick and Ballinasloe, and bring export consignments to the docks at Ringsend. But in 1872, having expanded to Victoria Quay, Guinness opened the wharf to which we have already referred. For many years after that its ten river barges, each carrying 68 tons and

Sir Benjamin Lee Guinness

167

crewed by men in navy blue, red-lettered jerseys, were a familiar Dublin sight. These have gone now, but the brewery's cross-channel ships, with blue hulls and orange funnels, are still part of the docks scene. They ply between Dublin and the Mersey, and are all registered in Britain.

Edward Cecil Guinness acquired his brother's half share in 1876, and ten years later the firm became a limited liability company, being floated at £6,000,000. By then it employed over 2,600 people, and its claim to be the biggest brewery in the world was undisputed.

Robert St

By then the two enormous buildings which we are approaching had been added to the southern side of the brewery. We can walk around the first of these by way of Portland St, Robert St and Market St. This is a fermentation building, and is eight storeys tall from the footpath. Rising from a rough granite base through a course of smooth granite, it shoots up into a cliff of brown, purple and red brick, nicely intermixed, and with a redbrick top. It has pleasing windows and stepped brick corbels. On the Robert St side is a line of four big graceful bow windows on the first floor, each based on a quarter sphere of granite. This building can be seen from as far away as the North Circular Road, its base being sixty feet above sea level. Back at the corner of Market St and Grand Canal Place, look south along the side of a huge brown malt store, noting the eight branches of the narrow gauge railway that formerly ran into this side of it. This is believed to be the largest brick building ever erected in Dublin, and possibly in Ireland. It is all of brick, including a honeycomb of malt bins inside, which are supported on pillars which stand in a vaulted basement. Though not as tall as its neighbour, to which it is connected by an overhead bridge, it is a very impressive block.

Guinness's is the only really big industrial undertaking in Dublin. To get the feeling of its size, and relate it to the size of the city, it is best to walk east from here along Market St, Bellevue and School St, turn left into Thomas Court and left again into Rainsford St. Soon on the right of Rainsford St we see Rainsford Avenue; this cul-de-sac running into the back of Thomas St is a rare example in Dublin of people being housed literally in the shadow of a huge industry. Rainsford St is the site of an eighteenth century theatre, but it lasted only from 1732 to 1736. The cobbled street brings us back to Portland St, then around to the right into Grand Canal Place again, which here forms a semi-circle to connect with the curiously named James's St Avenue, beyond the top of Echlin St. Going around the gentle curve, we see small houses, but the half-demolished state of the crescent is at odds with its surroundings. At the end of the avenue turn left into Upper Basin St, better known as

Basin Lane

Basin Lane. There are schools on both sides, the Christian Brothers' old grey building on the left being supplemented by a pleasing modern block further on, facing which is an Irish Sisters of Charity establishment varying between Victorian redbrick and modern yellowbrick, also quite pleasing. The apse of the redbrick chapel, curving onto the street, adds quiet dignity to the scene.

the Back of the Pipes

A door in a wall at the top of the street leads to the Back of the Pipes, and there is a linear park running off to our right, where the canal

Guinness's Brewery, the Market St building

has been filled in. An iron footbridge was dismantled in 1978. Crossing the park, follow the curve of the erstwhile canal around to the left. A partly ruinous building overlooking a yard looms up on the right. This is the former Marrowbone Lane distillery of William Jameson, once an imposing premises. It too was part of the DWD merger. Going down Long's Place, on the building's left, we come to what was formerly the premises of Plunket's, maltsters and malt roasters, established in the neighbourhood in 1819. Until 1817 porter was brewed from brown malt, but then a process of roasting malt in an iron cylinder was developed, and adopted quickly throughout the porter brewing industry. Plunket's, which survived until 1970, supplied many kinds of malt, not only to Guinness but to Watney, Bass and other breweries in Britain, and to American breweries. We turn right into Bond St, which abutted the old harbour, then left into Grand Canal Place, and through it and Echlin St back to James's St.

Over where the Guinness powerhouse stands was once the entrance of the Phoenix brewery, and near it stood Manders and Powell, a smaller brewery which was absorbed by the Phoenix in 1890. Just before the First World War the Phoenix itself was absorbed by Guinness, so the premises of both these firms are now part of the St James's Gate spread of over 60 acres. (It was the decision to divide production for certain markets between Dublin and Park Royal, London, that caused Guinness here to lose its place as the world's biggest brewery, reducing its claim to 'biggest in Europe'.) The Phoenix brewery, begun in 1780, came to be owned at one time by Daniel O'Connell Junior, a son of the Liberator. He mismanaged it and it passed to a John Brennan, who continued to produce 'O'Connell's Dublin ale', trading on the connection with the great public figure. For many years the label of this ale bottle carried a picture of the Liberator, and pictures of his monument in O'Connell St were also used. When Guinness took over the Phoenix, O'Connell's ale went on being brewed by D'Arcy's. The slogan 'largest brewery in Ireland (but one)' had also originated with the Phoenix, but was made famous by D'Arcy's. When D'Arcy's in its turn closed down, O'Connell's ale continued still, under the management of Watkins's in Ardee St.

The harp trade mark on the famous biscuit-coloured oval label of Guinness depicts the O'Neill harp, which is preserved in Trinity College library, and is popularly known as Brian Boru's harp. The firm claims that it developed the biggest brewery on earth without ever advertising, but when it eventually changed this policy it was so fortunate in its choice of copywriters and artists that after a while it produced at least one advertisement, which is preserved in the brewery, in which the product was clearly identifiable without the name 'Guinness' even appearing.

St Patrick's cathedral — Marsh's library — Kevin St — Carmelite church — Tailors' hall — St Nicholas Without — St Thomas's Court — weavers —Synge St — Portobello House — 'Little Jerusalem' — Cork St Fever Hospital.

We'll rig in Meath St Egypt's haughty queen,
And Anthony shall court her in ratteen.

— Dean Swift on native industry.

Dublin's Liberties were areas of special privilege and special immunity from city jurisdiction in civil, but not criminal, matters. Each had its own manor court, presided over by a 'seneschal'. The system originated under the Magna Carta, and the area concerned, whose geographical boundaries differed from time to time, was usually a spacious tract of land in the south-western part of the city. The Liberties included those of the Archbishop (St Sepulchre), Donore, Thomas Court (Earl of Meath), St Patrick's and Christ Church. The name 'St Sepulchre' had been given to the archbishop's palace, on the site of the present Kevin St garda station, Donore was a place name, St Patrick's and Christ Church referred to the cathedrals, and Thomas Court is a reference to the monastery of St Thomas Becket, whose lands were given to the Earl of Meath after the suppression of the institution, hence the alternative name. To add to the confusion caused by shifting boundaries and alternative names, there was also at one time a Liberty of Dublin, which included Donnybrook and stretched across the north side of the city from Conyngham Road to East Wall. But the term is usually accepted as meaning only those privileged areas in the south-west, and of these the biggest was the Liberty of Donore, with 380 acres, including Mount Argus and Mount Jerome and parts of Crumlin; the smallest was that of Christ Church, with one-and-a-half acres.

'The Liberties' in modern parlance is generally accepted to mean an area on the Liffey's south side bounded by Fishamble St, Werburgh St, Bride St, New Bride St, Long Lane, Malpas St, Blackpitts, Mill St, Ardee St, Pimlico, Thomas Court and Bridgefoot St. The Liberties Association, a body set up to safeguard the special character of parts of the area, mainly concerns itself with the 190 acres thus outlined, without categorically excluding places like Weaver Square and Chamber St.

We have already explored some of this area under other headings, and some of the places we visit in this chapter lie outside it, so that our present itinerary is something of a compromise between old and new. It will, of course, embrace St Patrick's cathedral and the former home ground of the weavers, both of which are parts of the essence of the popular conception of the Liberties.

St Patrick's cathedral

Begin with St Patrick's, overlooking its park in Patrick St. In the park, almost in the corner formed by the cathedral and street, is the reputed site of the holy well where people were baptised by St Patrick. The cathedral occupies the site of a Celtic church of St Patrick, and the theory that St Patrick himself founded this is supported by the fact that Celtic churches were not dedicated to non-Scriptural saints, except in the case of a founder. The river Poddle flows under Patrick St at this point, and the holy well was probably part of it. Sir Thomas Drew, at one time engaged as restorer of the cathedral, marked the likely site of the well on a map in 1890, and in 1901 a granite stone marked with a Celtic cross was excavated on the spot.

This stone, now preserved in the cathedral, probably dates from the ninth or tenth century, and probably stood originally over St Patrick's Well. Dr J. H. Bernard, a former dean of St Patrick's, points out in his *The Cathedral Church of St Patrick* that the cathedral's site is extraordinarily unsuitable for any great building, being the marsh of the Poddle, and thus making a crypt impossible; the lack of a crypt and the springs which perpetually gush through the moist earth around the foundations have for centuries damaged the building's fabric. To this day, water is still only seven and a half feet below the cathedral floor. A strong justification was needed for choosing the site despite this disadvantage, the obvious one being that the place was especially venerated because of its associations with St Patrick. Gregory, king of Scotland, on his expedition to Dublin in 890, is said to have visited the Old St Patrick's church, and it is mentioned in an 1179 bull from Pope Alexander III to Laurence O'Toole. In 1192 John Comyn, Anglo–Norman archbishop of Dublin, raised St Patrick's to the status of collegiate church, and it is commonly held that the church referred to in this upgrading was the new one, which was to become the cathedral, and that it had been begun in 1191. St Patrick's is in Early English Gothic style, and thus Dr Bernard claims that it cannot be dated as far back as 1191. But the Early English phase is generally accepted as beginning in about 1190. Dr Bernard, however, points out that the first authentic record of building of St Patrick's cathedral is dated 3 April 1225, and that earlier stonework may be from a gateway that led to the older wooden church, as Sir Thomas Drew suggested.

Archbishop Henry de Londres granted new charters to St Patrick's between 1218 and 1220. This man had held important ecclesiastical

St Patrick's Cathedral, Patrick St

Thomas Ryan—

posts in England, and disputes with monastic establishments there had brought him to distrust such establishments, including, of course, Christ Church. The location of another cathedral, outside the walls of the city, could provide him with a dean and a chapter more in sympathy with his own views. St Patrick's was raised to cathedral status in 1213 and in 1220 he added a dean to the three dignitaries, chancellor, precentor and treasurer, whom he had already established there. The cathedral was not dedicated until 1254, a year before the death of Archbishop Luke, Henry's successor. The present lady chapel was completed in around 1270.

The building is a beautifully proportioned Latin cross, consisting of nave, choir and transepts, all with aisles, and the lady chapel. It has had a troubled history. In 1316 a storm blew down the spire, then the cathedral was set on fire by the citizens, another part of the panic generated by the presence of Edward de Bruce and his army at Castleknock. Looters promptly took advantage of the confusion to remove some of the building's art treasures, the kind of thing that was still happening in Dublin during the 1916 Rising. In 1362 the north-west end of the nave was burned in a more serious fire, caused by 'the negligence of John the Sexton'. Archbishop Thomas Minot in 1363 petitioned the Pope to grant a 'relaxation of seven years and seven quadragene of enjoined penance to those who had lent a helping hand to the repair of the church of St Patrick', and he mentioned in this petition that the tower and bells had been destroyed. Archbishop Minot then built the tower which bears the present spire, though the spire itself was not added until 1749. This spire brings the height of the cathedral to over 230 feet.

Thomas Minot

Images of saints in niches in the choir, including one of St Patrick, were broken up by order of Thomas Cromwell in 1537, and in 1544 the stone roof fell in at the western end of the nave, destroying many old monuments. Edward VI reduced the cathedral to the status of a parish church and directed that part of it should be used as a courthouse, but the building was restored to its ancient privilege and status by a charter of Philip and Mary in 1555. In 1559 orders were given to 'new paint the walls, and instead of pictures and popish fancies to place passages or texts of Scripture on the walls'. In 1560, by order of Elizabeth I, a public clock was placed on the cathedral, as well as one each on Dublin Castle and the Tholsel. These were Dublin's first three public clocks, and the clock whose two faces we see now on the Minot tower at St Patrick's is the successor of one of them.

Early in the seventeenth century the cathedral was again being used for secular purposes. By 1633 the lady chapel was in ruins. A programme of repairs was undertaken after the restoration of the monarchy in 1660. The roof, which had become dangerous, was taken off in 1668, and the organs removed from the building. A new nave roof was built in 1671, using forty tons of timber from a wood in Shillelagh, Co. Wicklow. In 1681 a stone roof was erected over the choir, painted sky blue and dotted with gold stars. During Jonathan Swift's tenure as dean, from 1713 to 1745, no great repairs were undertaken, despite his keen sense of history and interest in preservation. Swift performed a notable service to the cathedral and its neighbourhood, however, by robustly dissuading Archbishop King from putting a brick spire on top of Minot's tower.

The 1681 work seems to have been rather ill-advised, for in 1774, when a plaster wall at the back of the altar in the choir was removed, it was found to have been hiding a lofty Gothic arch. More trouble was in store, for in 1787 the stone roof of the choir was found to be decayed, and five years later the south wall of the nave was found to be two feet out of the perpendicular. By 1805, when a report presented to the lord lieutenant estimated that even temporary repairs would cost £16,000, the nave needed a new roof, the north transept, which was used as the church of St Nicholas Without, was in ruins, the south transept was said to be 'tottering' and the choir was the only weatherproof part of the building. Between 1845 and 1852 Dean Pakenham, in the absence of any public grant, devoted his efforts to preventing the cathedral from falling apart. He found that the erection of great galleries inside the church had not helped towards its stability, apart from the fact that someone had removed the capitals from pillars to run timber beams into the walls.

A restoration of the nave roof began in 1863, and the following year the brewer, Benjamin Lee Guinness, stepped in with an offer to restore the church's fabric completely. This work took four years, and cost Guinness £160,000. He removed and rebuilt five bays of the south aisle of the nave, rebuilt the south wall in native granite, rebuilt the middle storey of the nave, renewed the clerestory and the south front of the south transept. He restored the nave roof, erected two flying buttresses at the north side of the nave, added two porches and built a new north transept, using the south transept as a model. The cruciform shape of the cathedral, long missing, reappeared. There is no doubt that St Patrick's would not be standing today had it not been for this gesture by the brewer.

But he was accused, by those who had not seen the cathedral before this restorative work, of destroying the greater part of its original character and beauty. The work was so extensive, said its critics, as to be even more 'disastrous' than contemporary work on English churches. The cathedral became known as the 'brewer's church'. It is said that in the service marking the restoration the dean began his sermon with the words, 'Today I take my text from Hebrews XX.' (XX is a symbol used by Guinness in the grading of stout.) But Frederick H. Mares, whose *Photographs of Dublin* appeared in 1867, wrote: 'The restoration has been most complete, and the glorious old pile presents, as nearly as possible, the same appearance as it did over 600 years ago.'

Later the maintenance of the cathedral was taken over by Guinness's sons, Lords Ardilaun and Iveagh, and Lord Iveagh undertook a full restoration of the choir between 1901 and 1904, under the direction of Sir Thomas Drew. In this work Drew found evidence of much earlier vandalism, such as the plastering over of walls and the hacking away of clustered shafts, around piers, to accommodate some octagonal casings.

St Patrick's, on the exterior, is 300 feet long and 156 feet wide along the transepts. It is a little over fifty-six feet high, from floor to roof, and is 21,300 square feet in area. There are eight bays on each side of the nave, four in the choir and three in each transept. On the north side, the three piers nearest the west end are part of Archbishop Minot's repair of the fourteenth century, and are higher and wider than their neighbours. Notice, on entering, how this has caused two arches to rise higher than the neighbouring string course, pushing up their own part of this course and leaving an unsightly break. These arches are in Cheshire stone, rather than the original Somerset limestone. The stone roof and four graceful arches of the crossing have been repaired, but never altered. The original groining is to be seen here and in the north and south aisles of the choir, the aisles of the south transept and part of the south aisle of the nave. In the aisle last mentioned, on the left of a Gothic door leading to the robing rooms of the clergy and choirboys, is a Carrara marble bust of Jonathan Swift.

Jonathan Swift

This bust, executed by an artist named Cunningham, once stood over the shop door of Alderman George Faulkner, Swift's Dublin publisher, and was presented to St Patrick's in 1775 by Faulkner's nephew. Over the door of the robing rooms is a slab bearing Swift's epitaph, and on the other side of the door one with the epitaph of Hester Johnson, better known to the world as Swift's Stella. Swift and Stella are buried near these epitaphs, in the nave, their tombs being marked in brass. The Swift epitaph was formerly attached to a pillar beside his tomb. Swift's tomb, like that of Strongbow in Christ Church, has had its authenticity disputed, but not as widely or with as much conviction. Some believe that he is buried beside the small St Moibhi's church in Glasnevin, a curious theory which we will meet when we pass that church in another chapter. In the north transept of the cathedral, the Iveagh window, designed by Frank Brangwyn, was erected in memory of their father by the children of the first earl of Iveagh. The spiral staircase leading to the organ chamber was designed by Sir Thomas Drew in 1901 and is modelled on a staircase in Mainz cathedral, a red sandstone building very different indeed from St Patrick's.

St Patrick's park

Leaving the cathedral, walk to its north side and enter St Patrick's park, with its walks, fountains and children's playground. The park was laid out for the poor of the district in 1903 at the expense of Lord Iveagh. The path along the north side of the cathedral was formerly Canon St, shortened when the park was laid out and later completely demolished. For many years this century it consisted merely of the side of an inn, at the Bride St end of the park. Near here was held the infamous 'bird market' on Sunday mornings, a street market in which linnets and other common birds were sold as something more exotic, having had their feathers painted. The street along the north side of the park is Bull Alley St where, facing the park, we can see some of the Iveagh buildings, another part of the redevelopment of the area, redbrick and Portland stone in an attractive Edwardian baroque style.

'bird market'

Bull Alley St
Iveagh buildings

Looking up at the cathedral from the north we notice the organ chamber at the north end of the choir, an addition of 1901 by Sir Thomas Drew. Look up also at Minot's tower, 147 feet tall from nave floor to battlements, and 39 feet square at the base, with Irish limestone

walls ten feet thick. When the present bells were installed in 1897 the floors of the tower, of Wicklow oak, which had been there since Minot's time, were replaced by concrete, and iron girders. The granite spire was designed by George Semple and is 101 feet high.

Going back around the cathedral's west end, see how the cathedral stands several feet below the level of Patrick St, which covers the Poddle. Passing it, we come to St Patrick's Close on the left, once called Guinness St. Going along it, we pass between the statue of Sir Benjamin Lee Guinness by John Henry Foley, sitting on its marble plinth, inside the railings on our left, and the cathedral choir school, with its blue Gothic door, on our right. Going around a gentle curve we pass the stone side of Marsh's library, again on our left, but if we look over our left shoulders as we approach its arched gateway, we see the snuff-coloured bricks of its front wall above us. It was built in 1703 to the design of Sir William Robinson, and opened as a library in 1707. Its official name is the library of St Sepulchre, but the more common name commemorates Narcissus Marsh, Archbishop of Dublin, who founded and endowed it. He had resigned as provost of Trinity in 1683 because he found the high spirits of the students oppressive, and a distraction from his own studies. The library contains about 25,000 printed books, including the personal library of Stillingfleet, bishop of Worcester, who died in 1699. There are also about 200 manuscripts. The library stalls are still as they were in the eighteenth century, giving the place an exceedingly quaint air, with chained books and decorated woodwork.

Continuing along the outside of the fine-cut stone wall of St Patrick's Close towards Kevin St, a horse trough is noted near the junction, whose obscured inscription tells us that it was erected in memory of Anne Louisa Woodward of Fethard, Co. Tipperary, Sophie S. Burgess and others, who devoted their lives to the protection of

St Patrick's Close

Marsh's library

179

animals. It seems odd that the inscription faces the road on the outer side of the trough, where it is less likely to be read, but this trough originally stood in the middle of Kevin St and was insensitively shoved aside in the motor age. A turn right here leads to the deanery of St Patrick's, a curious building. The central part, finished in 1782 by Dean Cradock, replaced the house in which Swift lived, which was burnt in 1781, and which was on the same site. The vaulted kitchens of Swift's deanery survive in the replacement, but Cradock's Georgian house has had wings added, in 1890 and in 1902.

deanery of St Patrick's

Kevin St

Back across the top of St Patrick's Close, Kevin St garda barracks stands on the site of an old archbishop's palace, the Palace of St Sepulchre, between the street and the L-shaped Marsh's library. The name of the palace was suggested by the 1184 Crusaders' project to recover the Holy Sepulchre from the Moslems. In 1326 the palace grounds are said to have contained the ruin of a prison, no doubt necessary to the administration of the independent jurisdiction of the Archbishop's Liberty. The palace housed the archbishops for over 600 years, and was handed over to the state in 1806. Apart from the gate piers, all that now remain of the palace are a sixteenth-century window and a mediaeval vault.

the 'cabbage garden'

Crossing Kevin St towards the right hand side of a curved block of redbrick municipal flats, we go up a laneway, Cathedral Lane, at the top of which we see through a gate a neglected graveyard, overlooked on its left by more flats, in New Bride St. This is locally known as the 'cabbage garden' or 'cabbage patch', and was a cemetery set apart for local people in 1666, and consecrated in 1668. The locals entitled to burial here were parishioners of St Nicholas Without, whose 'church', as we have seen, was really part of the cathedral. But also in 1666 a congregation of refugee French Huguenots took over the cathedral's lady chapel for worship, it having been granted to them three years earlier, and been repaired in the meantime. Their minister, M. Hierome, was chaplain to the duke of Ormonde, a fact which weighed with the cathedral authorities. The Huguenots were also granted burial rights at Cathedral Lane, first in part of the 'cabbage garden', then in an adjoining cemetery which was later known as the 'French burying ground', but has now disappeared. The 'cabbage' nickname probably describes the later use to which the graveyard at the top of the lane was put.

'Dutch Billies'

Back at the bottom of the lane, go left along Kevin St until number 35A, a three-storey brown brick house with a tapering top, is directly opposite. This house gives the best impression of any left in Dublin of what the weavers' houses of the Liberties looked like. These were called 'Dutch style', 'Queen Anne', 'Flemish style' or simply 'weavers' houses', and came to be known as 'Dutch Billies', the 'Billy' part being a reference to King William of Orange. Between 1680 and 1730 front-gabled houses existed all over Dublin. We have seen them already on the north side, in Phibsborough Avenue and at 48 Montpelier Hill, though they differ in many ways from this one in Kevin St.

The houses usually had either a curved or triangular top, but could also terminate in two triangles joined by a curve. Curved top parts were often deeper than on the house we see here. The top of the narrow part between the two long curves sometimes ended in another, shallow, curve, sometimes was flat and sometimes was capped by a triangular pediment. The narrow part sometimes, but not always, had a window, and from this a pulley could be extended for lifting and lowering goods; wool for weaving, as an example, was winched up from the street, the finished articles later being lowered for despatch. Similar houses, dating from the seventeenth century, are seen in Amsterdam and elsewhere in the Low Countries. Along Amsterdam's canals the pulley delivery system had obvious advantages. In Dublin this type of house became almost synonymous with the Liberties because, after the collapse of the woollen industry, the developers who were changing the face of the city elsewhere ignored this socially depressed area.

As we are about to go to Peter St, site of another former Huguenot cemetery and a Huguenot church, it should be mentioned here that the name Huguenot was first widely applied to French Protestants in the sixteenth century, and was probably a corruption of the German word 'eidgenossen', meaning 'confederates'. Mostly Calvinists, they were severely persecuted until granted a measure of tolerance by the Edict of Nantes in 1598. They were tolerated by Richelieu and Mazarin, but Louis XIV revoked the Edict of Nantes in 1685 and attempted to convert the Huguenots to Catholicism by force, so that 400,000 of them **Huguenots** fled from France, many crossing to England and some arriving in Dublin to join their fellows who, as we saw, had already established their chapel in St Patrick's cathedral. The cathedral link meant that most of them settled in the Liberties, where they engaged in weaving poplin (fabric hand-woven from pure wool and pure silk) on such a scale and with such skill that Dublin later became famous for this product. The Huguenots also worked in wool alone and in silk alone; nor was all Dublin weaving done in the Liberties; nor were all Liberties weavers immigrant Huguenots. But poplin from this area, woven on looms established, if not always worked, by Huguenots, became the classic Dublin fabric.

About 1688, not long after the big influx of Huguenots, woollen manufacturers from England began to move in and set up firms in the Liberties. They were attracted by the cheap labour and by the fact that the family of the earls of Meath, since the time of Charles I, had developed a breed of sheep famed for its wool. The earl of Meath's mansion was in Thomas St, and the new wool barons built large houses in the Liberties. The duke of Leinster would have built a large town house in the area if the wool trade had not collapsed a few years after it had been seriously set up, a tragedy inspired by William of Orange. Irish woollen exports to England, both from the Liberties and from the longer-established wool industry elsewhere in Ireland, were harming the English industry to such an extent that the English mills put pressure on the king, through the Lords, to suppress the Irish industry. This he did by having the supine Irish parliament impose an exorbitant duty on the Irish product. The Huguenots had by then been joined by many Dutch and Flemish Protestants. The fact that many of the woollen industry's proprietors were English did not matter in this industrial context. Out of business, they left Ireland, and their mansions became miserable tenements.

Peter St

Going back past the garda barracks, we turn left into Bride St and then right into Peter St. Here stood the seven-bay Queen Anne mansion of the Molyneux family, Molyneux House, erected in 1711, with dormer windows and a richly panelled interior. Facing the sombre

Adelaide hospital

Adelaide hospital, which was established primarily for Protestants and is still regarded as 'the Protestant hospital', is part of the premises of W. and R. Jacob, the biscuit manufacturers. Here stood the church called 'French Peter's', with its cemetery, officially St Peter's church of non-conforming French Huguenots. It was opened on 19 December 1711. In 1967 the remains of the Huguenots were removed from here and reinterred in Mount Jerome cemetery, and the Peter St site became part of the biscuit bakery.

church of Our Lady of Dublin

Passing the hospital, we come to the end of Whitefriar St, take a left turn followed by a right one almost immediately, and walk down to Aungier St, emerging with the church of St Peter on our right and the Carmelite priory and church of Our Lady of Dublin on our left. The Carmelite church, a large, fairly ornate establishment, has a deceptively non-ecclesiastical facade and entrance. It and the priory occupy the pre-Reformation site of a foundation of the same order. In the north chapel is a shrine dominated by a statue of Our Lady of Dublin, carved in oak in late mediaeval times. This statue, usually seen in the light of dozens of candles, is traditionally said to have come from St Mary's Abbey, and, after the abbey's suppression, to have been saved by an unusual ruse. The story is that it was rescued after partial burning, the back was hollowed out and the statue placed face downward and disguised as a hog trough. This may also be the statue from which the crown was borrowed for the 'coronation' of Lambert Simnel, the baker's son, in Christ Church cathedral.

Leaving this church we go down Aungier St, turn left into Longford St and head west through Golden Lane, Bull Alley St and Hanover Lane to the top of John Dillon St. Turning right here, we go down past the tiny St Francis Square, a name whose significance we will shortly see, and pass the brick arch that leads to the yellow granite path along the side of the church of St Nicholas of Myra. We are coming back here, but first we follow John Dillon St to Back Lane. In the lane,

Tailors' Hall

behind a gateway erected in 1714, we find the Tailors' Hall, Dublin's oldest surviving guildhall, built in 1706–1707. There are lovely long Queen Anne windows in the room where the guild formerly met, where the dark timber committee rostrum, with its serrated pediment, has been restored. The building contains attractive corkscrew banisters, of Jacobean style.

St Nicholas of Myra

Going back to St Nicholas of Myra by John Dillon St, we take the path to the courtyard in front of the church and admire its quatrastyle Ionic portico, clocktower and copper cupola. Inside, the church has a splendidly decorated ceiling and a fine altarpiece with eight short fluted Ionic columns. This church is the modern Catholic replacement of the St Nicholas Without part of St Patrick's cathedral. When the mediaeval parish of St Nicholas was extended outside the walls, no separate church

was built in its outer part, the north transept of the cathedral being used from the beginning. Later, when the cathedral was in Protestant hands, the parish of St Nicholas Without was merged with that of St Luke in a church which we will see further on. Thus there are now two churches of St Nicholas Without, the Catholic one which we see now, and the Protestant St Nicholas Without and St Luke. The saint is St Nicholas of Myra in each case.

Francis St

The street running past the front of the church is Francis St, and this and St Francis Square are explained by the fact that the church's site was formerly that of a large monastery of St Francis, peopled by friars known as Conventual Franciscans. This was established early in the thirteenth century, and stood until the friars were dispossessed by order of Henry VIII in 1540. It is recorded that in 1233 Henry III authorised a grant of 'twenty marks' towards the repair of the monastery. Being mendicants, the friars were assisted officially by the city of Dublin until their suppression, and unofficially by the citizens after that, when the monks found lodgings in houses in the neighbourhood for many years, before being re-established in a home of their own in Cook St and later at Merchants' Quay.

Iveagh Markets

Going down Francis St to the right we come to the handsome front of the Iveagh Markets, standing on the old site of Sweetman's brewery. Sweetman's went out of business in 1889. In the markets, clothes, household goods and even secondhand books are sold. A little further on, on the same side, is the blocked-up entrance to an old lane called Handkerchief Alley, whose nameplate survives on its southern side. Let us retrace our steps up Francis St to the church and to the corner of Carman's Hall on our right. The name honours a tavern in which the drivers of the Wexford stage-coach drank before and after journeys in the pre-railway days. Going along Carman's Hall, we find it crossed by Spitalfields, a name that came from England with the wool barons. We

Meath St

reach Meath St and cross the road. Just south of Meath Place notice that the shopfront at number 26A Meath St is built into an old archway. This was the entrance to an eighteenth-century Quaker meeting house. Further down the street on the far side is the Catholic St Catherine's neo-Gothic church, whose clocktower and spire are rather incongruous additions. Church clocktowers certainly are fashionable in this part of the city. This church was opened on 30 June 1858, replacing one that had become ruinous, after a fund-raising campaign that had begun in February 1852. The chairman of the first fund-raising meeting, Mr James Power, later succeeded his father as head of Power's distillery, and became Sir James.

Facing the church is Hanbury Lane; going along it we pass behind the older St Catherine's in Thomas St and come to a street, crossing our path, called Thomas Court. This is the site of the once prominent monastery of St Thomas Becket. It was a royal foundation of Henry II, set up by him primarily in atonement for his guilt over the murder of Becket in 1170 in Canterbury by four of the king's knights. As a royal foundation it had jurisdiction over the Liberties of Thomas Court and Donore, a large area. After its suppression the jurisdiction of the area passed to the Brabazon family, later earls of Meath. Going south along

An entrance to the Iveagh Market

Thomas Court and across its intersection with School St and South Earl
St, we bear left into Pimlico, another English name that came with the
wool barons, and come to Gray St on the left. As we go along this
thoroughfare we see at the corner of Reginald St a statue of the Sacred **Reginald St**
Heart with a sadly semi-demolished canopy. This was erected in 1929
by the parishioners of Meath St to mark the centenary of Catholic
Emancipation, and the canopy in its original form resembled those
which sometimes shelter statues of Victoria. Turn right here and walk
down to the Coombe. The Coombe was laid out in the heyday of the **The Coombe**
wool trade, and the name is derived from an Irish word meaning 'bent',
which the street certainly is. Going down it, we see over on the right a
preserved heavy gateway, all that is left of the old Coombe lying-in

hospital; the new 'Coombe' hospital is in Dolphin's Barn St, further out. The old Coombe hospital was founded in 1826 by Mrs Margaret Boyle, a wealthy widow, as there was then no maternity hospital on the south side of the city. A town house of the earl of Meath in Ardee St which had been built in 1719 was taken over as a nurses' home later.

In 1865 Sir Benjamin Lee Guinness and his son Arthur donated £2,000 towards building a forty-bed extension at Brabazon Row, at the back of the existing hospital, and £500 for a new dispensary. Arthur, who was to become Lord Ardilaun, became more deeply involved with the hospital, in 1874, when it was short of money for flood repairs. He suggested to the governors that they hand over the hospital to him, with the unexpended balance of the building fund, and he would complete the repair and rebuilding programme, then hand the hospital back to them. The only proviso was that he would select the architect and have a free hand, with no interference at all from the governors. This was agreed, and a virtually new hospital was handed back on 12 May 1877, ready for patients, the duke of Marlborough performing the reopening ceremony.

Another former Coombe building is the Weavers' Hall, built between 1745 and 1750 as headquarters of the weavers' guild, and demolished in 1965. A leaden gilt statue of George II by John Van Nost stood over the entrance in a niche, but was removed in the 1930s after it had fallen from its pedestal and the lead on the ankles was found to have rotted. The boots of the statue are in the civic museum in South William St.

On the same side of the Coombe as the preserved hospital gate, but further down, a path is seen inside a gateway, leading to the Protestant **church of St Nicholas Without and St Luke**, which stands at the Newmarket end of the path. It was built by Huguenots around 1707.

Going back up the Coombe, we find the last block of houses on this side named Watkins's Buildings, and turning left into Ardee St we find more of these, some smaller ones running off into a street behind the Coombe. In Ardee St is a brown Georgian house, facing up Cork St, with a granite-arched gateway beside the halldoor and a plaque on the building to say that it was a volunteers' garrison during the 1916 Rising. This is the former **Watkins's brewery**, founded in 1802 by Joseph and Richard Watkins, which went out of business in 1939. Here the famous O'Connell's ale was brewed after the demise of D'Arcy's brewery in 1926. The two Watkinses, Englishmen, took over a lease of the site, which runs 'forever', from the people to whom this lease had been granted by the earls of Meath. Sir William Brabazon, grandfather of the first earl, had been granted the property by Henry VIII, for this had been the site of the brewhouse of the monastery of Thomas Becket. Visitors to the brewery in the late nineteenth century clearly recognised storage cellars as former crypts. The houses we have seen bearing the Watkins name were built by the brewery, eighty of them, for its workers in the 1880s. Guinness, of course, also built houses for its employees.

Passing Cork St on our right we take another right turn into Chamber St, where Dutch Billies once stood. The turn facing Chamber St on the other side of Ardee St is Newmarket, which contains the malting firm of Minch Norton, last such firm in the Liberties. Going along Chamber St turn left into Weaver Square, which also had front-gabled houses, and cross South Brown St into Cow Parlour. South Brown St was the site of the famous poplin weaving firm of Thomas Elliott, founded in 1872, which moved to Cork exactly 100 years later. This firm produced tapestries for Aras an Uachtarain and for the throne room in Dublin Castle.

The name Cow Parlour may indicate that cattle were once kept in this quaint tiny street, but is more likely to be a corruption of a French name, possibly *coupe ourlet* (hem section) or *coupeur d'ourlet* (hem cutter), from a particular tailoring or dressmaking activity once associated with the place, attracted there by the area's weaving activity. This area was once called the Tenterfields, from the use of tenterhooks for drying. Going through O'Curry Avenue and Oscar Square, with its Marian statue on a neat lawn, we come to the corner of Mill St and turn right. **Mill St** Halfway along Mill St on the right is a three-storey brick house with two curious triangles, one over the porch and one over the central top window. This was a dower house of the Brabazon family and was built shortly after 1700. It then had a twin-gabled curvilinear top, but was much altered by the Victorian architect George P. Beater. The house, number 10, was once used as a mission hall, and was for a time a Christian Brothers' school. A doorway from Queen Anne times, possibly by the monumental sculptor William Kidwell, has been removed from the house but cemented to a building at the back. It has a beautiful scroll pediment. The house was once noted for its ornamental garden.

Continuing down Mill St we pass Warrenmount on our right and then turn right into Blackpitts, a long rambling street. Three **Blackpitts** explanations of the name are usually suggested. One attributes it to mass graves, legacies of a mediaeval plague, found here; another says it stems from pools formed by the river Poddle, and a third supposes that it comes from dark-stained vats, used by local tanners for curing hides. In the grounds of Warrenmount convent, on the right, is an old mill pond which is the only part of the Poddle still over ground between the two canals.

Turn left into Malpas St and go straight on into Long Lane, passing on the left the Bewley's bakery and opposite it, in the grounds of the Meath hospital, an old pedimented entrance to the hospital. We **Meath hospital** turn right and pass the modern front of the hospital, once also known as the Co. Dublin Infirmary, in Heytesbury St. Turning left again, we are in the quiet of Pleasants St, off which we take a right turn into Synge St. **Synge St** Soon on our right a small turn is worth exploring. It leads to a pocket-sized square called St Kevin's Cottages, with a miniature Marian shrine against a wall and a half-hidden row of cottages behind a gate. Coming out we go south along Synge St, passing the fine brick building of the Christian Brothers' school and cut-stone church of St Kevin on the corner of Harrington St. This area was once very popular with Jewish families, but many of them have now moved to outer suburbs. Crossing Harrington St, we see number 33 Synge St beyond it on our left, a brownbrick house of two storeys above a basement, where George

THE EARL OF MEATH'S LIBERTIES

Bernard Shaw was born in 1856.

    Shaw, like James Joyce, was the son of a drunkard, but, unlike Joyce, he did not emulate the parent. Shaw senior, between trips to the boozer, found time to be a snob; here in Synge St he found the young George Bernard playing with a friend, and, on discovering that the playmate's father kept a shop in which he sold nails, he informed his son that it was dishonourable to associate with people who were in 'trade'. Shaw senior owned a flour mill.

Portobello Harbour

    A turn to the left after Shaw's house brings us into Lennox St, and by turning right off this along Richmond Row we come to the Grand Canal at Portobello Harbour. The harbour is no longer here, but the nine-bay house with a fine portico is a former canal hotel, later converted to a nursing home. It was designed in 1805 by Thomas Colbourne, a Grand Canal Company engineer, when it was decided to make Portobello, instead of James's St, the terminus of the canal's passenger boats. The hotel was opened in 1807, and a short time later it was said that 'the beauty and salubrity of the situation, enlivened by the daily arrival and departure of the canal boats, render it a truly delightful residence.'

    Those who wish to see the birthplace of James Joyce in Brighton Square, Rathgar, may cross the canal by Portobello Bridge, go west along Grove Road past Cathal Brugha barracks to the next bridge,

Portobello House, Charlemont Mall

Robert Emmet Bridge, with a likeness of the patriot, and turn south into Harold's Cross Road. After a while the road is divided by a triangular park. Keep to the left, and at the end of Harold's Cross Road, having passed a petrol station on the left, turn left into the 'square', which is actually a triangle. Joyce's birthplace is at number 41, a two-storey **Joyce's** redbrick house with a bay window and neat lawn. **birthplace**

Coming back to Emmet Bridge on the canal, continue along Clanbrassil St across the South Circular Road to the corner of Vincent St, on the right. Turn right into it, noting the houses on the left, with single-storey redbrick fronts. Some of them have one storey in the front and two in the back. This style, and others we will meet in this area, date mainly from the 1870s. Turn left into Emorville Avenue, right into Ovoca Road, right again into Carlisle St, left onto the South Circular Road, left again into Emor St, right into Ovoca Road again, then left into Curzon St, along this into Arnott St, left into Vernon St and around the block formed by this street, Desmond St and McMahon St, back onto Arnott St where two right turns lead to Lombard St West, and along this to Clanbrassil St again. This may seem, on paper, like a route march, but is in fact a pleasant stroll, and gives an overall picture of the variety of styles in this small area. Note the characteristic of mixing single and double storey dwellings in the same block, also the small, railed gardens, occasional bay windows, some very heavy porches and some half-hidden basement floors in what at first look like one-storey cottages. Numbers 77 and 78 Lombard St are especially worthy of attention, each with a split-level halldoor and a two-storey bay window on one side only, but see how each house has preserved its individuality, one going classical with a pillared halldoor, the other remaining faithful to the predominant style of porch. Joyceans who visit Lombard St West will recall that Leopold Bloom used to live here before moving to number 7 Eccles St.

This district was formerly the home of many Jewish families, before it became fashionable to move to the outer suburbs, and there was a synagogue at number 46 Lombard St. It was part of an area nicknamed 'Little Jerusalem' among Dubliners, but probably not those Dubliners **'Little** living in it. **Jerusalem'**

Turn left into Clanbrassil St and right into the South Circular Road, heading south-west. The turns to the right are another part of what was 'Little Jerusalem', and they lead to the districts of Belleville, Fairbrother's Fields and the Tenters' Fields, the last of which we have already encountered. Past Griffith barracks on the left and then the synagogue, with its handsome quatrastyle facade, on the right, is the corner of Donore Avenue. Notice that the house on the far side of it has a **Donore Avenue** Gothic porch. Directly behind this, in Donore Avenue, is St Catherine's church, a late Victorian Church of Ireland building which expresses in brickwork ecclesiastical features more usually found in stone, such as a square tower. Bearing left along Donore Avenue we pass the charming little 1901 St Catherine's school in redbrick; this type of solid little suburban amenity from that period is well worth preserving, but is sometimes silently allowed to disappear. A similar one in Drumcondra was demolished without protest. Towards the end of Donore Avenue, after the Brown St junction, the wall of the old Cork St fever hospital appears on the right. Coming out into Cork St we are facing the top of Marrowbone Lane, and the area over to the left, behind the junction, is called Maryland, containing several roads of council housing with Marian names. To the right is the front of the old hospital, now called Bru Chaoimhin, and run as an old men's home by the Eastern Health Board. There is a handsome central three-storey block in brown brick, with a copper-domed clocktower, and the gables of other blocks, with fire escapes, face the street on either side. Further back an extension is visible, with a verandah, and across the street is the James Weir home for the nurses of the former hospital, a ponderous four-storey redbrick pile with a verandah over the street, built in 1903

Cork St fever hospital

but older in style. Cork St hospital, founded by Quakers and opened in 1804, was known as a 'house of recovery and fever hospital', and has had several extensions, the first major one being in 1817, when its amenities were overtaxed during a national epidemic of typhus, which lasted for two years. Dublin was hit by another outbreak of the disease in 1826, and in the winter of that year the hospital was so overcrowded that patients had to be accommodated in tents in the grounds, even during heavy snow.

Heuston Station, formerly Kingsbridge

Kingsbridge station — Dr Steevens's hospital — St
Patrick's hospital — St James's hospital — Royal
Hospital — Kilmainham jail — Inchicore —
Memorial park.

He gave the little wealth he had,
To build a house for fools and mad;
And show'd by one satyric touch,
No nation wanted it so much.

— Jonathan Swift, on his own bequest for the foundation of
St Patrick's mental hospital.

A MIXTURE OF STYLES

Heuston Bridge

The Liffey bridge formerly called Kingsbridge is now Heuston Bridge, and was renamed after the 1916 rebel Sean Heuston, whose bust we have seen in the people's gardens in the Phoenix Park. Built in 1827–28 to the design of George Papworth, it rests on two great supporting pillars of Egyptianesque design, which remind us somewhat of Broadstone station. On the south side of the bridge the long front of Guinness's lowest level runs up to the end of Victoria Quay, and beyond that the western view is dominated by the square bulk of Kingsbridge station, renamed, like the bridge, after Heuston, but still more often referred to by its older name.

Kingsbridge station

The granite main block at the front of Kingsbridge is a splendid building. Its engaged Corinthian pillars, festoons, balustrade and other decorations give it the appearance of a great Renaissance house. Though it bears the date 1844, its completion was delayed by a stonemasons' strike until November 1848. Its architect was Sancton Wood, of Bath, who had built an imposing Italianate terminus for the English Eastern Counties Railway at Shoreditch. He built Kingsbridge for the Great Southern and Western Railway, and the only similarities between it and Shoreditch are that the front of the station is formed by the company's offices, and passengers enter through a covered extension at the side. In Kingsbridge, this extension is a simple *porte-cochere* with eight pillars. Charles Hamilton Ellis, in his *Pictorial Encyclopaedia of Railways*, calls Kingsbridge one of the most meritorious railway buildings in Europe.

The train shed was designed by John McNeill, a Scot, and has about two-and-a-half acres of roof, resting on 72 cast-iron pillars, with connecting spans. Some of the pillars still carry the heavy brackets which were once part of an overhead system for lifting road vehicles on and off rail wagons. Near the most northerly platform, tracks formerly used by city tramcars which ran into the station are still in place. The station's Number 1 platform, on the south side, was built in 1872 to handle military traffic to 'garrison towns', and is still called the 'military platform'.

Visitors travelling by train from Kingsbridge will pass, on their left, the railway works at Inchicore also designed by Sancton Wood. These works produced, in 1939, the most powerful and famous locomotive class ever to run in Ireland, the '800' class. These were big steam engines of the 4–6–0 type (front four-wheel bogie, six driving wheels and no trailing bogie). The class was the second most powerful of its type in the world, superseded only by the 'King' class of the Great Western Railway in England. For train spotters, they closely resembled the Stanier rebuilt 'Royal Scot', which came later. Among the noted locomotive engineers who worked at Inchicore were R. E. Maunsell, H. A. Ivatt and Oliver Bulleid.

Dr Steevens's hospital

The nurses' home of Dr Steevens's hospital stands at the bottom of Steevens Lane, with the dispensary of 1900 behind it in John's Road. The home's Queen Anne look is another example of how eclectic the Victorian builders were. This is a building of 1897, yet in style and material it has absolutely nothing in common with its fellow-Victorian, the station across John's Road. It has three tapering superstructures fronting onto the lane and road, in three individual shapes. Yet it is far from ugly and even manages to make a pleasant impression, probably because its many windows help to give it a busy, living look.

Beyond it in the lane is the main front of the hospital, Dublin's second oldest, founded in 1720 and fully opened thirteen years later. It was designed by Thomas Burgh in a pleasant early Georgian style, and its dormer windows and octagonal white clocktower, with weather vane, give it a distinctive charm. Notice the great stone surround of the main door, and the fan-topped Georgian windows in the clocktower. Going through the entrance block one arrives in an amazing little cloister bordering a quadrangle. Dr Steevens's treats many emergency cases, but the atmosphere in the quadrangle is as different as can be from the hurly-burly world of general hospitals on popular television. There is even a quaintness in the handrail knobs, shaped as human hands.

It has sometimes been called Madame Grissel Steevens's hospital, and was founded by a lady of that name, who was, however, a 'Miss' and not a 'Madame'. Dr Richard Steevens had left his estate to his sister Grissel with the stipulation that when she died a hospital should be built with the residue, but Miss Steevens began work on the hospital immediately on receipt of the legacy. After the hospital was built she lived in an apartment there. Grissel Steevens was the unwitting victim of a story popular in Dublin which told of a beggarwoman who, accompanied by several of her children, called at a house for alms and was told by the lady of the house to 'be off with your litter of piglets', whereupon she cursed that lady, who later gave birth to a child with a pig's snout. Miss Steevens, the story ran, was that child, and though she was often seen sitting at her window, with no deformity, the tale persisted.

Dr Steevens's Hospital, Steevens' Lane

Jonathan Swift was a board member of Dr Steevens's hospital, and Stella was its benefactress, leaving £1,000 towards the support of a chaplain there. In 1953 Guinness's brewery presented wireless equipment to the hospital on the occasion of the golden wedding anniversary of the firm's chairman, the earl of Iveagh, as a mark of appreciation of the hospital's services to the brewery staff.

St Patrick's hospital

Adjoining this hospital's grounds are those of another, St Patrick's hospital, with which Swift has more memorable connections, as a bequest of his financed its foundation. It is reached by climbing Steevens' Lane to the top, where a gateway on the right shows a path between trees leading down to the main block. Swift left about £11,000 for the establishment of this psychiatric hospital, which was founded in 1745, the year of his death, and opened twelve years later. It is one of Ireland's leading institutions in this field, and is noted for the treatment and study of alcoholism, for which it has special facilities. Rather ironically, the brewing process in Guinness's can sometimes be smelt in the hospital's wards and grounds. It has been said that Swift's premonition of his own insanity — it overtook him a few years before he died — prompted him to found St Patrick's, but it is more likely that his decision was inspired by a visit to the Bethlehem hospital for the insane in London, where he was appalled by the conditions in which the patients lived, and which he nicknamed 'Bedlam'. He resolved to found a better type of institution for the mentally ill in Dublin, where they would be treated as patients and not as criminals.

More than an eighth of all admissions to psychiatric hospitals each year in the Republic of Ireland are to St Patrick's, and in latter years a special unit for adolescent treatment has been set up. The hospital is the teaching centre of psychiatry for Trinity College, the professors and lecturers being members of the hospital staff. Since 1919 St Patrick's has also been a training centre for nurses, and since 1956 for social workers. The entrance block of the hospital is the original sombre stone building of 1745, with its unusually long corridors, but modern buildings have been added, and most of the admission wards were laid out since World War II. The institution has a convalescent hospital in another Georgian house, St Edmondsbury, near Lucan, and also has a unit in the grounds of St James's Hospital in the upper part of James's St.

Beside the St Patrick's entrance gate is the city end of Bow Lane West, which curves towards Bow Bridge on the Camac river. Near this end of the lane a former maltings is seen on the left, ruinous but still wearing the distinctive 'hat' of these buildings. Further along, we pass Kennedy's Villas on the right, which name has nothing to do with the late American president, then a flight of steps named Cromwell's Quarters on the left leads up to the western end of James's St, where this runs into Mount Brown, Henry Cromwell, fourth son of Oliver, was governor-general of Ireland from 1655 to 1659, living on the site of the present magazine fort and having jurisdiction over lands as far south and east as 'Cromwell's Quarters', the Royal Hospital not having been built and the Phoenix Park not having been laid out and enclosed at that time. The view across the road from the top of the steps has the oldest part of the St James's hospital site on the left, with an unusual housing estate called Ceannt Fort, consisting of eight hilly roads, to its right. St James's was formerly St Kevin's hospital, and before that it was the South Dublin Union. The site originally accommodated a workhouse, set up under an act of 1702, and this also embraced a hospital for foundling children, 'to prevent the exposure, death and actual murder of illegitimate children'. Catholics complained that its prime purpose was to take Catholic infants and raise them as Protestants. The high rate of infant mortality in the hospital also attracted unfavourable attention. In the first quarter of 1795 alone, 440 of the 540 children admitted died there. In 1797 the Irish House of Commons appointed a committee to inquire into the management of the hospital, the result being that the administration of the place was reformed the following year. An act was passed establishing a new corporation of governors for the foundling hospital, but things, apparently, did not improve. The British House of Commons in 1829 heard that 41,524 children had died in the thirty years to 1826, either in the hospital or while being 'nursed' in the provinces under the hospital's aegis. On the recommendation of the House, the hospital was closed.

Going back down Cromwell's Quarters and turning left, the

Bow Lane West

Cromwell's Quarters

St James's hospital

Camac is crossed at Bow Bridge, the nearest point to the city from which the little river can be conveniently seen. The Camac enters the Liffey beside Kingsbridge (Heuston) station, having passed under the station. West of the bridge, the road is called Bow Bridge for awhile.

Kilmainham Lane

West of Irwin St, where Bow Bridge gives way to Kilmainham Lane, the scene becomes surprisingly rural, as the road passes between the Camac on the left and a high earthen bank on the right, mostly grassy and with overhanging bushes. The Royal Hospital, which is invisible from here, is beyond the top of this bank. Ahead, on the left, a row of cottages appears, and the old Kilmainham jail, now a museum, is seen in the distance. The road now divides, the left fork going down sharply to the Camac. Keeping to the right of the fork, a flight of stone steps is observed running down to meet the lower path, then a pub is passed, and beyond it a gap in a castellated wall leads to more steps, which run down a grass bank to join the lower road where this meets

Rowserstown

the quaintly named Rowserstown Lane. Rowserstown is merely three small streets, but they form a tiny detached village here in the Camac valley between Kilmainham Lane and Old Kilmainham. A brick bridge over the river separates Rowserstown Lane from Kearns's Place, and this leads up to Old Kilmainham on the southern bank. Turning right here, walk towards the most westerly part of the South Circular Road. A right turn onto the South Circular Road leads to a broad stone bridge over the Camac, with trees rising from the banks on either side.

On the north side of this bridge the road runs straight to where it crosses the Liffey at Islandbridge, formerly Sarah Bridge, passing on the way between Kilmainham jail and the main entrance of the Royal Hospital. The latter is ahead on the right, at the western end of Kilmainham Lane, which we left at Rowserstown. With its pretentious tower, it has often been called 'gingerbread Gothic'. The stone part of the gate, as was noted earlier, was taken stone by stone from the junction of Victoria Quay and Watling St and re-erected here. The tower is meant to be the dominant feature, for in its Watling St days it was called the Richmond Tower, but its use as a gate has focussed attention on the arch.

Royal Hospital

Through the gate a path is seen leading to one of the four great sides of the Royal Hospital, the only monumental seventeenth-century building now in Dublin. It was designed by William Robinson — though Sir Christopher Wren is often given the credit — and built between 1680 and 1685 at a cost of about £24,000. It was the brainchild of the viceroy, the duke of Ormonde, to open here a home for army pensioners on the lines of Chelsea hospital. The pensioners wore a uniform which made them easily recognisable in the neighbourhood, where they were colloquially known as 'Chelsea pensioners' despite their Dublin address. In the building, which now contains many items belonging to the National Museum, including coaches, carts, trade guild banners and a loom from Elliott's poplin works in South Brown St, is a chapel with a fine plaster ceiling and excellent wood carvings. The wood carvings have been attributed to Grinling Gibbons, who worked for Charles II and George I, but are in fact the work of James Tabary, a French sculptor who lived in Dublin. Their attribution to Gibbons is

Royal Hospital, Kilmainham

Thomas Ryan

probably part of the Wren myth, as Gibbons worked for Wren on the
choir of St Paul's Cathedral in London. The Royal Hospital, which was
used for a time as a police barrack after its original occupation ended,
may now be visited only by special permission of the Office of Public
Works, which has done a great deal of restoration there. With a fine
clocktower, the building contains a large quadrangle, in the centre of
which several discarded statues moulder on trestles, including that of
Queen Victoria, sceptre in right hand and orb in left, which once sat
outside Leinster House.

Inside the Royal Hospital's Kilmainham gate, and to the left of the

Bully's Acre

path, are two cemeteries. The bigger of these is Bully's Acre, 'bully'
being a corruption of 'bailly' or 'bailiff', and this is the oldest cemetery
in Dublin. It is said to contain the grave of Murrough, son of Brian
Boru, marked by a stone. Robert Emmet was buried here in 1803, and
while his body is officially recorded as having been taken away for
reburial, it is believed by some to be still here. This cemetery also
contains the shaft of the old Kilmainham high cross, marking the official
place for the public reading of important documents. The other
cemetery, adjoining the northern part of Bully's Acre, contains graves of
'Chelsea' pensioners and some British troops killed in the 1916 Rising.

The road running east along Kilmainham Lane and west along
Inchicore Road is a continuation of the ancient high ridge on which
Christ Church is built. It is also part of the line which divided Ireland in

two halves about 1,800 years ago. Dublin, or 'Eblana', is said to have been noticed by the geographer Ptolemy about the year AD 40 as a city, but scarcely an important one. Over one hundred years later Mogh, king of Munster, defeated Conn of the Hundred Battles and forced him to agree to the division of the country, Conn's half being north of the line on which we now stand, and Mogh's half south of it. The eastern end of the line was fixed at High St about the year AD 177, and the line ran west to Galway. The halves were called *Leath Mogha* (Mogh's half) and *Leath Coinn* (Conn's half), sometimes written as Leth Quinn. The name Munster, incidentally, is a corruption of a word originally meaning 'belonging to Mogh'. Mogh belatedly foresaw the increasing importance of Dublin's harbour, which the line had left in Conn's half, and reneged on the treaty.

Kilmainham courthouse and jail stand at the city end of Inchicore Road. The courthouse, a granite building with a pleasant garden at its side, still bears the royal arms, but Kilmainham jail, beyond it, rising behind its dark, depressing wall, has become a shrine of Irish independence. Much voluntary labour was expended on the restoration of this ugly building, and on its conversion to a museum commemorating the leaders of the 1916 Rising who were executed there, but its demolition and the erection of a simple memorial would have been in better taste. In an era when buildings of worth are being demolished, the preservation of a jail with no aesthetic value is ironic.

Kilmainham courthouse and jail

Charles Stewart Parnell and Isaac Butt were among the prisoners here. The chapel of the prison may be seen, as may the cells and the execution yard. The yard is a gravelled quadrangle with thick walls and a massive dark-brown timber door. Its only furnishings are an Irish tricolour on a staff and two black-painted timber crosses. A few strands of ivy high on a wall are the only signs of life, and a plaque bears the names of Patrick Pearse, James Connolly, Sean MacDiarmada, Con Colbert and the other leaders who died here.

The Camac flows behind the prison, and we should follow it and go west along Inchicore Road. A turn left into Grattan Crescent brings us to a gate on the right leading to the Inchicore railway works, but this gate, always open, is merely an outer one, and inside it are several terraces of houses, built for railway workers by the Great Southern and Western Railway. The engine sheds at Inchicore went into operation in April 1846, with thirty-nine men employed, a far cry from the 1,000 or thereabouts now employed on the seventy-three-acre site. Workers' housing was a problem at the outset in Inchicore, as the area was largely rural, so the company built its own houses, with a dining hall, library and recreation centre, and a dormitory house for provincial drivers staying overnight. As the work force grew, so did the need for more houses, and we see several styles in Abercorn Terrace, St Patrick's Terrace, Inchicore Terrace South and Granite Terrace, showing the piecemeal development, redbrick, brownbrick, concrete-washed facades with Gothic doorways, and houses built entirely of granite, except for redbrick corners and door and window surrounds.

Inchicore railway works

Returning to the junction of Inchicore Road, turn left into Sarsfield Road, pass under a railway bridge, then pass a convent on the left. Isolated in an open grassy area on the right, near a pub, are three small streets between two end roads, looking like the beginning of an estate that was suddenly abandoned. Phoenix St, West Liffey St and Park St are here, but they are collectively referred to as the Ranch. Keeping to the left, walk back towards the city along Colbert Road, past the memorial park and cenotaph honouring men killed at war in the British forces, designed by Sir Edwin Lutyens.

the memorial park and cenotaph

St John's Road lies ahead, across the South Circular Road, and as we enter it there is a fine view of the Wellington monument to the left. Kingsbridge station is at the end of the road, and soon its sparrow-hued ridge-and-furrow goods sheds appear on the left. A little further on, still looking left, a glimpse can be had of the vivid red bricks of St Bricin's Hospital on the far side of the Liffey. Turning right into the Military Road, with the heads of the trees meeting in the middle, go up for another view of the Royal Hospital, its posts crowned with the torsos and heads of suits of armour.

St John's Rd

By coming back around the front of the station and walking onto Heuston bridge, the Camac can be seen joining her big sister through an arched opening at the side of the station.

Kilmainham Jail

The Casino — St Moibhi's — Delville — Botanic
Gardens — Glasnevin cemetery — Dunsink —
Rathfarnham castle — St Enda's — Bottle Tower
— RDS.

*Dublin is splendid beyond my utmost expectations. I can go
round its walls and number its palaces until I am grilled
almost into a fever.*

— Sir Walter Scott.

So far, we have been examining what lies in the city between the Royal and Grand canals, or just a little outside them, but now the route leaves this inner area and goes around the outside of Dublin. Too long for a walk, it is an ideal drive for a fine day, and quite an interesting one even on a normal Irish day. The first item of major importance to be seen is the famous casino of Lord Charlemont in Marino, on the north side.

Fairview parish church

Beginning at Ballybough bridge, the route to the casino runs through Fairview Strand, passing the Jewish graveyard on the left with its little house whose plaque tells us that it was built in the Mosaic year 5618, actually 1857–58. Fairview parish church, a Gothic building of 1855, stands just beyond the corner of Philipsburgh Avenue, formerly Ellis's Lane, and once the main road through the suburb of Annadale, most of whose residents were Jews. Turning left into the Malahide Road

Marino Crescent

at Marino Mart, Marino Crescent, with its park in front of the terrace, is seen on the right. Bram Stoker, author of *Dracula*, was born in the crescent, at number 15 in November 1847, and Martin Haverty, author of a *History of Ireland*, also lived there, at number 21. Left of the lower part of Malahide Road, in Marino Demesne, stood Marino House, built for the 'Volunteer' earl of Charlemont by his step-father, Thomas Adderley. The crescent was built in 1792 and it is said that its builder, a painter named ffolliott from Aungier St, put it up deliberately to block the view of the sea from Marino House, having had a dispute with Lord Charlemont.

the casino

Further up Malahide Road, the casino stands in the grounds of the Irish Christian Brothers on the left, beyond the corner of Griffith Avenue. A special permit from the Office of Public Works is needed to view the interior, which suffered some damage during years of neglect. The original furniture has long gone. The outside of the building, however, is superb. Surrounded by twelve Tuscan columns, eight of them in the four porticoes and four at the corners, it is based on Palladio's idea of the symmetrical villa, and also incorporates his notion of a temple facade running all around a building. Urns adorn the roof and lions guard the approaches to the corners. The building has a central heating system in its walls, operated simply by lighting fires in the grates. The ancient Romans had similar systems. Lord Charlemont had the casino, often referred to as the temple, built between 1765 and 1771, at a cost of £60,000, from plans sent by Sir William Chambers from England. Norbert Lynton refers to it in *World Architecture* as one of the most perfect buildings of the Renaissance, but he also calls it a 'little pleasure house', and indeed this word 'little' is often, but mistakenly, applied to it.

This is possibly because the isolated building, dwarfed by its own ornamentation, gives an appearance from even quite near at hand of being built on the scale of the 'garden furniture' popular at the time of its erection. Balustrades, pediments and festooned panels hide the top storey, and the columns and urns stress the structure's mathematical precision. Only by mounting the steps that cross its surrounding basement area, and standing beside it, do we realise that it is quite a large villa. There is ample space inside, yet one is given a feeling of enclosure rather than exposure.

The Casino, Malahide Road

The nearby redbrick building of the Christian Brothers, formerly the O'Brien Institute for boys from one-parent homes, is a pleasant example of late nineteenth-century French domestic Gothic.

From Malahide Road go west along broad Griffith Avenue, with its four rows of trees, to Glasnevin and turn left down Ballymun Road. Stop opposite the Institute of Industrial Research and Standards and walk along Church Avenue, with tiny whitewashed cottages on the left, to the gate of St Moibhi's churchyard, dominated by the little church with its squat tower. A glance right will show parts of the Bon Secours hospital, a modern institution built on the grounds of Delville, once the home of Dr Delany, chancellor of St Patrick's cathedral, a fellow of Trinity College, friend of Jonathan Swift and sometime Dean of Down.

Occupying, with the hospital, the site of a sixth-century monastic settlement, the present main part of St Moibhi's church was erected in 1700, but the tower dates from 1680. There have been some structural alterations in this century and in the last. An older church on the site fell into ruin about 1630. Dr Delany is buried in the churchyard, though his tombstone was hidden by ivy until about 1976. He and his wife worshipped in this church, as did Swift, and a blocked-up gate behind the church indicates that there was a direct path from Delville to St Moibhi's.

Griffith Avenue

St Moibhi's churchyard

Bon Secours hospital

Delville

Mrs Delany

Delany built Delville in 1722 and went to live there full-time in 1734. He married the former Mrs Pendarves in 1743, and she soon became noted for her vast appetite for entertaining, and for the huge meals she provided for her guests at Delville. Mrs Delany had also been a friend of Swift before her marriage. He was a regular visitor to Delville, which has given rise to a rumour that he is buried with Dr Delany in St Moibhi's churchyard and not in St Patrick's cathedral; supporters of this theory obviously believe that the social stigma which attached to insanity in the eighteenth century led to the nature of Swift's illness being falsified, and that this falsification was somehow carried through and applied to the time of his death and his place of burial. But the theory lacks logic. What is certain, however, is that he had a printing press in Delville, on which he produced those of his pamphlets which commercial printers found too dangerous to handle.

The original monastic settlement was established by St Moibhi, and among its residents were St Columba (Colmcille), sometimes called the 'apostle of Scotland', and St Ciaran, and as we go back out onto Ballymun Road, we see a school dedicated to the latter. Go down Ballymun Road and turn left at Glasnevin Hill. Almost immediately on the right is the long front of a former farmhouse, the gate into the old farmyard still in place. Down on the left is the Bon Secours hospital entrance; keep right here, down the hill cross a bridge over the Tolka

Our Lady of Dolours church

river passing the modern black triangle of Our Lady of Dolours church. This replaces an old wooden chapel beside which the 'Inkbottle School', founded by Dean Swift, stood until 1901. Swift had designed the school himself, in the exact shape of an inkbottle.

botanic gardens

A little further on, the gates of the national botanic gardens appear on the right. These gardens, now covering more than fifty acres, were founded here in 1795 on a sixteen-acre plot by Dr Walter Wade of the Dublin Society (later the Royal Dublin Society). The land had been bought from the family of Thomas Tickell, biographer of the essayist Joseph Addison. A tree-lined walk in the gardens is named the Addison walk, the area of the gardens having been a haunt of Addison and his friend and collaborator Richard Steele, founder of *The Tatler* and later knighted, who was a Dubliner. The gardens, which are bounded on one side by Prospect cemetery, the largest in Ireland, and on the other by the Tolka, replaced earlier plots at Ballybough bridge in 1732 and at Great Martin's Lane, now Railway St, in 1735. By the time the Glasnevin gardens came under state control in 1878 they were already quite famous. Opened primarily for the study of agriculture and horticulture, they became a retreat for a public in search of beauty and tranquillity. With flowerbeds, rockeries, Californian redwood, Monterey pine and black Corsican pine. Chinese tulip trees, purple beech, greenhouses of cacti, waterlilies and banana plants, a beautiful rose garden arranged around an antique sundial and the possible glimpse of a darting red squirrel for those who come early and quietly enough, these gardens are one of the most enthralling spots in the city. Marble statues including one of Socrates, near the rose garden, came

Thomas Moore Rose

from Iveagh House in St Stephen's Green. Inside the gardens' entrance slightly to the left, is the Thomas Moore Rose, a vegetative descendant

of the Co. Kilkenny rose which inspired Moore to write the lyric of 'The Last Rose of Summer'. And at the superintendent's house is one of the few thornless climbing roses in the British Isles.

To go to Prospect cemetery, drive down the road facing the gardens, turn right, and soon after a pub named the Botanic House take a sharp right turn onto Finglas Road, taking care to ignore a smaller road which splits this road junction, Hart's Corner, in two. This smaller road would lead to an old gate of the cemetery, now closed. The cemetery wall, on the right of Finglas Road, still has watchtowers in position, which were once manned by armed guards to discourage body-snatching. The small road which we passed in the middle of Hart's Corner was opened at the suggestion of Daniel O'Connell to avoid a turnpike on Finglas Road, at which funerals had to pay tolls. Glasnevin cemetery, as this is better known, was opened in February 1832 for the burial of Catholics.

Glasnevin cemetery

Glasnevin cemetery originally covered nine acres, but has now spread to over 100 acres, and burials there are not confined to the members of any one church. The burial ground occupies lands on both sides of Finglas Road. Inside the main entrance a mortuary chapel is seen, and not far away, to the right, is the great capped tower of Dalkey granite which marks the tomb of the Liberator. Known as the

O'Connell monument

O'Connell monument, although there is another such monument in O'Connell St, the tower was designed by George Petrie and is 168 and a half feet tall. Daniel O'Connell was largely instrumental in having this cemetery established, and he was buried here in 1847 with great ceremony, in an area known as the O'Connell Circle, further from the main entrance than the present tower. It was later decided to lay out a new O'Connell plot to Petrie's design, which incorporated not only this tower, based on the Celtic round towers of Ireland, but a chapel recalling the earliest known Christian style of architecture in Ireland, and a Celtic cross, with O'Connell to be reinterred in a crypt at the tower's base. The tower and crypt were completed in 1869, and in May of that year O'Connell was reburied there, but the unforeseen height of the tower precluded the completion of the design in the allotted space, without presenting a cluttered appearance.

The present main entrance replaced the older one after the turnpike had been abolished. The gate, and the mortuary chapel, opened in 1879, were designed by James J. McCarthy. In the newer part of the cemetery, away to the left of the chapel, is the tomb of Charles Stewart Parnell, a simple mound surmounted by a huge, uncut stone.

Our route from the cemetery is north-west along Finglas Road, then left along Ballyboggan Road between the Tolka and the edge of a modern housing estate. At the end, turn right along Ratoath Road, and cross the Tolka at Cardiffsbridge, keeping to the left. As the houses peter out, turn to the left along Dunsink Lane. After less than a mile, the gate

Dunsink observatory

of Dunsink observatory appears on the left, and a low building with an unusually high area of copper dome, visible from the road, clearly tells of the uncommon nature of the work going on here. The observatory may be visited on certain Saturday nights from September to March, inclusive, and at other times by appointment. It was established under the terms of a bequest of Provost Francis Andrews of Trinity, who died in 1774. Work began on Dunsink in 1783 and it was opened in late 1785 or early 1786, papers based on work there being published in 1788.

The first astronomer appointed was Rev. Henry Ussher, who was succeeded by John Brinkley, an Englishman, and he by the brilliant William Rowan Hamilton, who was only twenty-one years old at the time of his appointment, but who had been proficient in working out the calculations of eclipses and occultations since he was sixteen. Hamilton's appointment was not a success, as he spent more time at mathematics than astronomy, angered the college board by taking in pupils to supplement his income, and wrote about comets in the *Dublin Penny Journal*.

When Hamilton died in 1865 he was succeeded by a German named Francis Brunnow, who between 1866 and 1868 erected the domed building to house a new telescope. The dome, which weighs six tons, is arranged so that it can be rotated during observations. Robert Stawell Ball, from Granby Row, Dublin, took over from Brunnow, and he is remembered for devising a system whereby the public clock on the ballast office in Westmoreland St and a time ball in the port were controlled from Dunsink. This time ball was dismantled in the late 1940s, and is preserved in Dunsink. In 1947 Dunsink was taken over by the school of cosmic physics of the Dublin Institute for Advanced Studies.

Going on along Dunsink Lane, we cross the Tolka and then the Royal Canal below Blanchardstown; before leaving the Tolka, it is **Blanchardstown** worth mentioning that this river receives a tributary called the Pinkeen some way north-west of here, near Mulhuddart, explaining something that has puzzled strangers for generations, why Dublin children never use the name 'minnow', but always call this fish a 'pinkeen'. Over the canal, cross the Navan road and go on by Beech Park Avenue and College Road, with the grounds of Castleknock college on the right, **Castleknock** including the preserved castle ruin. Soon after this, on the left, a tall clocktower comes into view, and the first impression it gives is one of total unsuitability to its surroundings. But this is a mistake, for it is really a water tower, erected in 1800 to store water pumped from the Liffey to the farm at Farmleigh, residence of Lord Iveagh, in whose grounds it stands. The clocks on the east and west faces of the tower are an artistic afterthought, but not a mere mannerism, as their mechanism was installed by Sir Hugh Grubb, a celebrated maker of astronomical instruments, and they contain a chiming mechanism. The tower includes a weather cock and has a lofty viewing balcony, supported by granite corbels, on all sides. The tower was built by the engineering section of Guinness's brewery. We go on past Mount Sackville convent and down by Knockmaroon Hill and Martin's Row to the Liffey bridge at Chapelizod. Joseph Sheridan Le Fanu lived here, and his novel *The* **Chapelizod** *House by the Churchyard* is set here. The 'izod' part of the village's name may refer to Isolde, who may have been the daughter of the Irish King Aengus, who reigned in Arthurian times. Turn right at the traffic lights at the end of Martin's Row and go straight on along Ballyfermot Hill

Cherry Orchard hospital

Clondalkin round tower

Walkinstown

Kimmage Manor

Rathfarnham Rathfarnham Castle

and the built-up Le Fanu Road, turning right off the roundabout at the end of this onto Ballyfermot Road, which runs west past Cherry Orchard hospital on the left and then taking the next left and following a long, winding road which ends in a T junction. A short distance to the left here, the Grand Canal is bridged, and Ninth Lock Road runs into Clondalkin, site of another sixth-century monastic settlement.

Contrast the round tower here, at the side of the road, with the one we saw in Glasnevin. The Clondalkin tower probably dates from the eighth or early ninth century, and is all that is left of the settlement. Notice how it stands on a base broader than itself, and how the steps to the door begin several feet from the ground, so that when the occupants had hauled up the ladder it was difficult for an enemy to follow, especially if he was weighed down by arms, armour or both. Also, an occupant could come out and stand on the platform outside the door, if necessary, in the process of repelling unwelcome guests. These towers were used first as a look-out and then as a refuge in time of attack, but one shudders to think of what life was like during a protracted siege for the defenders cooped up inside.

Several of these towers survive in Ireland, such as those in Glendalough, Co. Wicklow and Cashel, Co. Tipperary, but this in Clondalkin is one of the most accessible, being on the side of a street, and is among the better-preserved examples, even its stone cap being intact. The monastery which existed in this place was plundered by the ubiquitous Vikings in 832, before they had made any significant advances on Dublin. In 853 the Danish king Aulaffe, or Amlave, having arrived with a powerful fleet and forced all the Danes in Ireland to submit to his rule, made a truce with the Irish princes and adopted Clondalkin as a favourite residence, but twelve years later his establishment was burned out by the Irish, who killed about 100 leading Danes in a raid. The doughty tower survived, as it has now survived urbanisation. It also survived an eighteenth-century explosion in a local gunpowder works, which wrecked a mediaeval church whose ruins are in the Church of Ireland graveyard across the road.

Turn left into Main St and continue along Monastery Road and the Naas Road until a V-junction is reached, taking the right fork along Long Mile Road, and turn right off this into Walkinstown Avenue. Then go straight ahead at a roundabout along St Peter's Road and Greentrees Road, straight on again past Kimmage Manor, on the left, to another roundabout, and still straight ahead along Templeville Road and across Templeogue Road into Springfield Avenue. Here the River Dodder is crossed, and beyond it our route turns right, along Fairways, then left along Butterfield Avenue a right turn is made into the main street of Rathfarnham. We see Rathfarnham Castle on the left, but a fine entrance and wall have disappeared in road widening here. The castle now belongs to the Jesuits, and is much changed from the original building of the late sixteenth century, erected here by the powerful Archbishop Adam Loftus. The Dublin hills, steps to the Wicklow mountains beyond, can be said to begin here, and Rathfarnham was used as an outpost from which to discourage any designs by mountainy men on the city. A skeleton force could be stationed in the castle, to be augmented by a full garrison in times of trouble, as it was in 1641, when part of the city wall collapsed while rumours of a plot to seize Dublin Castle were rife.

Rathfarnham Castle has had many owners, including Thomas, marquis of Wharton, a profligate and idler who was viceroy in Ireland for a while, but took his duties so lightly that he felt four months a year was long enough to spend in the country. His son Philip, duke of Wharton, came next as master of Rathfarnham, but in 1724, while still in his twenties, he was in such financial trouble through gambling and drink that he sold the castle to the Right Hon. William Conolly, **William** Speaker of the Irish House of Commons, for £62,000. Conolly is best **Conolly** remembered as the owner of the magnificent Palladian mansion of Castletown, with its splendid long gallery, out at Celbridge, Co. Kildare, and it was the possession of this mansion that made it easier for him to dispose of Rathfarnham Castle, for which he had little use, to Right Rev. John Hoadly. Hoadly died at Rathfarnham in 1746, after which it passed to Mr Bellingham Boyle, and then to Nicholas Loftus, second earl of Ely, a direct descendant of its builder. In 1852 Lord Chancellor Blackburne became its owner. By then the original Gothic windows had been modernised and a stone coping had replaced the Elizabethan battlements.

Grange Road runs south-east from here and then turns right, passing the Loreto Abbey on the left, originally the home of William Palliser, who built a mansion here in the early eighteenth century, though there have been many additions since then. Go straight on, pass a petrol station, and a pair of gate posts surmounted by lions appears on the right. The gateposts, notice, are marked with two names, the Hermitage and Sgoil Eanna, meaning St Enda's school. This was the **St Enda's** home of the school founded by Patrick Pearse in 1908 'with the object of **school** providing a secondary education distinctively Irish in complexion, bilingual in method and of a high modern type, generally, for Irish Catholic boys'. Religious segregation in schools was, and is, quite common, but catering to only one creed and only one nationality is unusual. In the ideological context of the type of education Pearse wished to provide, however, it was quite a natural stipulation. St Enda's brought financial stress to Pearse, and he went to America on a fund-raising lecture tour on its behalf. It has been said of St Enda's that the education there was geared to militarism, but it must also be said of Pearse that he was a reformer who anticipated many modern developments in his teaching methods. Pearse left the school for the last time to take part in the Easter Rising of 1916; at that time the school had sixty pupils. Afterwards the school buildings were occupied by British troops. The last of the Pearse family to live there was Margaret, Patrick's sister, who died in 1968. The work of restoring the building, in its forty-four acres of parkland, and converting it to a museum, began in 1970.

Going through the gate and up to the old school building, we see a three-storey granite Georgian mansion, with steps and a two-storey Tuscan portico, and curving side terraces. The room on the right of the halldoor was Pearse's office. A previous owner of the Hermitage was a

Col. Hudson, who fought at Waterloo, and his horse is buried in the grounds here. In the house are the original fireplaces, that in the main hall having an eighteenth-century oak surround. After the house was handed over to the state in 1970, and urgent work such as re-roofing completed, the Office of Public Works brought a craftsman out of retirement to revarnish this fireplace, and the halldoor, in the correct original style. The garden of St Enda's has now been laid out in the shape of a Celtic cross.

Going back past Loreto Abbey to where we turned off, turn right and drive along Nutgrove Avenue. The grounds of the Castle golf course are on the left, and these were originally part of Rathfarnham Castle demesne. Beyond the golf course, Whitehall Road is on the left, named after a house called Whitehall which stood in isolation here before the area was built up. Going along this road and keeping to the left, see a stone tower coming into view, broad at the base and narrow at the top, with a spiral stairway on the outside. Its topworks remind one of **the 'bottle tower'** the neck of a bottle, and it is known locally as the 'bottle tower'. Before the area was built up, however, it was called the 'inkbottle', from those old broad-bottomed 'unspillable' containers of this fluid, and before that again it was accurately known as Hall's barn. In the winter of 1741–42, described as a time of 'hard frost', Major Hall, the owner of Whitehall, a fine five-bay house, built this tower as a barn, employing local men, the object being both to provide him with a barn and give employment to the local poor, then in great distress. There is a similar structure near Castletown House called 'the wonderful barn', built by the Conollys, and Hall probably copied this. Some of the structures built in Ireland and in Britain simply to provide work for the poor are referred to as 'follies' because of their apparent uselessness, but the bottle tower, being a practical building, did not qualify for this description. It has often been mistaken for a shot tower, a structure made for the manufacture of shot by dropping molten lead through a sieve into cold water, but is far too low to have been used for this.

Rev. Jeremy Walsh, curate of Dundrum, later lived at Whitehall. The bottle tower now survives in the garden of number 30 Whitehall Road, and a smaller, similar tower is seen behind it.

Churchtown Coming back onto Nutgrove Avenue, continue along it to its junction with Churchtown Road Upper. Turn right and then immediately left into Churchtown Road Lower and go along this, skirting Milltown golf course, on the left, until the Dodder is again **Clonskeagh** crossed. Turn right and follow Milltown Road to Clonskeagh, a pleasant drive which passes the grounds of Shamrock Rovers football club. At Clonskeagh Road we cross into Eglinton Road, which brings us **Donnybrook** to the end of Donnybrook Road, where we turn right and again cross the winding Dodder. A large modern bus garage is straight ahead, but our route runs to the left, where there is a broad V-junction. Keep to the **Ballsbridge** left along Anglesea Road, which winds down to Ballsbridge and brings **Royal Dublin** us out beside another Dodder bridge, with the great Royal Dublin **Society** Society showgrounds on our right in Merrion Road, and the sprawling Irish Hospital Sweepstakes offices across the road from them. Walk down for a view of the showgrounds, unless a show is in progress, when

they may be better seen from within. Many thousands come here each year for the Dublin Horse Show and the Spring Show, and to smaller, more specialised exhibitions. The society was founded on 25 June 1731, in the rooms of the philosophical society of Trinity College, to improve the condition of the country and raise the status of the agricultural population. Its first headquarters was in the parliament house in College Green, now the Bank of Ireland, then in Grafton St and Hawkins St in turn before moving to Leinster House, where it remained until 1922. The showground here in Ballsbridge was begun on a fifteen-acre site in 1879, and now covers fifty acres, being also the society's headquarters.

Pembroke town hall

The Victorian Gothic granite and brick building at the corner of Merrion and Anglesea roads is the former Pembroke town hall, which later became a technical school. Beyond it is the long granite facade, in a muted classical style, which embraces the central, east and west halls of the RDS showgrounds, with the figure of plenty in the tympanum over the main entrance, festooned urns, and medallions with bovine, ovine and equine heads on the outer pavilions. The first architect engaged to lay out the showgrounds, after a lease of 500 years had been obtained from Lord Pembroke, was George Wilkinson. Since then there have been many additions, and many changes. Directly across the road from the main entrance a branch line from the Dublin to Wexford railway once terminated, especially laid to facilitate the carriage of livestock to and from the showgrounds. The area now occupied by the new bank offices, east of the sweepstake offices, was formerly leased by the RDS to the famous bloodstock sales firm of Goff's, which had previously been in Lower Mount St and has now moved outside the city. A drinking trough at the roadside here is a relic of the site's former character. On the showgrounds side, beyond the main facade, brick pillars punctuate an ivy-clad wall. The north paddock hall is here, and looking between it and the granite buildings, one sees a quaint weathervane on a clocktower, in the shape of a horse and rider. Going on to the corner of Simmonscourt Road past the Sandymount hall, once simply called the sheep hall, Thomas Prior House can be seen on the facing corner.

Thomas Prior House

This curious Victorian building, built in 1881, is now dedicated to a founder member of the Dublin Society, but it was originally a school for the daughters of deceased Freemasons. The school was founded in 1792, the present building being opened in 1882 and extended in 1892 and 1894. A large sextant symbol is noticeable near the top. The classical fountain on the lawn seems, at first glance, out of place, but then we notice how casually eclectic the whole character of the place is. There are brown and red bricks and red sandstone, circular, oval and rectangular windows, and a white slatted octagonal tower with a copper dome, topped by a swallow-tailed weather vane, with a five-point star cut-out. In the background, near the monastery of St Damian, the pinkish bricks of the RDS Simmonscourt hall, topped by another horse and rider weathervane, add to an extraordinary mixture which could not possibly retain its unity in a location nearer the city centre.

On the road back to the city across the Dodder, we pass a striking circular building, to the left, which gives the impression of being surrounded by a moat, at the junction of Northumberland Road and Elgin Road on the city side of the bridge. This is the American embassy, begun in 1962 and finished in 1964, to the design of the American architect John McL Johansen, and his Irish collaborator, Michael Scott.

American embassy

It is truly a product of its age, the freedom of expression being somewhat reminiscent of Frank Lloyd Wright's Guggenheim museum in New York, though the coil motif is not here, or Pier Luigi Nervi's 1958 Palazzetto dello Sport in Rome. In the embassy this freedom has not been abused, and inside, that slight 'lost' feeling experienced in round buildings is quickly dispelled by the layout. It may not have the romantic aura of the French embassy at Ailesbury Road, or of the Belgian in Shrewsbury Road, an air which lovers of exciting fiction feel should be associated with all such missions, but it is a pleasing addition to the landscape at a time when many new buildings show a sheer contempt for imagination.

Before concluding this tour and going back to the city, come back a little on the embassy side and turn up to Herbert Park, one of Dublin's most beautiful, laid out for an exhibition in 1907.

Herbert Park

In the Dublin Mountains, the Hell Fire Club

Glossary

Of Architectural and Building Terms used in this Book

Apse Semi-circular or U-shaped end of church, usually behind high altar.

Arcade Line of arches supported on piers or pillars.

Balustrade Line of miniature pillars supporting a handrail.

Byzantine Fifth-century Constantinople style; the use of round arches is a characteristic. It mixes classical and oriental elements.

Capital Upper part of a pillar.

Campanile Bell tower.

Clerestory Upper window level, above an adjacent roof.

Colonnade Line of columns.

Composite Roman order combining Corinthian stylised leaves with Ionic scrolls.

Console Ornamental scroll-like bracket supporting frieze, cornice or balcony, or used as keystone.

Corinthian Classical order with ornate capital, using stylised acanthus leaves.

Cornice Projecting shelf along the top of a building.

Doric Simple classical order of pillar with fluted shaft and no base.

Dutch style Domestic building style using tapered or triangular top on front elevation, often built in Queen Anne reign or shortly afterwards.

Fenestral Pertaining to windows, perforated. May include opening covered by a material other than glass.

Fillet Flat bands of stone between flutes.

Flutes Vertical channels or grooves in pillar.

Gothic European mediaeval style, revived in second half of nineteenth century as neo-Gothic; characterised by pointed arches and rib vaulting.

Groin Ridge at meeting of two vaulting sections.

Georgian Neo-classical building style in reigns of first four Georges, usually applied to domestic buildings.

Ionic Classical style using scrolls or volutes in capitals.

Italianate An Italian style using arches, balustrades, square turrets and sometimes long flights of steps, popular with some nineteenth-century railway architects.

Keystone Wedge-shaped central stone at crown of arch.

Lintel Horizontal stone or beam over door.

Marble Literally a hard limestone of pleasant and patterned colour, taking a brilliant polish. In common usage, it applies to other highly polished coloured stone, such as pink granite.

Obelisk Tall square tapering stone, with pyramid at top.

Portico Colonnaded porch, sometimes merging with the facade.

Palladian Style in which a dominant central classical building is flanked by lesser ones; originally an arched opening flanked by flat ones.

216

Pavilion End sections of classical building made distinctive by projecting them, raising level or using pediments. Originally an ornamental building, such as a summer house.
Pediment Top, usually triangular, part of portico.
Piazza Space enclosed by pillars.
Pilaster Flattened pillar attached to a wall as decoration only.
Romanesque Style which preceded Gothic, with round arches and vaulting, and usually thick proportions.
Regency A restrained early nineteenth-century classical style.
Tuscan Roman order similar to Doric, but with a base and no flutes.
Tympanum Triangular area enclosed by a pediment.
Vault Stone ceiling. Barrel vaults are arched, usually semi-circular, but they may be pointed. Groin and rib vaults are sectioned, usually quadripartite. A stone rib differs from a groin in that stone ribs can be built separately as a skeleton.
Venetian Victorian style characterised by groups of round-arched windows.

BIBLIOGRAPHICAL NOTE

The reader who wishes to pursue the study of Dublin has no shortage of material from which to choose. For a comprehensive and massively researched account, one can do no better than J. T. Gilbert, *A History of the City of Dublin*, (3 vols.), Dublin 1861, happily reprinted in 1978. A shorter and more popular account is offered in Desmond Clarke, *Dublin*, London 1976, which has, of course, the advantage of dealing with the century that has elapsed since Gilbert wrote. Dublin's heroic period as a great classical city is superbly chronicled in Maurice Craig, *Dublin 1660–1860*, London 1952, Dublin 1969 (paperback), a delightful book which wears its erudition lightly. An older but equally respected volume is Constantia Maxwell, *Dublin Under the Georges*, London 1936, 3rd ed. Dublin 1946. The literary city is highlighted in V. S. Pritchett, *Dublin, A Portrait*, London 1967, an impressionistic but beautifully written book. For a highly personal account by a native Dubliner, Eamonn Mac Thomáis, *Me Jewel and Darlin' Dublin*, Dublin 1974, is recommended. Its account of the lives of ordinary Dubliners in the 1930s and '40s is especially useful in gaining an overall picture of the city and its people. Elgy Gillespie ed., *The Liberties of Dublin*, Dublin 1973, is a well-illustrated book dealing with an area whose traditions and customs have aroused much interest in recent years. Finally, for those interested in learning more about the outskirts of the city, two books can be mentioned. Weston St John Joyce, *The Neighbourhood of Dublin*, Dublin 1912, is still readily available as a result of a recent reprint. The same holds true for Dillon Cosgrave, *North Dublin, City and County*, originally published in Dublin in 1909, but available in a paperback edition since 1977.

INDEX